PERGAMON INSTITUTE OF ENGLISH (OXFORD)

Language Teaching Methodology Series

The Sociolinguistics of Learning and Using a Non-native Language

Other titles in this series include

ALTMAN, Howard B and C VAUGHAN JAMES
Foreign language teaching: meeting individual needs

BRUMFIT, Christopher J
Problems and principles in English teaching

CARROLL, Brendan J
Testing communicative performance: an interim study

DUFF, Alan
The third language: recurrent problems in translation into English

FISIAK, Jacek (ed)
Contrastive linguistics and the language teacher

FREUDENSTEIN, Rheinold
Teaching foreign languages to the very young

FREUDENSTEIN, BENEKE and PONISCH (eds)
Routes to language learning: teaching foreign languages in industry

JOHNSON, Keith
Notional syllabuses and communicative language teaching

KELLERMAN, Marcelle
The forgotten third skill: reading a foreign language

KRASHEN, Stephen
Second language acquisition and second language learning

LEONTIEV, Aleksei A
Psychology and the language learning process

LEWIS, Glyn
Bilingualism and bilingual education

NEWMARK, Peter P
Approaches to translation

ROBINSON, Pauline C
ESP (English for Specific Purposes)

SHARP, Derrick W H
English at school: the wood and the trees

STREVENS, Peter
Teaching English as an international language

TOSI, Arturo
Immigration and bilingual education

See also *SYSTEM: the International Journal of Education Technology and Language Learning Systems* (sample copy available on request)

The Sociolinguistics of Learning and Using a Non-native Language

LEO LOVEDAY

Doshisha University, Japan

PERGAMON PRESS

Oxford · New York · Toronto · Sydney · Paris · Frankfurt

U.K.	Pergamon Press Ltd., Headington Hill Hall, Oxford OX3 0BW, England
U.S.A.	Pergamon Press Inc., Maxwell House, Fairview Park, Elmsford, New York 10523, U.S.A.
CANADA	Pergamon Press Canada Ltd., Suite 104, 150 Consumers Road, Willowdale, Ontario M2J 1P9, Canada
AUSTRALIA	Pergamon Press (Aust.) Pty. Ltd., P.O. Box 544, Potts Point, N.S.W. 2011, Australia
FRANCE	Pergamon Press SARL, 24 rue des Ecoles, 75240 Paris, Cedex 05, France
FEDERAL REPUBLIC OF GERMANY	Pergamon Press GmbH, 6242 Kronberg-Taunus, Hammerweg 6, Federal Republic of Germany

First edition 1982

Library of Congress Cataloging in Publication Data

Loveday, Leo
The sociolinguistics of learning and using a non-native language.
(Language teaching methodology series)
1. Language and languages—Study and teaching—Social aspects. 2. Sociolinguistics. I. Title. II. Series.
P53.8.L68 1982   401'.9   81–23499

British Library Cataloguing in Publication Data

Loveday, Leo
The sociolinguistics of learning and using a non-native language.—(Language teaching methodology series)
1. Language and languages—Study and teaching
2. Language acquisition   3. Sociolinguistics
I. Title   II. Series
401'.9   P53
ISBN 0–08–028668–2

Printed in Great Britain by A. Wheaton & Co. Ltd., Exeter

204550

To
my parents with gratitude

Foreword

Recently there has been a deluge of literature and programmes that are sociolinguistically based, often with the aim of assisting disadvantaged speakers of a language, in particular non-standard English. Thus, sociolinguistics and bilingual education have, above all in the USA, come to be associated with discriminated and dislocated minorities.

However, it is quite erroneous to believe that sociolinguistics is merely a tool for accomplishing a kind of linguistic 'social work' and this book is an attempt to demonstrate the subject's general value and vital importance for those involved in teaching a non-native language to all types of learners. Whether it be English in Hong Kong, French in Manchester, Swahili in Ohio, Welsh in Wales, Russian in Sophia or whatever, the implications of sociolinguistic work are of immediate and direct relevance to every language teacher.

Unfortunately, a great deal of distrust and frustration seems to exist between language practitioners and language theorizers. This is partly due to the general but unfounded supposition that the theorizer knows more. The communication gap between teacher and theorist is also widened through the use of sometimes frustrating jargon, unfamiliar name-dropping and limited access to specialist, academic publications.

Furthermore, it often seems to be the case that lacking experience of classroom reality, theorists fail to understand the problem of applying their often too abstract findings. This book is essentially an attempt to overcome these difficulties by presenting the most vital and profitable discoveries which are important for learning a non-native language in a clear and concise manner. All the references are given within the text itself and it is hoped that this neither slows down nor interferes too much with the flow of the argument.

Thus, the book aims at providing insights into the social dimensions of assimilating, employing and imparting a linguistic system different from that natively learnt. However, the presentation here is not merely descriptive but constitutes an argument for a humanistic and pluralistic understanding of language as essentially an act of meaning. A new framework for considering the dynamics of bilingualism and a symbolically-orientated explanation of the concept communicative competence together with a comprehensive and critical review of the most exciting sociolinguistic research currently carried out is what awaits the reader.

Kyoto, 1982   LEO LOVEDAY

Contents

x   Contents

1
What is sociolinguistics?

If the main concern of this book is the social dimension of learning and using a non-native language, the primary question which must first be answered is what exactly does the subject *sociolinguistics* refer to and what does it offer.

The hyphenated name of the discipline immediately points to its two central concerns: society and language. Simply put, it investigates and theorizes on the relationship between these two areas, which is a relationship long tabooed by a traditionally dehumanized linguistics. What then is this relationship between language and society?

In fact, we are all familiar with the complex links between society and language, although perhaps not immediately on a conscious level. It is common knowledge that people speak differently according to their background and that it is frequently possible to relate aspects of a person's speech to his place of origin or education or social group or generation or even occupation, among others. Moreover, (we all alter the way we speak according to whom we are with and this can depend on how intimate we feel our interlocutors to be or on the actual circumstance we find ourselves in, e.g. some may speak to close relatives (spouses, parents, children) quite differently in public than in their own home.)

On top of this, we judge people not only on the basis of what they say but how they sound, especially when meeting someone for the first time. Although this popular knowledge about language and its speakers is really a collection of stereotypic associations which may be more fiction than fact, we apply it constantly in our daily encounters. Such knowledge and linguistic behaviour was, however, long considered unworthy of study by linguists and teachers of non-native languages. The reason seems to have been the result of an exaggerated respect for the written forms of language, on the one hand, and an over-narrow interest in the historic development of language, on the other. Then in the middle of the 1960s there was a re-discovery of and a new awareness for the inextricable links between language and social behaviour by principally American scholars. Up until then those who studied language were not at all concerned with patterns of language use and its accompanying belief system but were much more interested in establishing language as an absolutely independent entity.

Sociologists, amazingly enough, have traditionally focused their attention on social stratification and organization without taking the different ways groups spoke or communicated into account. Fortunately, both linguistics and sociology have today developed beyond their classical limitations and together with other social sciences such as anthropology have helped to father the discipline *sociolinguistics* which now sees itself as an autonomous enterprise rather than as a sub-section of something else.

Sociolinguistics, however, is not only concerned with the linguistic indicators of social background mentioned above. It is also very interested in (1) the various conventions we follow in order to organize our speech with each other that are oriented towards social goals. In fact, many conversational and interactional structures have been found to exist as part of, for instance, telephoning, joke telling, narrating stories, classroom talk between students and teachers and so forth. A considerable amount of research of this nature is associated with a school of sociologists who have a rather awesome name. They are *ethnomethodologists* which simply means people who study the methods and means that social groups employ to achieve their objectives. They believe that social reality cannot be captured by statistical tables but is actually 'constructed' in the process of interaction. Among the leading ethnomethodologists working on language are Sacks (1972) and Schegloff (1972a, b). Other investigators in the same field do not regard their research so sociologically and instead see themselves more within the linguistic camp. Their work is generally called *discourse analysis* and under this category belong the studies on the structuring of teacher–pupil interaction (Coulthard 1977) and with special reference to the non-native language classroom (Heaton 1980). Another group of analysts of the patterns for arranging oral messages are anthropologists who study myths, folktales, riddles and rituals with reference to the society in which they are produced.

A different domain from the structure of communicating language is (2) the study of how *social norms and values affect linguistic behaviour,* e.g. Basil Bernstein's theories (1971, 1973) on the divergent speech styles of working class and middle class English children which are seen to result from differing attitudes towards explicitness. Research into the social reasons for linguistic behaviour is not, of course, restricted to the stylistic differences between different groups within one society but also deals with communicative variation between different linguistic and ethnic communities.

Many non-native language teachers are probably aware of the way norms governing speaking in the native language can conflict with those for speaking in another. Yet this area has received very little attention until quite recently although, as we all know, perfect grammar and pronunciation are rarely enough for effective mutual understanding in a non-native language. Much sociolinguistic work has been carried out on this aspect under the concept of *communicative competence* which was coined by Hymes (1972, 1974b). This perspective derives from anthropological concerns with the cultural frames in which language moves and has led to the creation of its own school in sociolinguistics known as the *ethnography of speaking* (Bauman & Sherzer 1974).

(3) The *variety and diversity of language related to the social framework of its speakers* constitutes a central domain of sociolinguistics. It might at first seem synonymous with the field described above under (2) but the difference lies in its much more traditionally sociological aims. There are many linguistic markers providing social information ranging from an accent which includes features such as nasalization and pitch to choice of vocabulary as well as the grammatical system. In some multilingual communities the languages spoken themselves may provide indications of the social status of its speakers. Linguistic diversity as a topic for investigation is the primary objective of sociolinguistics. The most notable contemporary British research here has been that of

Trudgill (1974) on the social differentiation of Norwich English and, more recently, Milroy's (1980) study of the social networks reflected in Belfast English. Investigations in this sphere are, of course, very relevant to the non-native language learner since he/she should be able to recognize the social and regional forms of the language to be acquired as well as possess an awareness of the beliefs and prejudices attached to the various forms if he/she wishes to properly understand and use the non-native language.

(4) The *political use of linguistic resources* is a further object of sociolinguistic study. Institutions such as the Academie Française which attempts to officially prescribe what is acceptable and what is not in French or the 'purification' of the German language under the Nazis or even the rather dubious language compensation programmes for deprived black American children are all examples of the political exploitation of language. On a much larger scale are the spelling reforms of Communist China aimed at democratizing the access to the complicated writing system or the adoption of Gaelic as a national language by the Republic of Ireland when it was the mother tongue of only 3% of the population. In fact, language choice is a matter of considerable sociopolitical consequence in a great many countries of the world today. Naturally, educational policies regarding which non-native language is to be taught in schools can also be sociopolitical. For instance, there is the relatively recent decision to teach Maori to New Zealand whites, the widespread teaching of Russian in the Eastern bloc and the desire to introduce a local, indigenous language in the school curriculum of new African states. Much of contemporary research in this area is directed towards educational decision making and generally goes under the name of *language planning*. The field is particularly associated with Fishman (1968b) who has been a founding figure in sociolinguistics with his studies on the problems of multilingual communities. Additionally in this category is the work on pidgins and creoles whose historically low-status has been promoted through their sociolinguistic treatment, e.g. the establishment of neo-Melanesian, originally an English-linked pidgin, as one of the official means of communication in contemporary New Guinea.

(5) The *social aspects of being bi- or multilingual* are, without doubt,

very important for learners of non-native languages. Most studies in this area have concentrated on minority groups within different countries, usually assuming certain political undertones connected to a wider recognition and acceptance of such groups cf. Gumperz (1977, 1978) on the possible breakdowns in communication between Londoners of Indian origin interacting with speakers of English as a native language. Other sociolinguists have been interested in the way non-native speakers switch around their languages, using one only for a particular activity. This phenomenon has been called *code switching*. Other studies have examined the social motivation for borrowing items from one language into the other. A further strand of research concentrates on the how and why of bilinguals' remaining loyal to one of their languages. A historical case of this is why Cornishmen gave up their Celtic tongue but the Welsh managed to maintain it.

Within all the five domains outlined above, the sociolinguists concerned will differ in the amount of emphasis they place on the linguistic, social, anthropological or applied aspects of their work and may even disagree about their categories and approaches. In fact, the territory that sociolinguistics covers is vast and the roads linking its various provinces have not yet been firmly laid. There already exist a number of introductions to the discipline: Trudgill (1974), Bell (1976) and Hudson (1980) but an alternative to leafing through these is for the reader to gain an awareness of his own linguistic behaviour, attitudes and experiences in and outside the classroom and compare these with the themes presented here.

If any abstract diagram of where the sociolinguistics of non-native language learning and using lies within the web of academic interests then it might look something like Fig. 1.

The shaded space within the dotted area representing sociolinguistics marks our field of focus which emerges where the circles of the disciplines linguistics, sociology/ethnomethodology/social anthropology and foreign language teaching converge. Among the themes of this shaded area are the social dynamics of speaking two languages, the as yet underestimated classroom implications of the connection between culture and language, the much quoted but not fully explicated

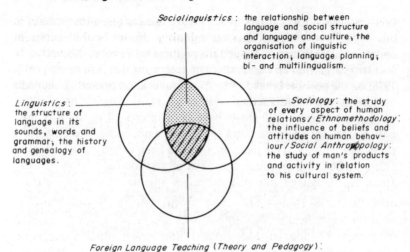

Sociolinguistics : the relationship between language and social structure and language and culture, the organisation of linguistic interaction; language planning; bi- and multilingualism.

Linguistics : the structure of language in its sounds, words and grammar; the history and genealogy of languages.

Sociology: the study of every aspect of human relations / *Ethnomethodology*: the influence of beliefs and attitudes on human behaviour / *Social Anthropology*: the study of man's products and activity in relation to his cultural system.

Foreign Language Teaching (*Theory and Pedagogy*): the application of linguistic, psychological and sociological theories and insights for educational purposes.

Fig. 1. *The sociolinguistics of non-native language learning in relation to academic fields.*

notion of communicative competence in a non-native language and the growing legitimization of social and regional non-native varieties of a language.

As stated at the outset, the aim of this book is to convey knowledge about the sociolinguistic aspects of learning a non-native language while foregoing the aura of scientificness created by jargon. However, two abbreviations appear throughout which save space and theoretical complications. These are the terms *L1* and *L2*. An L1 is used to refer to a first language which some call a 'mother tongue' or 'native language' but the latter expressions can cause confusion in cases where, for instance, two languages are learnt simultaneously as in a bilingual family or if the L1 speaker is regarded as an ethnic outsider, e.g. certain children who are neither natives of the community nor learn their mother's tongue. An L2 is sometimes a term for a non-native language that is employed essentially to communicate with other non-natives of the language within one sociopolitical unit, e.g. English in India. It can also describe a second language that is a channel for communicating with 'foreigners' who are usually not members of the L2 speaker's national, ethnic or racial group. In this book the concept L2 is used in the sense of a non-native language, whether it is naturally or formally acquired and whether it is learnt for intra- or extra-group communication. Its fundamental meaning is a language that has not been learnt in early infancy.

The reader will also come across two related terms: *target* and *source* language. A target language clearly implies a far less complete state of linguistic perfection than that suggested by the term L2. A source language does not contain the notions of acquisitional priority and singularity as the term L1. Although target/L1 and source/L2 are used here interchangeably, their theoretical distinctions already highlight the difficulty of describing what is generally taken for granted or ignored: the social environment and conditions in which a non-native language is acquired and applied.

2
The social dynamics of becoming and being bilingual

According to one of the leading sociolinguistic authorities on bilingualism, Fishman (1978, p. 42), monolingualism is a myth fostered by centuries of Euro-Mediterranean linguistic experiences and derived concepts such as universalism, rationalism and liberty. To the contemporary Western mind bilingualism connotes provincialism, oppression and irrationalism.

The subject of bilingualism has only just begun to be treated seriously and above all in America where hyphenated Americans (Norwegian-, Yiddish-, Italian-, Japanese-, etc.) set about explaining and presenting their linguistic and social reality. Most research in the area has dealt with the purely linguistic, political and psychological aspects of bilingualism but the focus of attention is centered more and more on its social dynamics.

Bilingualism

In fact, it is extremely difficult to give a precise definition of bilingualism. There exists extreme heterogeneity in the level of proficiency, nature of acquisition and social background of bilinguals. For a long time they were regarded as anomalies by linguists who felt the natural state of affairs was to grow up speaking one language. The general layman's understanding of the term is a person who has command of two languages and, particularly, someone who has not had to learn the L2 in an institutional setting but is naturally exposed to it in childhood. Linguists, on the other hand, have experienced great difficulty with the concept and have come up with various classifications, some of which have proven to be more confusing than productive due to the problems of knowing exactly how a bilingual mind operates.

The most common distinction which has since been heavily attacked is the separation between *compound* and *coordinate* bilingualism. The coordinate bilingual, contrary to what the term might suggest, is not supposed to be able to coordinate between his languages so that he is bad at translation because he possesses two completely independent and mutually exclusive language systems which do not allow for cross referencing. The compound bilingual, in contrast, has compounded or fused his two language systems, resulting in his constant recourse to the classification of experience in one of the languages which is usually his first acquired one but this must not necessarily be so. It is possible to imagine the case of someone who is so immersed in an L2 environment that he comes to use his L2 as his principal system of reference, even when speaking his L1. The compound bilinguals are the type of bilingual that is most likely created by formal teaching which does not employ the 'direct method' or which continually translates back into the L1. Exactly how valid the psychological aspects of these terms are has been the subject of extensive research. Many studies have, in fact, demonstrated that it is best to consider these two states of bilingualism as extreme points on a continuum if they are relevant at all (see Macnamara 1970; Diller 1970; McCormack 1977).

Other terms which have been coined include the following:
   balanced which describes speakers who are fully competent in both languages. This is more of an ideal than a fact since most bilinguals are more fluent and at ease in one of the two;
   subtractive refers to the situation of a bilingual minority (frequently immigrants) who are dominated by a society speaking a different language which can lead to the deterioration and eventual loss of their L1. This is what the original American concept of the 'melting pot' hoped to achieve in its *a priori* postulate of the minority's adoption of the majority's language and life-style;
   additive is a recent term for two socially useful and prestigious languages which are both viable and are considered complementary and enriching.

In connection with these last two classifications of bilingualism, it is worth noting the results of a recent investigation on two groups of

French Americans in New England, one of whom received all their elementary education in English and the other of whom received a third of their curriculum in French (Lambert 1977). After five years, the children in the partial French schools clearly outperformed those in the all English schools in tests involving various aspects of *English* language skills as well as academic content (mathematics learnt partly via French). "They apparently have been lifted out from the typical low standing on scholastic achievement measures that characterize many" minority linguistic groups in the USA. The French-schooled children had a more positive self-conception of their bilingualism which they perceived as "additive" rather than "subtractive".

From a sociolinguistic standpoint, of course, the fundamental issue is not how does the bilingual mind work but rather who are bilinguals, what are their relationships with natives and each other and how do social attitudes affect linguistic behaviour and learning?

First of all, we have to decide what being bilingual means. Is it someone who is equally proficient in both languages? Is it someone who can speak but not write a language? Is it someone who knows a dead language like Latin or an artificial one like Esperanto?

Well, there is no generally accepted linguistic definition of the term but it does seem to increasingly refer to anyone with more than a beginner's knowledge of a non-native language. Exactly how much more is not certain but open to various interpretations.

Of course, it would be quite idealistic to restrict the term to those who can speak, read and write two languages equally well not only because there still exist languages for which no written forms have been developed but because, as anyone with experience of L2 learning and using knows, it is practically impossible to achieve or maintain an absolutely equal level of competence in two systems simultaneously. Perhaps a realistic conception of a bilingual is someone who can function with a degree of efficiency in two language worlds but nowadays the non-fluent L2 user is considered "a more typical, if not ideal, representative of bilinguals" (Segalowitz & Gatbonton 1977).

Moreover, nearly every bilingual feels that he can express himself in certain situations and at certain periods better in one particular language than the other. For example, he may feel he could court or pray or write an official letter more successfully in one language. But a bilingual is not always simply more 'at home' in one language than another. In the Philippines, for instance, for which the most common estimate of the languages spoken lies at 87, most Filipinos have a definite preference for reading their newspapers and magazines in English, even though English is not the first language they learn and is seldom employed for spoken activities (Sibayan 1975). On the other hand, at the market place or among friends, the local ethnic language is preferred but in formal contexts English is used or possibly Filipino, the second *lingua franca* of the islands. The linguistic choices and their social matrix grows more and more complicated once one starts to investigate it.

Bilinguals who employ their languages in daily life have been found to use them to express particular feelings such as solidarity or social distance. Often one language serves a 'high' function such as the officialdom, media and education while another serves a 'low' function such as shopping, speaking with friends etc. We have already seen this in the Philippine example above. Many other cases could be cited: in a number of South American countries Spanish is the 'high' language while local Indian languages tend to be the 'low'; in Tsarist Russia French was the 'high' and the Russian so low that some of the aristocracy did not even bother to learn it.

The power of knowing a high L2 is revealed in the following anecdote from a Kenyan university student about the contemporary linguistic situation in his country

> My brother was arrested by the police and sent to the chief for making beer without a licence. The chief rejected his plea in our local language that he be forgiven. I then went to the chief's centre. Nobody was allowed to go in and there was a policeman at the door. I spoke English to the policeman and said I wanted to see the chief. I was allowed in. And it was my English during my talk with the chief that secured the release of my brother. (Scotton 1978, p. 733.)

This example shows how languages are linked to notions of status which we discuss below. Actually, the imputed superiority of a specific language over another is a widely observable phenomenon today as in the past and the story of bilingualism can also be interpreted as the story of a power struggle and ensuing repression. Much of what has been written about bilingualism in modern times, especially in America, has concerned itself with the supposed impaired intelligence of bilinguals. This had arisen from erroneous generalizations related to large scale immigration and social dislocation that accompanied it. But such negative evaluation of bilingualism can still be found.

However, there has recently been an upsurge of interest in cultural and linguistic diversity and pluralism, stemming from widely shared liberal attitudes; the American 'melting pot' theory is currently being renounced for the conception of a culturally and linguistically mixed unit such as the Canadian 'mosaic'. Bilingual education is now interpreted increasingly as special provision for children whose linguistic background differs from the dominant ethnic group of a society (see Carey 1974; Fishman 1976; Perren 1976b; Alatis 1978).

Bilingual education

Bilingual education has existed since antiquity. Recent discoveries of bilingual tablets show that children were taught to read and write in Eblaite and Sumerian 5000 years ago. Throughout the Greek empire schools were set up by non-Greek speaking parents for their children to be educated in the language and, similarly, the children of Celtic and Germanic tribes were taught in Latin following the colonization of Europe by the Roman legions. The Roman boys, on the other hand, were expected to learn the language of the much admired Hellenic civilization, Greek (Lewis 1977).

In medieval times, Latin remained the language of the educated across the whole of Europe and the idea of teaching in the native language was regarded as positively shocking and revolutionary when it was suggested by the French jurist, Jean Bodin, in the sixteenth century (Mackey 1978).

However, bilingual education has not been merely limited to the Middle East and Europe. When Europeans emigrated to the New World, provisions had to be made for their children to be educated in their national language. Institutional education in a language other than that of the home has been the norm in certain parts of Africa ever since the first Koranic schools teaching classical Arabic were created at the beginning of the fifteenth century. Colonial education extended the languages to English, French, Portuguese, German, Dutch and Spanish, some of which still continue as the medium of instruction. In Asia, too, education has long been associated with the writing of a script often not available in the L1 of the majority, e.g. Chinese and Devanagari. Millions of children in India and the Soviet Union have received a bilingual education for centuries.

The actual factors which lead to bilingual education are varied. It may occur because of political dominance (as originally was the case for Latin and English) or it may be culturally for its own sake (to appear 'educated') or administrative (where in order to deal with the local government a knowledge of an L2 is required) or economic (to have access to the job market) or military (e.g. the German occupation of France) or historical (the continuation of English in India) or religious (e.g. Latin for Catholics, Classical Arabic for Moslems and Sanskrit for Buddhists) or demographic (as with a *lingua franca* such as English where the likelihood of contact by means of the language is considerable) or ideological (Swahili is not spoken by any portion of the mainland population in Tanzania as an L1 but it was chosen as an official language not only as a nationalistic gesture but also to maximize equality of opportunity). A study by Fishman *et al.* (1977) suggests that further factors may also be involved as found in the promotion of English as world *lingua franca:* urbanization, industrialization or economic development, educational development and world-power affiliation.

It is, of course, very important to distinguish between learning an L2 within an institutional setting and learning it in daily social inter-action. The difference lies in the learner's conception of what he is doing. In the former the language is generally regarded as an 'end' or a product in itself while in the latter it is the 'means' or vehicle to achieve communicative goals, a point which will be taken up in Chapter 3.

Although this distinction has not so far been emphasized, what now follows is mainly orientated towards the institutional acquisition of an L2.

As Fishman (1976, p. 99) states

> . . . students, teachers, parents and politicians alike react differently to a language, in the classroom and outside it, depending on whether or not it is their mother tongue, whether or not it is powerful on the world scene, and whether or not it has long been authoritatively codified and attuned to the needs of modern technology. Presumably bilingual education that involves languages with plus ratings on all of these attributes will have 'easier going' than bilingual education involving language with minor ratings.

While bilingual education has been carried out 'for its own sake' or 'educational effects', there are many other instances where an L2 has been forcibly imposed on a particular linguistic group. For example, in rural areas of Paraguay the language of the community is Guarani, unlike in the urban centres where it is Spanish. Yet these rural children receive their entire education in Spanish and are even forbidden to use their L1 during recreation. This, of course, is due to the unquestioned assumption that Spanish represents a 'higher' culture. When teachers were confronted with the suggestion that Guarani be introduced as a school subject, they were shocked and declared it as a waste of time (Rubin 1968). But one need not travel to South America to see such prejudices at work.

Gaelic was not allowed in Scottish schools until 1918 and then it took another 40 years to become the medium of instruction. Welsh children had to suffer the same enforced bilingualism until the 1953 decision of the education ministry. Interestingly enough, the English language was itself forbidden in the schools of thirteenth-century England where French, the language of the Norman élite at that time, was used together with Latin (Lewis 1965).

Many of the above examples highlight the frequent association between a language and the virtues or vices of its speakers. Their language stands for their social identity. This frequently made link between ethnicity and language can sometimes cause resentment and conflict in learning an L2. It should not be forgotten that the 1976 Soweto riots in South Africa which led to the deaths of blacks and whites were provoked by the government's insistence that the blacks receive their education in Afrikaans, a language related to Dutch spoken by many of the whites.

Language has long worked as a primary symbol of defining affiliation to social groups. Of course, many other symbols also serve to identify ethnic belonging (appearance, food, dress, shelter, artifacts, worship, etc.) but language seems often to carry special significance.

On the other hand, there are many examples where a separate ethnic identity has been maintained without a specially marked ethnic language, e.g. the majority of the present-day English-speaking Irish, who gave up their Celtic language. It is interesting to observe how speakers may sometimes alter their ethnic identities when changing their languages. A recent investigation by Gal (1979) looks at the way Hungarians living in what is now Austria have, due to political and demographic changes, become almost monolingual Germans in three generations and how the younger children feel themselves to be Austrian or, at least, try to convince other Austrians they are.

Another study, this time on French learners of English in Canada (Taylor, Meynard & Rheault 1977) discovered that the learning of an L2 could pose a threat to the ethnic identity of the learners and in such circumstances negatively effect its acquisition. Furthermore, it is worth noting how ethnic groups who have lost their language set about re-acquiring it as a symbol of their ancestry and ethnic pride, for instance the Welsh, the Irish and, more recently, the Maoris in New Zealand.

The sociology of bilingualism

(i) *Attitudes of the learner*

Already in the example just cited concerning the French learners of English in Canada we have glimpsed the influence of social factors on the acquisition of an L2. In fact, a multitude of variables have been found to exist many of which are sociolinguistic in nature.

Robinson (1971) has suggested that one reason why girls seem to perform better than boys in bilingual education is due to the supposed 'femininity' of all linguistic work. This is, however, not applicable to all cultures for, as Preston (1962) notes, in Germany reading and learning are approved masculine activities. In a few studies on bidialectal or bilingual minority groups it has emerged that women tend to be much more conscious of standard norms and prestigious forms in their language than men. For example, in rural Norway it is the women who are first to adopt the new terms into their regional speech (Oftedal 1973) while along the Austro-Hungarian border young women are opting out of the peasant community by refusing to speak the local Hungarian dialect and refusing to marry the men folk who do (Gal 1979). In Greece, women belonging to an originally Albanian-speaking community, have been reported as favouring the L2, Greek, and using the latter more than men (Trudgill & Tzavaras 1977). Similarly, Mexican-American women were found to be more standard in their pronunciation and grammar when they spoke English (Hartford 1976).

Whether these findings have something to do with the view that females have to be much more conformist in their speech (and appearance) than men in order to survive in society as reflected in a female's linguistic hyperformality and hypercorrectness (Lakoff 1975) remains yet to be affirmed.

There exists much work on the relationship between socioeconomic status and achievement in school subjects (see, for example Barker-Lunn 1971) but the effect of social class membership on the development of L2 skills has not yet been fully investigated. There are, however, some indications that a positive attitude towards learning an L2 (where its learning marks the learner as 'educated') is associated with high economic status. This is what Burstall et al. (1974) found for French learning in English primary schools. This is not necessarily the case in every community since the acquisition of an L2 does not automatically coincide with the acquisition of higher status.

Richards (1978a) raises the question of role awareness as a learner in an institutional context as a negative influence on participation and effort in the classroom: "When the teacher is the instigator of communication, asking questions, instructing, demonstrating, etc., the learner may appear to be a nonfluent language user" (p. 100). However, if a peer-teaching situation is allowed whereby the learner assumes an active role, the level of fluency may be much higher.

Doubtlessly related to this active contextual role is the finding of recent studies that complex linguistic skills can be acquired in the absence of formal instruction if regular and favourable social interaction occurs between the learner and members of the target community. Thus, Dittmar & Klein (1977) in their examination of the acquisition of German syntax by Italian and Spanish immigrant workers found that out of the extralinguistic variables: age at time of immigration, duration of stay, contact with Germans at work and contact with Germans at leisure time, it was the latter that proved the most significant for the level of L2 proficiency. Additionally, Obanya (1976) discovered that immigrants to Ibadan learned Yoruba as an L2 because of their need to survive in the L2 environment and mix socially as well as occupationally with Yoruba speakers. This social motivation behind efficient L2 learning led to the implementation of a very successful programme in California to help Vietnamese immigrants. It was based on the belief that an immigrant finding a job in an English-speaking world in which he was accepted by the host group would acquire English skills. The students were given a ten-week language course and then individually placed in occupational settings appropriate to their training and interests.

For d'Anglejan (1978) one of the causes for failure to acquire an L2 is often the lack of contact with target language speakers available to the learner due to restricted social interaction. The classroom cannot provide the same social stimulus and pressure as a realistic context and the learner should be directed to or placed in communication situations with well-disposed natives.

As we have seen with the resurrection of dying languages by ethnic activists, the speaking of a particular language can frequently serve as a symbol of sociocultural identity. This aspect has been taken up by researchers on bilingualism who claim that success in an L2 depends on the attitudes of the learner towards the new group and his personal feelings about ethnic identity. Two basic motives for learning an L2 are suggested by the investigators. One is the desire to be better educated and advance oneself through bilingualism, thereby regarding

L2 acquisition as *instrumental* or an object that is not necessarily valuable in itself but as a passport to prestige and success. The other motivation is *integrative* and relates to the learner's wish to learn more about the other cultural community "as if he desired to become a potential member of the other group" (Lambert *et al.*, 1972). Findings which take intelligence and aptitude into account show that students with an integrative orientation were markedly more proficient in L2 learning than those instrumentally orientated (Gardner & Lambert 1959; Gardner 1960; Anisfeld & Lambert 1961).

The implications of this theory for the classroom are self-evident. If L2 learners are going to learn better if they identify more with the target community, then the teacher should be wise enough to encourage any such contact through pen friends, exchange visits, cultural events and so on. Furthermore, where students are generally attracted to L2 learning by the thought of being able to communicate with native speakers, this should be exploited to the maximum since Lambert's work has shown that the motivational orientation towards the target language group helps as much as general linguistic ability. Gardner & Lambert (1972) actually suggest the technique of 'public defence' whereby the L2 learner has to defend rhetorically the target community in the classroom. Research has apparently shown this to have a favourable impact on students' perceptions and stereotypes of the target group.

The work on the social dynamics of learner motivation is, of course, related to the attitudes of students towards the L2 and its speakers. In an investigation into the factors affecting the successful learning of Hebrew in Canada, Lambert (1967) found that the extent of a Jewish student's desire to become acculturated in the Jewish tradition and culture provided a sensitive indicator of progress in Hebrew. Further support for the validity of integrative motivation comes from a longitudinal study on English schoolchildren learning French which compared the early attitudes and achievements of one group before and after a visit to France with that of another group who did not travel to the target community. Those who had come into contact with the L2 environment had reached a level of achievement superior to the rest of the experimental sample and expressed a markedly stronger preference for the spoken aspects of learning the language.

There also exists a growing body of research which indicates that L2 learners are neither wholly integrative nor instrumental in their motivation but that these just represent the extreme points on a scale of attitudes. Moreover, those who proposed the theory have now distanced themselves considerably from it.

Nevertheless, it is interesting to link the theory with another investigation carried out at a London grammar school during the Second World War which discovered that until France fell the children felt German much more difficult than French but then found French also increasingly difficult and when, at the height of Western friendship with the Soviet Union, Russian was introduced it became the favourite language and was considered by the children as much easier than French and especially German (Adler 1977). Of course, from a purely structural stance German is the closest out of these three languages to English, belonging as it does in the same language family.

In cases where the L2 is stereotypically associated with speakers of a group with relatively low socioeconomic status the amount of integrative motivation is understandably not particularly strong among general learners. In the USA, for example, the teaching of certain foreign languages is frequently associated with minority ethnic groups such as the French in Vermont and New Hampshire or the Spanish in California and New Mexico. The social attitudes towards the local speakers of these second languages makes the teachers' task difficult. They have, first of all, to impart a positive attitude towards the local L2-speaking community in order to overcome the students' unwillingness to identify and thereby motivate themselves for L2 learning. Obviously, a sympathetic presentation of the target community should be a fundamental task of all L2 teaching but these circumstances present a special challenge.

From this one can see how languages are often rated according to the prestige of their speakers at a particular moment and place. In Israel where many different language groups have come together, informants were presented with a list of the major languages spoken in their country and were asked to indicate beside each language whether it had 'very high', 'high', 'medium', 'low' or 'very low' status in their eyes. Their agreement in the matter was considerable: (1) Hebrew/English, (3) French, (4) Russian, (5) German, (6) Arabic, (7) Spanish, (8) Yiddish, (9) Polish, (10) Ladino/Hungarian, (12) Turkish, (13) Rumanian, (14) Persian. When another group of informants from all over Israel were asked to answer the same questions, their ratings closely corresponded to the original responses. Moreover, when the first group were presented with a list of settlers from various countries (who used the languages on the list) there was a high correlation between the prestige of the languages and the prestige of the settler groups who spoke them (Herman 1961).

Much contemporary sociolinguistic research has shown that all language groups have covert stereotypical perceptions and reactions to those outside themselves. These, of course, are significant for the L2 learning process. Thus, Lambert *et al.* (1972) discovered that American students learning French held negative stereotypes of the target community considering its members to be cruel, dishonest and less reliable. This was related to the presence of a local French community in the students' area.

In fact, one psychologist maintains that "what acts as the language learning block . . . is precisely the awareness of differences rather than an emphasis on an underlying similarity" (Rosansky 1973). In connection with these ideas is the suggestion formulated on the basis of the resemblance between pidgin languages and the pidgin-like forms produced in the early stages of L2 learning that the extent and persistence of the pidginized forms in L2 learners' speech depends on his "social and psychological distances from the speakers of the target language" (Schumann (1978a). It is worth noting that when pidgins start carrying integrative and expressive functions, e.g. when pidgin speakers marry a speaker of the target language, the language becomes more complicated and expands into a creole (Smith 1972). In other words, if a speaker seeks realizable integration with another community speaking a different langauge, his L2 learning will be much more elaborate and less pidginish than if he merely uses it as an instrument. Richards (1972) views the close approximation to L2 norms as depending on the degree of interaction and integration that the learner can achieve in the target community. He illustrates his hypothesis with the fate of German and Puerto Rican immigrants to America. German immigrants to Texas were not poor and did not live in ghettos. They suffered no handicap and learnt English easily and well; although a certain amount of German remained in their English it resulted in no obvious social discrimination. The Puerto Ricans in New York had limited access to social and economic channels and their variety of English has become fixed and socially stigmatized; they see themselves locked into a society where their chances (and resulting motivation) to learn English are low. As in many bilingual communities, these non-standard L2 varieties also serve as a marker of ethnic identity so that speaking the L2 in a standard fashion has come to be regarded as 'traitorous' and may be compared with the attitudes of certain non-standard native speakers.

Indirect evidence for the *pidginization hypothesis* is plentiful. In the New Amazon, for example, missionaries have insisted on using only Spanish with the Columbian Indians which has instead reinforced the maintenance of indigenous languages (Sorensen 1967). Lambert & Tucker (1972) also found that a group of English-Canadian children learning French through an 'immersion' programme (where they attended an all French school) began to re-introduce English-like pronunciation into their French after a few years because they felt that the acquisition of an outgroup language diminished their loyalty to their own ethnic group. Perhaps the more positive attitude of girls to language learning mentioned above (Burstall 1978) is also connected to this. Could it be that girls are socialized in such a way that they find it easier to muster the 'empathic capacity', the ability to identify with other people's feelings and appreciate details of their behaviour, which is such a significant factor for fluency in an L2 (Taylor *et al*. 1971)?

Other studies have shown that after the age of ten there is a decline in favourable attitudes towards members of external ethnic groups accompanied by an accelerated development of the stereotyping process and an increase in loyalty towards the peer group (Lambert & Klineberg 1967; Allport 1954). Furthermore, psychologists (Inhelder &

Piaget 1958) have stated that before 12 years a child manifests "an astonishing degree of ignorance and a striking insensitivity, not only to his own designation . . . as Swiss, French, etc. . . . but towards his own country as a collective reality" (p. 348). This has led some to link the generally recorded poor performance of L2 learners from adolescence onwards in comparison to L2 learners before puberty with an increased awareness of ethnic identity (Hakuta 1975).

The acquisition of a native-like command of an L2 can, to various degrees, be seen as involving an encroachment on one's sense of ethnic identity. There is some evidence which suggests that as a person begins to master a second language, he or she develops feelings of alienation or *anomie* (Lambert *et al.* 1963). In such instances the learner hovers between two ethnic groups, neither fully identifying with one nor the other. Although this state seems to be more associated with minority group members learning an L2 within the environment of a dominant L2 community, it does seem to have some general applicability.

This is demonstrated by the case of a nine year old Punjabi boy living in the UK who had been repeatedly placed in a remand home for stealing (Chapman 1976). Whenever he was sent home, he stole again with the declared intention of returning to the remand home. He refused to communicate with a Punjabi interpreter saying that he did not like the language and pretending to only understand English even though his L2 knowledge was inadequate. He was the youngest of four children who all spoke English (his two elder brothers much better than he and his younger sisters). His parents could speak no English and were incapable of understanding the problem.

This section clearly shows that language does not exist in a social vacuum but is firmly fixed in the way of life, beliefs, practices and value system of its speakers. It is, above all, man's instrument of social integration. As we have seen, problems may arise when the social integration which should follow from language learning is not desired by the learner or the target community. However, teaching an L2 without its ethnic component does not appear to offer many advantages since the learner's satisfaction and success have been found to be higher when the language represents a particular ethnic group (its culture, history, literature, identity).

Not all the social factors affecting L2 learning have been entered into here but the learner's attitudes have been concentrated upon. In the following chapters we shall examine the indispensability of a familiarity with the cultural background of an L2 for satisfactory understanding and communication, the negative consequences of institutional concentration on language as form rather than as the transmission of meaning and the counterproductivity of traditional L2 teaching resulting from misguided norms of classroom interaction and a basic hostility towards error.

(ii) *Attitudes of the target community*

Whatever the type and degree of bilingualism, in many situations the L2 speaker's main concern is how he will be received by the target community—which is as often as not the very reason for his learning their language.

Strangely enough, it is generally not his grammar or his command of educated vocabulary that seems to bear the most weight for the majority of the L2 community in spite of the fact that this is what L2 teachers devote most of their class time to. In fact, studies have shown that the more native-like the L2 speaker's accent sounds the more favourably regarded he will be by the L2 community (Giles 1978). Of course, the general level of proficiency attained is also taken by the target community as a gauge of the learner's degree of commitment to it (Genesee and Holobrow 1978).

Among various historical, economic and cultural factors, the ability to relate to and accept non-ethnic members seems to depend in personal encounters on the extent to which the non-ethnic member is prepared to make linguistic concessions towards the outgroup. Generally, ethnic groups feel that an outsider who tries hard to sound like them is expressing a favourable disposition towards and approval of them. In connection with this, it has been discovered that children speaking in an L2 receive greater tolerance than their adult counterparts from the target community (Herman 1961; Hatch 1980). This is obviously related to the fact that native children lack a high degree of fluency in the language. In fact, research has clearly indicated that members of immigrant groups, desiring another ethnic group's approval and admittance to integrate, shift their L2 speech towards them. It is well known that certain immigrant group members do their best to eradicate any traces of their L1 accent, not only to avoid discrimination but also to prove their commitment to what the L2 symbolizes (Ryan & Carranza 1977). Of course, this is also closely linked to the social connotations of the L1 deriving from attitudes towards its speakers held in the target community. A further aspect of this is the humour enjoyed in the target. community when hearing authentic or imitated L2 accents, the function of which has been interpreted as simultaneously boosting ingroup solidarity and deprecating the outgroup (Bourhis *et al.* 1977).

According to Williams (1970), reactions to speech can be linked to a set of beliefs providing stereotypes which influence the listener's behaviour and thereby become social reality. This can be reflected in the way the L2 speaker is addressed by the target community. For instance, it has been observed that in West Germany northern Europeans, Americans or Australians tend to be addressed in public exchanges with the polite plural 'you' (SIE) as comparable Germans but southern Europeans and Africans with the less polite singular form (DU) (Clyne 1975). Furthermore, sometimes pidginized forms especially reserved for marking or making fun of the foreigness of a speaker, e.g. *today he no come* are actually used by natives to L2 speakers perceived to have lower socioeconomic status (Valdman, 1977a).

It is, however, quite wrong to believe that native-like oral proficiency will guarantee total acceptance by the target community. In fact, the community may well frown upon the too native-like mastering of an L2 or find it threatening. For example, an Englishman fluent in French imagined that he would be welcomed by French-speaking Quebeckers (Gannon 1980). Instead, each attempt he made to communicate in French was frustrated by either a response in English or, which he found worse, by an apparent inability on the part of his listener to understand him. He was later informed by a Francophone friend that his French was 'too good' and created suspicion so that if he wished to communicate in the French-speaking parts of Quebec he should also use English as the occasion demanded.

Another Englishmen who learnt to speak fluent Japanese at the turn of the century commented on the target community's reaction in the following manner:

> seeing that you speak Japanese, they will wag their heads and smile condescendingly, and admit to each other that you are really quite intelligent much as we might do in the presence of the learned pig or an ape of somewhat unusual attainments. (Chamberlain 1904, p. 382.)

An American-born Professor of Japanese, Miller (1977), writes that if a foreigner speaks halting Japanese he will be praised and flattered but fluency shunned since it "provides overt evidence of large scale, long-lasting and extremely serious invasion of sociolinguistic territorial interests". A leading Japanese sociolinguist, Suzuki (1975), has tried to show how strong the Japanese belief that "foreigners ought not, properly, to understand Japanese at all", although he adds that this applies mainly to Caucasian L2 speakers. Koreans, Chinese, south-east Asians and Indians are exempt from these expectations and their fluency is taken for granted. Jordan (1980) claims that a fluent Japanese-speaking American may sometimes evoke discomfort and unpleasantness for the Japanese: "How often the statement is made that a Western face and colloquial Japanese are in conflict. This reaction can be explained at least in part by surprise that results from lack of experience" (p. 228).

However, this reaction is not a purely Japanese phenomenon. The Englishman's reaction to a too perfect pronunciation in an L2 speaker has been described as that of a host who sees an uninvited guest making free with his possessions (Christophersen 1973). This anti-integrative, ethnocentric attitude towards L2 speakers has been called "communalist" by Mazrui (1975) in contrast to "ecumenical" linguistic communities which transcend the boundaries of racial or ethnic definition. Mazrui writes that British imperialists were so possessive about the English language that they insisted on speaking Swahili to Africans who knew fluent English, even though they both spoke inadequate Swahili: "it became a point of honour sometimes to maintain the linguistic distance between the Englishman and his coloured subject as a way of maintaining the social distance between them."

Among "ecumenical" communities can be included the French, the Arabs and, to some extent, Americans. According to Lawrence (1940) the French feel complimented when foreigners imitate them unlike the English who take it as a parody. Christophersen (1973) states that this is also true of Americans who direct their mistrust not to those who can speak their language but to those who cannot. Even though one would expect the Arabic community to be extra-communalist as the English one has tended to be, Arabs define 'Arabhood' as an Arabic speaker whether native or not, who is Muslim; its central defining characteristics are linguistic and religious not pigmentational.

Positive attitudes within the target community towards bilingual speakers may be fostered by political factors such as have already been outlined above. For example, in the Soviet Union which promotes the ideologically motivated 'merging of the peoples' (russification) and the eradication of "archaic nationalistic characteristics and traditions which are inconsistent with the manifestation of the communist epoch" (Lewis 1972, p. 316) non-ethnic Russians who show a preference for the Russian language (as an L2) are favourably regarded by the target society.

In an experiment conducted with French and English Canadian listeners Taylor (1971) has shown how an L2 can be used as a symbol for inducing cooperation or conflict: one of three versions of the same message recorded in French-Canadian English, French and in partial English and French were presented to English Canadians who were asked to evaluate the speaker and tape record their own response. The more the French-Canadians adjusted to the language of the target (English) community, the more he was judged favourably, especially in terms of his "considerateness" and his efforts "to budge the cultural gap". When the French Canadian spoke in French, the English Canadians responded with a message back in English; when the speaker used a mixture of the two languages, he received the same in return; finally, when the French Canadian was seen to make an attempt to 'converge' with English, the English Canadians tried to reciprocate by speaking French. Not only do these findings demonstrate the significance of bilingualism in interethnic relations but they also point to the positive symbolic value that the use of an L2 can assume in particular target communities as a gesture of solidarity.

(iii) *Attitudes of the learner's community*

Another study of the lingusitic situation in Canada illustrates the same attitude from another angle. The competence with which an adult speaks a non-native language was shown to influence the social and political attitudes attributed to him by others of his native community. Thus, French Canadians who were very competent in English were regarded to be pro-English and undesirable as group leaders by fellow French-Canadians (Gatbonton-Segalowitz 1975). This negative evaluation of a competent L2 speaker as a kind of ethnic 'traitor' is by no means uncommon.

Forster (1970), for instance, tells of the reaction of a medical colleague who heard his English-born godfather speaking fluent French to a French visitor in England, which was: "Well, Williams, I have always thought that you were a profoundly immoral man, and now I am convinced of it."

Similarly, novelists in India who write in English are impugned for using a foreign language and their incapacity to express the inwardness of Indianness and for selling their artistic conscience for financial rewards (Kachru 1978). Of course, when a community is concerned about the maintenance of its ethnic tongue because it is being threatened by another language, then the learning and using of an L2 by its members may justifiably be considered as betrayal. In such situations we again see language serving as an ethnic boundary marker to be defended. Linguistic renegades received perjorative labels for betraying the ingroup's integrity and self respect (Khleif 1979). For example, young Albanian-Greeks call those who attempt to change a conversation from Albanian into Greek (and are members of their native community) "a clever boy" or "queer" (Trudgill & Tzavaras 1977). However, younger Albanian-Greek bilinguals hesitate to speak their

L1 in public and ask their parents not to. This ambiguity is related to the Greeks' stereotypic association of Albanian speakers as 'backward' and 'rural'.

This avoidance of using an L1 brings us to the situation where speakers deny knowledge of their L2. In New York, women of Puerto Rican origin deny knowledge of English because their community holds the belief that a 'good' woman is helpless and belongs in the home—English is learnt on the street (Padilla 1958).

Related to this is the denial of one's native language. Thus, certain young Australian speakers of the aborigine language, Guugu Yimidhirr, deprecate their L1 in the presence of non-aborigines and claim to know little of it (Haviland 1979). This is the tragic result of associating their L1 with their undervalued and persecuted ethnicity and culture so that their denial of its knowledge is an attempt to prove and affirm their new L2 identity.

Schumann (1976) describes the difference between "good" and "bad" L2 learning situations as dependent upon the degree of social distance perceived to exist by the learners between themselves and the target community, although it is, of course, a mutual affair. If the target community is dominated or subordinated by the learners' community in a political, cultural or technical way, then the learners are not likely to be interested in learning the target community's language. A class of interpreters will usually evolve to mediate between the two such as is the case of Americans in Saudi Arabia. In cases where a bilingual community is found, the L2 speaker faces a number of options, depending on the degree of cultural similarity between the two communities: assimilation, acculturation or preservation. If assimilation is chosen, the L2 speakers give up their native life-style and values and adopt those of the target community. If acculturation is opted for, they merely adapt their life-styles and values but maintain their own cultural patterns for ingroup relations. When they completely reject the life-style and values of the target community, they set up an 'enclosure' framework (separate institutions, associations, endogamy, for example) in order to achieve preservation. Therefore, it follows that L2 learning is most successful when assimilation strategies have been chosen. Another factor is the intended length of residence in the target community which can determine whether the reduction of social distance will be desired through extensive, long-term contacts, in turn affecting L2 acquisition.

In fact, all these social variables often occur together and exist on a continuum. For instance, the L2 learning situation of Red Indians in America is "bad" because the learners' community considers itself and is considered subordinate to the target community; they wish to preserve their own cultural patterns and have been forced to live on reservations fostering their internal cohesiveness and social distance towards the Anglo community.

American-Jewish immigrants to Israel, on the other hand, present a different story. They consider themselves politically, economically, technically and culturally equal to Israelis (a view which is reciprocated by the target community) and seek long-term residence so that all these factors promote social proximity and facilitate L2 acquisition.

Partly related to this notion of social distance and its consequences on language learning is the significance of parental support and parental evaluation of the relevance of the L2 for their children's employment (Gardner & Santos 1970; Hakuta 1975). In Kenya, for example, where Swahili is taught as an L2 but English extensively used by the upper class, Scotton (1978) found that at a school attended by the children of high-ranking Kenyan officials very few passed the examinations in Swahili. Her only explanation for this is the low evaluation of Swahili by pupils and their parents—Swahili has not been made an examination subject necessary for entry into secondary school.

Gulutsan (1974) describes the case of a Canadian boy who first hated learning French as an L2 and who lived in a working class neighbourhood where it was regarded as 'useless' and 'impractical' by the community and, especially, his peers. The environment did not enhance or justify his L2 learning. His parents, however, encouraged him to continue while his other schoolmates gave up learning the language for technical studies. Just as he was about to abandon with French completely, his family moved to another district of the town. The school offered no facilities for vocational training and instead stressed academic work. In this school he did not feel he was missing out on anything during the French lessons since everyone had to study it. The children also seemed to like the subject and the parents of his few friends often spoke an L2 and at times travelled extensively. The school also sent groups of children to Quebec during the summer. The boy's attitude towards L2 learning, of course totally altered. What the case illustrates is how important peer group influence, the school's orientation and the native community's values are. The families in the lowest economic strata of the town expressed strong disinterest and remarked on the uselessness of L2 learning while the highest economic strata favoured it.

Different from attitudes which see the L2 as a step to social advance-ment or a clue to sophistication is the view which regards L2 learning as something perfectly natural and far from spectacular. It might come as a surprise but this perspective is common among so-called 'primitive' peoples for whom the knowledge of two or more quite unrelated languages is taken for granted. This is because they do not share the widespread western belief in the uniqueness and particularism of a language. Here are two exotic examples which, in turn, possibly question our usual conception of language. In the north-west Amazon, a wife has to come from another tribe, which invariably means another linguistic community (of which they are several in the area) resulting in the everyday fact that most children remain bilingual or trilingual in speech until adolescence as well as having to learn a local *lingua franca*. Moreover, in adulthood they may acquire more languages (Sorensen 1967).

A similar state of affairs where it is considered normal for community members to carry on daily conversations in two or three languages is the sub-arctic region of Alaska. Here the two languages occurring in a single conversation may be either French, English, Chipewyan or Cree (Scollon 1979). What is significant here is that the people of the community realize and accept that they are an ethnic conglomeration. In both the Amazonian and Alaskan examples none of the languages have yet come to exclusively symbolize ethnicity.

Sometimes the attitudes towards the L2 are not at all clear cut. Lewis (1978) has described the ambivalence towards Welsh as an L2 by bilingual

Welsh-English speakers. These simultaneously held beliefs such as "I should not like English to take over from Welsh" and "English will take you further than Welsh" reflect the approval of Welsh in principle but the reluctance to act on that approval so that Welsh is not encouraged by parents except for their children to use with grandparents.

In connection with the fears of the death of their L1, minority bilingual communities over the last few years have increasingly voiced their demands for their children to be educated bilingually. This may be because the parents are worried that they will no longer be able to ensure total communication with their children (generation and culture gaps) or, feeling insecure in the dominant target community, wish to maximize their group's channels of opportunity which can be endangered by the shift away from the L1. Or, as we have stated above, they wish to maintain their L1 as a symbol of their ethnic heritage.

From what we have presented in this section it should be obvious that the attitudes of the learner's native community towards the acquisition of an L2 can significantly determine the learner's motivation and success.

A cautionary tale

Much of what has so far been said could be summed up simply as prejudice. As we have seen, there is prejudice against L2 speakers who speak badly and prejudice against those who speak too perfectly. The L2 learners may themselves regard the target community with antipathy because of the latter's socioeconomic status, sociocultural background or even its apparent rejection of them. In America, the word 'bilingual' has become a polite euphemism for members of a deprived linguistic minority and bears a negative connotation (Macnamara 1970). Thus, the state of bilingualism itself may be a subject for prejudice, although such an attitude seems to be receding among young people who increasingly favour linguistic and cultural plurality.

It seems that to overcome all prejudices a bilingual has to provide considerable linguistic proof of his loyalty to either of the communities whose languages he speaks. However, in order to receive a favourable reaction in the target community, it is not only necessary to adopt L2 grammatical and phonetic patterns but also facial expressions, gestures and even outlooks. The L2 teacher is thus involved in something much more than the mere transmission of linguistic information. He is producing would-be natives.

Much space has been devoted here to the question of acceptance and rejection on the basis of a language. Although it is, of course, extremely important for immigrants desirous of integration to be able to function adequately in an L2, it should be pointed out that linguistic perfection is not the most absolutely essential criterion for cross-lingual communication for as the celebrated anthropologist, Margaret Mead (1964), has so often discovered, something more is required in such contact situations:

> I am not a good mimic and I have worked now in many different cultures. I am a very poor speaker of any language . . . when I work in a native society I know what people are talking about and I treat it seriously and I respect them, and this in itself establishes a great deal more rapport, very often, than the correct accent. I have worked with other field workers who were far, far better linguists than I, and the natives kept on saying they couldn't speak the language, although they said I could . . . you see, we don't need to teach people to speak like natives, you need to make the other people believe they can, so they can talk to them, and then they learn (p. 189).

These comments by Mead not only emphasize the necessity for a supra-ethnic sensitivity for the target community but it also throws into question the need for sophisticated L2 skills for daily communication. Some believe it would be better if we all spoke one language but ethnicity is an inevitable attribute of human organization. New ethnicities arise, old ones alter, others disappear. The ethnicity becomes more reasonable and tractable when recognized but grows stronger when denied or oppressed (Fishman 1976). The supposedly supra-ethnic languages of wider communication such as English are not free of ethnicity. Mazrui (1975) argues that the universalization of English must lead to its de-Anglicization and de-racialization but seriously questions its present ability to "bear the experiences of a black man".

If a de-ethnicized, world-wide *lingua anglica* seems unrealistic, an alternative could be the preparation and education of all speakers to communicate with those who speak their language as an L2. Tucker (1977), for instance, wonders whether American society is ready to receive American bilinguals. He sees the central problem as lying with the dominant (target) community and not the minority (learner). But it is sociologically unlikely that a dominant group would, even through education, renounce applying its long upheld and often inexplicit perceptions of identity in order to successfully integrate non-ethnic L2 speakers. Or, in the words of an anthropologist, Sumner (1906), "stateways cannot change folkways". .

The task of everyone involved in interlingual, intercultural and inter-ethnic encounters, therefore, is to prove the value of diversity, the richness in difference and the something that the monolingual speaker of a language of wider communication can only rarely sense: "that this human world might become a network of interlocking and simultaneous memberships and loyalties" (Fishman 1976, p. 9).

3
The cultural dimension of a
non-native language and its study

The previous chapter revealed how, among a host of other factors, success in L2 learning can depend on a willingness to understand and follow the ways of the target community. It also highlighted the 'natural' ethnocentricism of groups to perceive themselves as more favourable and psychologically distinct from others (Tajfel 1978). Moreover, language is often taken as evidence for this distinctiveness. Different languages and different ways of living are frequently believed to go hand in hand. Thus, it is not uncommon to hear statements such as "German is a logical language" or "The English are democratic because they only have one form for 'you'". These kinds of comments are, of course, related to the prevalent conception of language as a reflection of culture.

First of all, one ought to be clear about what is meant by culture here. It does not refer to theatre going or the possession of a refrigerator. It refers to something rather abstract and difficult to grasp immediately as one is part of it. It involves the implicit norms and conventions of a society, its methods of 'going about doing things', its historically transmitted but also adaptive and creative ethos, its symbols and its organization of experience. Another way of understanding culture is to conceive of it as knowledge:

> As I see it, a society's culture consists of whatever it is one has to know or believe in order to operate in a manner acceptable to its members, and do so in any role that they accept for anyone of themselves. (Goodenough 1957, p. 167.)

Naturally, such knowledge is rarely conscious let alone verbalized for this would, in part, lead to the breaking of its spell. Now why is cultural knowledge significant for the L2 learner? In much of L2 teaching today cultural knowledge tends to be equated with classical literature and, although the importance of the crucial dependency of linguistic skills on cultural premises is fashionably proclaimed, much has yet to be achieved to really impart the cultural dimension of a non-native language. However, the movement towards the teaching of communicative competence (to be discussed in the next chapter) constitutes a step in this direction.

The lack of concern about teaching culture probably has something to do with the fact that no one has as yet been able to adequately describe the workings of a cultural system. It would seem that we are partly prevented from explaining it due to culture's inbuilt tabooing of any such explication. But does this mean we should not bother?

In fact, some believe we should not but I am among those who feel we must. Exactly why the effort is worth making is patent when one realizes how inextricably intertwined language is with culture.

Linguistic and cultural relativity

The relationship between language and culture has long been an area of study within anthropology, one of the parent disciplines of socio-linguistics. To understand this relationship, it is necessary to tackle the anthropological concept of *cultural relativism* which gained currency at the beginning of this century in the discipline. According to this concept, each culture presented a unique, coherent system that shaped and moulded individuality in its own special way. The American theories about cultural relativism were really an argument against contemporary ideas about racial and biological determinism. However, it proved very influential and over the years was applied to language, which was seen as playing a central role in cultural life.

(i) *The Sapir–Whorf hypothesis*

The most extreme formulation of linguistic determinism is that of Benjamin Lee Whorf (1956) who claimed that different languages embody different models of the world. By contrasting what he called "Standard Average European" with certain Red Indian languages,

Whorf tried to illustrate how differing concepts of matter, time and space were represented in the grammatical structure of these languages. This thesis still provokes much controversy due to its apparent untestability; both the concepts involved, grammar and world-view, are mentalistic and, therefore, particularly difficult to verify. Whorf argued that language actually determines a speaker's perception of reality and in this way perpetuates cultural differences. To give an example, he associated the absence of tense forms in the Red Indian language, Hopi, with an outlook on life that was "timeless" and "ahistorical".

Although the philosophical dynamics of grammar are still a mystery, it is well known that in some languages social forces impinge on the pronominal and verbal systems. In Japanese, for instance, the subject can often be deleted and an honorific form employed. For the one verb 'to give' there are several different forms available: *ageru, kudasaru, yaru, kureru* and the right choice depends on the particular configuration of contextual relationships perceived to hold between (1) the giver and receiver, (2) between the speaker and giver and receiver, or (3) between the hearer, giver and receiver. Traditional grammar approaches are not able to account for this interconnection between a social 'reality' and a linguistic system because they try to explain language without referring to anything outside it (Loveday 1982a). Another example is the existence of a 'mother-in-law' style in certain aboriginal languages of Australia, which require two completely different forms for their entire vocabularies, one employed when taboo relatives such as mothers-in-law are within hearing distance and the other for when they are not (Dixon 1972). These few illustrations prove how part of a perceived social world enters into the structure of a language.

Whorf's mentor was the famous anthropologist, Edward Sapir, who had often alluded to the close relationship between the vocabulary or lexicon of a language and the cultural environment in which it evolves and in which it is embedded:

> The understanding of a simple poem, for instance, involves not merely an understanding of the single words in their average significance, but a full comprehension of the whole life of the community as it is mirrored in

the words, or as it is suggested by their overtones. Even comparatively simple acts of perception are very much more at the mercy of the social patterns called words than we might suppose. . . . We see and hear and otherwise experience very largely as we do because the language habits of our community predispose certain choices of interpretation. (Sapir, 1949b, p. 162.)

Of course, the culturally determined system of perception encoded into our language is essentially a historical product. The system was developed long before the speaker's time and can often be regarded merely as the creation of convention and tradition. Nevertheless, Sapir's comments are partly illustrated in a study of the different associations provoked by the same word in Japanese-American bilinguals (Ervin-Tripp 1968, p. 203) (Fig. 2).

Fig. 2. Japanese English bilinguals' responses to stimulus words.

"Moon"		"New Year's Day"	
Japanese	English	Japanese	English
moon viewing	sky	pine decoration	new clothes
zebra grass	rocket	rice cake	party
full-moon	cloud	feast	holiday
cloud		kimono	
		seven-spring herbs	
		shuttle cock	
		footwarmer	
		friends	

L2 learners have to imbibe, as the L1 speakers above have done, the individual tang of the words from the customary situations in which they occur. They have to assimilate possibly varying cultural connotations of linguistic items. The concept of a beautiful woman might conjure up to a desert Arab male sensuous images of a 250 pound lovely, while to an American male, lexically equivalent words in English might connote a slim, but disproportionately big-busted creature.

There is a body of research that is very concerned with these aspects of language, which are not made explicit but are intended to be accessible to the hearer. It examines the assumptions, beliefs and attitudes held by a speaker about his world which underlie and render his message intelligible. This covert information technically goes under the name of *presuppositions* (Lyons 1977).

Every utterance contains presuppositions of some kind and many are culturally relative. In fact, grammaticality can depend on them. For example, the phrase "There's a tiger in that cave who eats children" is anomalous while "I have a cat who eats chocolate" might not be if the speaker associates human features with a domesticated cat, i.e. the conventional presupposition of the relative pronoun 'who' occurring with a being that in English culture cannot possess human qualities is violated in the first sentence with the tiger but not adhered to in the second. Obviously, native speakers and perhaps teachers of their own language take such culturally determined presuppositions for granted and often leave them for L2 learners to incomprehend (Loveday 1981a).

What should have emerged from above is how language and culture are interdependent and how language can express and reflect a particular 'reality'. Whether it actually forces a version of reality on us is a perplexing question which is best left to philosophers and psychologists. It would be rather incredible to imagine that speakers are unable to perceive phenomena that have not been formalized in their language. After all, varied and conflicting philosophies, religions, scientific theories, and *Weltanschauungen* have all been capable of expression in the same language, e.g. English, Arabic, Russian and Chinese and many more, which proves that there is nothing inherent to the linguistic system which constrains cognition. Furthermore, the development of mathematical notation and the terminology of science may be seen as an attempt to overcome the limited 'reality' of natural language. It is important to realize that discoveries and inventions of western science have not been expressed in western languages at all but in a special supra- and interlinguistic scientific symbolism (Haugen 1977). Additionally in this connection, everything may be translated from one language into another if no limitation of space is imposed and full explanation and circumlocution is allowed.

However, in a superficial sense (and with a superficial speaker too!)

language may be said to provide a ready-made model of experience but to what degree speakers allow themselves to be limited by the linguistic model is by no means established.

(ii) *Classificatory systems*

Most current research on the embodiment of a culturally related world view in language concentrates on the categories developed in a language for perceiving and ordering 'what's out there'. Thus, the vocabulary employed to categorize phenomena such as plants, kinship, disease and animals are taken as a guide to the 'reality' of the community. Our linguistic and cultural classificatory systems may not necessarily correspond closely to that of modern science. In fact, it is a tenet of this kind of research that categories cannot be equated cross-culturally.

The Kwaio of the Solomon Islands label fresh water as one substance, salt water as another; they place birds and bats in one category in contrast to moths, butterflies and the like; they class fish and marine mammals together; and they label with a single term colours westerners call blue and black (Keesing & Keesing 1971). Is this primitive science or simply a different set of contrasts to carve up the world of meaning with?

In many east Asian, American, Indian and Oceanic languages there exists the usually obligatory use of a linguistic form known as "numeral classifiers" so that when something is counted, it is classified according to a particular quality such as shape, class-membership, state or process. In Japanese. for example, when counting a hanging scroll it is necessary to add the suffix *-fuku* after the number and when counting a framed, non-hanging calligraphy *-ka*. Something liquid has a different numeral classifier from something solid as does something strung from something 'lumped' or something stretched over a frame. What is significant here is how these features have been selected out by members of a culture from the multitude of phenomena in the world and encoded into the grammar of a language.

Another aspect of such classificatory systems is that its users tend to consider them "literally exhaustive" and "objectively correct"

(Fishman 1971c) and one investigator, Kantrowitz (1967) has demonstrated how socioculturally particularistic classifications can even be constraining (in the Whorfian sense just outlined). In this study the vocabulary of race relations between white and negro prison inmates in America where some negroes call a white who does not discriminate *a free thinker* but whites call such a person a *nigger lover;* in turn, a negro who is not aggressive towards whites is called a *free thinker* by the whites but a *devil lover* by blacks. Here language does not only reflect social beliefs and values; it also helps to reinforce them.

An insightful illustration of how the existence or absence of linguistic categories can influence perception and behavior is provided by Maw (1971), who comments on the colours by Ugandan children in her painting lessons. In the children's first language (Luganda) 'blue' does not exist as a colour category and has been borrowed from the English. When painting, the children "seemed to use the colour as a general substitute to fill up spaces (rather as English children sometimes use brown) and to replace any colour they had not got. . . . Blue did not seem to exist in its own right. So one day, as a preliminary to their painting someone resting on a hot day, I asked the class what colour the sky was. After a long silence someone said red. A number of the class agreed, and I said, "Well, it could be red sometimes at sunset, for example. But what else could it be?' Someone else said white and got more agreement. I said it could be white when it was very cloudy, but this day was supposed to be hot. What other colour could it be? No further suggestions came, so I took them outside to look. All chorused 'blue' in tones of relief and revelation" (pp. 222–223).

Although linguistics was long interested in the question of sociolinguistic relativity, when transformational grammar established itself in the mid-sixties under Chomsky (1965), relativity became interpreted as a "negation of the psychic unity of mankind" (Mathiot, 1979a) and was abandoned in favour of the universal approach to language. Linguistics had already been drifting away from the cultural dimensions of language ever since the 1930s when Bloomfield's behaviouristic school (1933) dismissed linguistic meaning as inaccessible to science.

Today, however, with transformational grammar and universal linguistics in the doldrums and the growing awareness of sociolinguistics, the question of the interpenetration between language and culture is emerging as fundamental once again.

(iii) *The ethnography of speaking*

The anthropological tradition of viewing language and culture as interrelated systems has continued unbroken up until today. But it is no longer the structure nor the lexicon of the language that is taken as a reflection and agent of cultural forces but the *use* of language and *speech behavior* itself. A new school of research has developed, led by Hymes (1962), known as 'the ethnography of speaking', whose aim is the "formulation of descriptive theories of speaking as a cultural system" (Bauman & Sherzer 1974, p. 6). So cultural relativism has shifted away from the purely formal aspects of language and has been extended to linguistic activity.

As yet only a few studies analyzing a community's linguistic behaviour in terms of its culture exist. Typical investigations are those such as that of Albert (1972) who links various patterns of verbal behaviour in Burundi, Africa, to hierarchical conceptions of the universe and society as well as to other aesthetic values. Philips (1974) describes the norm of unstructured, freely expressive behaviour on a Red Indian reservation in connection with the Indian ideal of individuality and self-determination. Reisman (1974) explains the convention of simultaneous talking in conversation over a considerable period by several speakers on the West Indian island of Antigua in terms of a self-assertive, competitive, cultural attitude (it is not arguing). Bauman (1974) attributes the basic silence of Quaker ministers to their spiritual beliefs and Godard (1977) relates American telephone openings to the ideal of free expression. Loveday (1982b) relates strategies of addressing and referring to participants as well as the distribution of speaking rights to certain values and norms of Japanese culture, such as the hierarchic ordering of status and the establishing of identity on a collective basis. It should be added that the ethnography of speaking is also interested in the different ways communities structure and organize their verbal activities and the following chapter is totally given up to this topic.

An illuminating piece of research by Agar (1975) on the language of drug addicts indicates how surface knowledge of the addicts' vocabulary is insufficient for understanding their conversations. Even though the researcher spoke the same language, English, he did not share their cultural code, that is to say, he did not know the underlying 'logic' and belief-system:

> After learning about 300 argot terms, I could render acceptable para-phrases of almost any given sentence that an addict might utter in interaction with other addicts. Yet even with this understanding I remained confused about the overall meaning of larger segments of ongoing interaction. My understanding was acceptable for sentences in isolation, but not for sentences in use. Other information was necessary (p. 42).

Hymes has argued that language and speech have a special patterning that is socially determined and just like other social organizations, politics, religion and economics cannot be taken for granted as somehow 'given' or everywhere the same. The scientific focus on the factors involved in verbal behaviour such as the circumstances, the participants, their intentions, the planning of their acts and how they deliver them, norms of interaction and the linguistic varieties employed will lead to a richer understanding of the cultural dimensions of language.

(iv) Sociocultural determinants of language

The discipline sociolinguistics enjoys a dual heritage, deriving from both anthropology and sociology. Unlike the basic concept of the former, *culture,* the latter focuses on society or *social structures.* Sociologists have not generally dealt with the notion of culture partly because they have been able to take cultural principles for granted and partly because in many modern societies "ordered social life goes on despite great diversity in cultural codes" (Keesing & Keesing 1971, p. 26). If society refers to people as a unit, then culture refers to the patterns of mental processes that regulate and influence the way the unit works. The abstract force of culture has not been central to sociology and a substantial portion of sociolinguistics has followed this self-imposed limitation and concentrated on variation within a social system in terms of the linguistic indications of age, occupation, sex, ethnicity, group membership (class, caste, etc.) and how language reflects social stratification (Sherer & Giles 1979).

Although the findings of such sociolinguistic investigations further substantiates the interdependence between language and society, its relevance for learning a non-native language is important but very specific since the sociolinguistic details vary from community to community. We can, therefore, not deal with this research here since our aim is to provide a broad overview of the subject without handling the teaching of any one particular L2. Nevertheless, L2 speakers should be familiarized with these sociocultural determinants of language which will lead them to a deeper and more satisfying level of comprehension and communication in the target community. Some textbooks drawing upon some of these findings have already appeared (Hughes & Trudgill 1979).

Instead let us turn to a few areas of sociological sociolinguistics which provide general insights for L2 learning and teaching. For example, there is the important question of social change resulting in language change. Friedrich (1966) has shown how transformations in Russian society (the emancipation of the serfs, the revolution and two world wars) have contributed to structural changes in the relationship between family members, relatives and household staff and led to linguistic changes in the words used to describe the relationships. A similar study by Witterman (1967) of changes in Javanese terms of address reveals how post-war independence, industrialization, urbanization and the resulting modification and abandonment of traditional role relations has led to the discontinuation of certain address terms and the broadening of others. The now classic study of Brown and Ford (1960) brought to light the historic shift in meaning from power to solidarity in the European dual second person pronouns (tu/vous, du/Sie).

It can often be the case that the linguistic contents of L2 courses tend to refer to an earlier stage of sociocultural development. Contemporary English textbooks can still be found with the occurrence of *sir* in conversations with people who are neither customers nor schoolmasters. But it is not only the socially outdated language of the textbooks that is responsible for archaic forms. Frequently the ideas of linguistic conservatives and purists, commonly through the language teacher, are also at work (see Chapter 5).

For example, in contemporary English there is now a tendency to replace the third person pronoun, 'he' for general reference with 'they' (Mackay 1980). Such a development is generally frowned upon or ignored in the L2 classroom.

Bernstein's (1971, 1973) theories lie between the purely sociological and the strictly anthropological sociolinguistics. He characterized two different speech styles within the English community that are related to class. The style called the 'elaborated' contains longer sentences with a more varied and explicit vocabulary and developed logical connections which are often left implicit in the other 'restricted' style. The latter tends to contain formulaic expressions such as "Don't you know" and "isn't it so" appealing to the hearer to fill in from background knowledge those parts of the message which have not been spelled out. Bernstein relates these two styles to the social world of their users: the restricted style is employed by members of a small, closely-knit group sharing a high sense of identification, similar experiences and mutuality of expectation while the elaborated style is more individualistic or context-independent (Kay 1977) in the sense that it relies little on the contribution of background knowledge on the part of the hearer and is suited to communication of unfamiliar and novel content to someone with whom one has little in common. In fact, Bernstein's work demonstrates how language adapts and evolves in relation to the sociocultural system it serves. The implications of Bernstein's theory have been misunderstood by teachers of pupils who are thought to use the 'restricted' style because the latter is taken by educators as inferior to the 'elaborated'. L2 teachers do not generally differ in this respect and generally tend to restrict the handling and use of the L2 in the classroom to the elaborated mode. The consequences can be a heightened sense of artificiality and a violation of certain everyday conversational principles (see Chapter 5).

(v) *Bilingualism equals biculturalism*

Today it is perhaps easier to see how erroneous the belief is that perception and experience is wholly determined by language. Taken literally, linguistic determinism would mean that speakers of two structurally different languages would have two different versions of reality. It would also imply that bilinguals would have to be skilful cognitive jugglers able to alter their world-views as they switched languages (Macnamara 1970).

However, the theory is best understood as an attempt to stress the very important point that different linguistic communities have unique ways of viewing the world and that their languages give us systematic clues to what those views are (Fishman 1978a). The theory was also conceived as an attack on the excessive pride of English monolinguals and of those who would save the world by popularizing English.

What is essential to realize is that a world-view underlies *all* of cultural behaviour of which language is but a part; culture is not solely re-presented and reinforced by the latter. However, it is generally the linguistic channel via which culture and its accompanying thought-world is *felt* to be active. This feeling is acutely described by an Englishman below:

> When I speak German to Germans, I automatically shift my orientation as a social being. I spontaneously adapt myself to the atmosphere characteristic of their status, outlook, prejudices. The very use of the customary formulae of politeness injects a distinct flavour into the conversation, colouring attitudes and behaviour. Some of these modes of expression, to be sure, are merely meaningless formulae, but by no means all. The retention of titles, in European fashion, for example, colours mutual relations, as does the free and easy American way of dropping them altogether. (Lowie 1945, p. 257.)

These introspective observations reveal how speaking another language may involve adopting another outlook on life. It is not the L2 *per se* which calls for this but the body of beliefs and practices contained in the L2 culture which are reflected and expressed in linguistic interaction.

Thus, when the French-born American novelist, Julian Green (1941), found it impossible to translate one of his books from French into English, he commented that "It was as if, writing in English, I had become another person". Actually, it is not so much that a new personality or different attitudes are adopted in an L2 but that a new constellation of relationships, a new configuration of topics to be discussed, and ways of discussing them may arise in the different language setting.

However, the use of another language does not automatically mean the existence of another culture. Diebold (1961) has shown that an Indian community in Mexico could share extensively in the culture of the dominant Spanish community while maintaining its native language.

That a language embodies the attitudes and values of its speakers and that these may not be the same in the L1 and the L2 is indicated in the following set of responses produced by Japanese-American bilinguals (Ervin-Tripp 1968, p. 203):

1. When my wishes conflict with my family . . .
(in Japanese) It is a time of great happiness
(in English) I do what I want
2. I will probably become
(in Japanese) a housewife
(in English) a teacher
3. Real friends should
(in Japanese) help each other
(in English) be very frank.

What has so far been said should have clearly proven that being bilingual must to a certain extent entail being bicultural in every case where the two languages exist in separate communities, i.e. where a community does not use the L2 and L1 in conjunction.

In spite of the interpenetration of language and culture, many have been loath to recognize the significance of this relationship. Until very recently the majority of language teachers have followed the isolationist and autonomous attitude in linguistics, avoiding considering a language-in-culture approach. This has resulted in virtually no research or theorizing in the pedagogic area, apart from some work on the educational problems of usually deprived minorities with a cultural world different from the dominant one (Cazden, Vera & Hymes 1972). Let us now turn to the cultural dimension of a second language from a teaching perspective.

Culture in language teaching

(i) *Classroom culture*

L2 teaching does not occur in a sociocultural vacuum. The students of the classroom themselves belong to a culture and where this differs from the L2 teacher's or the L2 teaching style, certain difficulties may appear. Dumont (1972), for instance, describes the unexpected problems encountered by Anglo teachers of English on a Red Indian reservation in America as follows:

> When classes began we did not expect the intensity of the constrained and cautious behaviour of the students nor the long and sometimes embarrassing periods of silence. Teachers requested, pleaded with, shouted at, commanded, badgered, and cajoled students to talk. When they did their replies could barely be heard or else the word was mouthed. . . . Inevitably, the days were long periods of desk work, teacher monologues, or lectures and rhetorical questions.

Outside their lessons, the children were noisy, bold, daring and insatiably curious. The cultural conflict arose because of contrasting cultural evaluations of silence and the teacher's function: for the children silence was appropriate in situations where the unexpected might occur (such as in class) and they believed that learning from peers was more important than when it was teacher-directed.

With reference to Latin American students learning English in an American setting, Jaramillo (1973) tells of the possible conflict arising from different cultural expectations. Thus, Latin American students first require more verbal contact for making acquaintance with each other in the class, which costs time that the Anglo teacher is not often prepared to give. They also dislike individuals being picked out for questioning but prefer a more collective approach. Female students will rather not participate if they feel to be in competition with males. The students surprise/displease the teacher in their different attitudes towards spatial distance and body touching (they are less distant than Anglos) as well as their louder and more spontaneous expression of emotion. On the other hand, the teacher is expected to instruct by 'memory' (i.e. not refer to books in class time, nor say ''I don't know") and maintain a certain level of formality; he should not sit on the edge of his desk nor smoke.

Toelken (1975) describes some of the problems involved in Red Indians writing English composition. Their responses of "impossible" and "illogical" to the topics announced by the instructor were assumed to be symptoms of 'arrested literacy'. However, deeper understanding revealed that assignments such as "Write an autobiographical description" were felt to be non-topics by some students who came from tribes who believed that a person became someone only with age and experience:

> others felt that to write on such a topic would be revealing too much—something like mentioning one's own name (taboo). The topic "What are your plans for the future?"—often given as a first theme by instructors who felt that everyone who came to college must have in common some view of his future—was greeted with great puzzlement by the Indian students, some of whom felt it was like 'tempting fate' to write on such a subject, while others felt again that it was a non-logical area not susceptible to rational discourse. (p. 280).

Other aspects of essay-writing such as logical organization, avoidance of repetition, the notion of certain tactical fact-sequences were theoretical dilemmas for many of the students.

Very little attention has been paid to the cultural behaviour and beliefs of L2 teachers themselves and how this affects their attitudes towards language and teaching. Jorden (1980) discusses the contrasts in language instruction and learning between Japanese native teachers and American students whereby the widespread Japanese assumption that foreigners will *not* be able to speak is shared by the teachers, resulting in self-fulfilling low classroom expectations. Moreover, L2 speaker shortcomings are not only expected but excessively tolerated and even regarded as "reassuring" according to Jorden.

If any readers have taught speakers of cultures different from their own they are probably well aware of the problems, prejudices and antagonism evoked by conflicting cultural attitudes in the L2 classroom and the necessity to overcome this through cultural awareness.

(ii) *The teacher as cross-cultural interpreter*

One of the most often cited and cherished goals of language teaching is the promotion of international and cross-cultural understanding. This being the case, it follows that a great deal will depend on the teacher's handling of the cultural dimensions of the L2 and especially on his treatment of it in relation to the L1 culture.

An L2 is a carrier of an alien culture and may in certain cases constitute a threat to the students' ethnic identity (cf. the section Attitudes of the learner, Chapter 2, pp. 15–23. Thus, the teacher has to be a skilled and sensitive cross-cultural interpreter capable of reducing the learners' ethnocentricism without damaging their self-image. This is especially the case with immigrant learners. One simple way of accomplishing this is to let students present their way of life, e.g. by asking students to interview each other about their (various?) native culture(s) or to bring representative objects such as food (Lindsay 1977; Di Pietro 1978).

The teacher of an L2 who is also a native of its community is really involved in practising the philosophy of "I'm OK—you're OK" while attempting to make L2 learners recognize and sympathize with a different system of behaviour and values. The teacher has to prevent students from experiencing the typical chain reaction of different → inferior → hostile (Ball 1979). The L2 culture has to be taught without judging by the yardstick of the L1 culture.

The above is, however, easier said than done for, confined to a single culture, one readily conceives of other cultures in terms of deviations from one's own. On top of this, it should not be forgotten that our own culture rewards us for producing certain patterns and avoiding others. We often recoil when cultural differences are pointed out. It is natural for non-natives to superimpose their own cultural framework on another and much easier to recognize what a cultural pattern is not than what it is. The basic problem for teachers is to decide what is an important and worthwhile cultural aspect. Gladstone (1972) suggests that teachers ask themselves two questions: "Is this information needed by students for the proper understanding of the custom or concept and am I sure about this detail?" If the answer to either is no, then the teacher should not bother about imparting or discussing the particular aspect. It is, after all, not possible to be conscious about every cultural detail.

Few L2 teachers are familiar with the sociology or anthropology of their own or the target community. Yet it is vital for them to learn about the characteristic L2 way of life in order to be able to explain linguistic behaviour. This is no more obvious than when translation is attempted without any understanding of cultural background. Of course, it is impossible to know everything about another culture but, as Jaramillo (1973) emphasizes, we should, at least, be aware of our own preconceived notions, be observant and demonstrate a sincere interest in it rather than impressive expertise.

Of course, learning about another culture may involve unpleasant discoveries and these ought to be explained sympathetically in terms of the social system in which they operate. For example:

> our rationalization is that it is 'uncivilized' to kill one's sister just because she was intimate with a man. What we often don't know and have difficulty in accepting is that such patterns fit into larger ones . . . and that what is being guarded is not the sister's life (though she may be deeply loved) but a centrally located institution without which society would perish or be radically altered. This institution is the family. In the Middle East the family is important because families are tied together in a functional interlocking complex. The accompanying network (and obligations) satisfies many of the same functions that our government satisfies. The sister is a sacred link between families and, like the judge in our own culture, she has to remain above reproach. (Hall 1974, p. 142.)

Surely such insight into the workings of the target community are indispensable. In transmitting these the L2 teacher must, however, avoid perpetuating stereotypes and clichés but try to represent the L2 culture as it is. Recently, Seeyle (1977) has outlined seven skills for intercultural communication which he believes can be tested. These are:

the sense of culturally conditioned behavior, e.g. that the picture of two male Arab diplomats holding hands in public expresses friendship; the interaction of language and social variables, e.g. an 8 year old talks differently from an 80 year old, a dock worker differently from a professor, a southerner differently from a northerner;

conventional behaviour in common situations, e.g. linguistic formulae for greetings, congratulating, reducing anxiety, etc.;

the evaluation of statements about a society, e.g. that the student must learn to differentiate judgements that serve the ethnocentric bias of the native community from those that have an adequate empirical base;

cultural connotations of words and phrases, e.g. the associations evoked by "moon" given on p. 37 in Fig. 2 which derive from the special festival day in Japan where children spend part of the night moon-viewing or admiring the full autumn moon;

the acquisition of the skills needed to locate and organize L2 cultural information from the library, mass media, personal observation;

the demonstration of intellectual curiosity and empathy towards the target culture.

It is quite wrong to believe that sustained contact in the target community can replace the teacher here in the attainment of cross-cultural awareness, as the numerous examples of the mutual cultural ignorance of different ethnic groups living side-by-side attest. What is absolutely necessary is a readiness to respect and accept, and a capacity to take part in the target way of life so that participation is reinforced by rewards that matter to the participant. Of course, these characteristics will depend on the flexibility of the individual learner. There exist communities who do not offer much gratification for respecting and participating in others which are socially, culturally or ethnically different. Such communities are usually monolingual, monolithic and nationally established. In such a native environment, the teacher's role will be far from straightforward but all the more vital if the goal of mutual understanding is to be reached.

For Hanvey (1979) there are four stages of cross-cultural sensitivity: the recognition of superficial or visible cultural traits that are interpreted as exotic and bizarre deriving from tourism and textbooks; the awareness of significant and subtle cultural traits that contrast markedly with one's own arising from culture conflict situations and interpreted as irrational or frustrating; the next phase is the same as the last mentioned one but differs in that it is intellectual so that the cultural symbols are cognitively credible and, the last stage where one is subjectively familiar with how another culture feels from the standpoint of the insider which, of course, only comes from cultural immersion. This ultimate level has been called *transspection:* "transspection is an effort to put oneself in the head . . . of another person. One tries to believe what the other person believes, and assume what the other person assumes. . . . Transspection differs from analytical 'understanding' . . . [it] tries to learn a foreign belief, a foreign assumption, a foreign perspective, feelings in a foreign context, and consequences of such feelings in a foreign context. In transspection a person temporarily believes whatever the other person believes. It is an understanding by practice" (Maruyama 1970).

Although most L2 teachers will probably maintain that they cannot teach towards this supreme level, it was often carried out in colonial contexts, admittedly for the indigenous elite. However, if transspection seems too lofty an aim the teacher can certainly pave the way to its attainment. Some suggestions for this now follow.

(iii) *The cultural input*

Up to now most language teachers have pursued the approach of 'purist linguistics' which views language as the vehicle for a highly restricted kind of communication—important and exalted though it may be—and concentrated on the employment of the L2 by a small minority of gifted individuals, novelists and poets, overlooking its potentialities as a reflection of the entire culture of those who speak it.

Although it has long been believed that cultural knowledge can only be gained and absorbed in the natural setting of the target community, there is no evidence to suggest that mere exposure will contribute to effective understanding and functioning in a different cultural environment and it is surely more likely to be the opposite if the would-be communicators have not been prepared in advance.

There are doubtlessly quite a few teachers who object to the idea of having to teach culture. They see their principal task in providing students with purely linguistic skills. But will the diligent learning of words and phrases, the laborious memorization of irregular verbs, the deciphering of the frequently trivial and unauthentic texts lead to true cross-cultural awareness?

In spite of the continuous calls for the teaching of the cultural dimensions of a non-native language, there have been few proposals as to how this could be implemented. Whatever the specific objectives of L2 teaching may be, one of its fundamental goals must be to impart an ability to comprehend fully and with satisfaction what the target community means in speaking and writing. This must entail the comprehension of a distant and different way of organizing experience.

Moreover, as has been seen above, language reflects and expresses the cognitive code of a particular community. If a teacher is going to provide an adequate explanation of the meaning of an item in the L2, this can only be done by referring to cultural knowledge. If the teacher does not do this, the lack of clarification of underlying assumptions may even lead to contempt and hostility on the part of the learner who applies his own cultural frame as a yardstick. In this matter the teacher can rely on the natural curiosity of the students for the target community. The explanation does not necessarily have to take place in the L2 and it should be appropriate to the intellectual state of the learners.

Since the native culture of the learner acts as a filter for assimilating the alien one, one suggested method is to compare the L2 cultural and social patterns. Marquez (1979), for example, contrasts one domain of cultural-linguistic knowledge and behaviour, the kinship of the Philippines and the USA, in relation to the Tagalog and English forms which refer to the domain. The study shows how in Tagalog kinship overrides affection and equality while sex differences are rarely made and status is ascribed rather than achieved in contrast to the sociolinguistic system in American English. Marquez sets out to prove that cultural comparison is possible in spite of the complexities involved and to show how such "results should be useful to the language teacher who earnestly wants to teach more than mere grammatical mastery, for such mastery is not enough" (p. 323). He maintains that his proposed model of contrastively analysing culture could be applied to other domains such as addressing, greeting,

leave-taking, style and lexical domains such as religious terms, household vocabulary (clothing and culinary), government and politics, education and friendship and many more.

Obviously, much of L2 teaching time has to be given up to explaining and practising purely linguistic elements. A rather old but nevertheless significant analysis of the cultural context of L2 teaching texts by Marckwardt *et al.* (1953) discovered that such texts could be placed in four categories: (1) elementary material presenting cultural information in a disorganized and unrelated fashion; (2) cultural miscellanies with a preoccupation with the picturesque and trivially bizarre; (3) comprehensive cultural histories with a propagandistic slant; and (4) literary texts that were not intended to elucidate culture but to develop skills in criticism. Furthermore, these particular categories could be related to the teaching of certain languages, e.g. the approach in the third category was typical of French teaching. The investigators felt all of the material to be grossly inadequate and to perpetuate cultural clichés. They drew up a set of questions teachers should consider concerning the content of material:

1. Does the material focus upon characteristic and significant aspects of the foreign culture?
2. Can the material be so organized that the student will leave the course with a fairly clear idea of some salient aspects of the foreign culture?
3. In using this material, can important traits or themes be compared or contrasted with typically . . . [L1 community] behaviour? And can this be done in a manner leading to a better understanding of . . . [L1 community] life?
4. Is the student stimulated to search for historical or other explanations for values which differ from his own?
5. Do the materials foster an awareness of the validity of the mode of life in any given society?
6. Is the material free from dubious or undesirable value judgements?
7. Does the material lead by implication to a clearer understanding of the nature in a general sense? (pp. 1217–1218).

Although teachers may frown upon it, the most profitable material for teaching the culture of the target community is popular in nature. Particularly insightful are products of the mass media such as soap opera, cartoons, 'light' novels, the boulevard press, etc. This material is not always easy to interpret because it requires deep familiarity with and comprehensive exegesis of the culture in question. All such material should be chosen with an eye to the subcultural diversity of the target community, e.g. its socioeconomic, religious, regional, generational and ethnic sub-cultures so that students do not end up thinking of the target culture as one uniform set of experiences and values.

Related to this is the proposal to use mail order catalogues to teach culture in the L2 classroom by Scanlan (1979). By looking at the objects depicted and the similarities and differences to the learner's native culture, insights can be gained not only into the material manifestation of culture but also the ideational. Thus, by considering the meaning of the models presented in terms of age, corpulence, hairstyles and so forth the class can arrive at a certain level of cross-cultural awareness. This heightened awareness occurs while the students grow more sensitive to their own society in their thinking about the contrasts.

Finally in this section, a note on the long practised method of classroom translation is required. Translation destroys the interrelationship between language and culture. *Real* native texts can rarely be rendered satisfactorily and their artificial simplification for translation purposes or even the writing of them by textbook-writers to fit the learner's 'reality' results in the false conceptualization of the L2 cultural world as merely "a somewhat blurred and indistinct version of their own, rather less expressive and lacking in nuance and vitality" (Rivers 1972, p. 267). However, translation could be profitably used to bring out the divergent values attached to words and their referents, to show how the possible equivalents in the L1 are 'culturally-loaded' in sometimes a completely different manner and how circumlocution is necessary if the concepts are to be effectively rendered. In short, translation can be a useful tool to make students conscious of the different ways languages and their related cultures encode experience.

There exists a widespread belief that the cultural knowledge to be transmitted in the L2 classroom is only available to a native of the L2 culture. But this is not necessarily so. A non-native may in some cases be more aware of deficiencies in his students' grasp of the target culture because of his intimate knowledge of their cultural sphere. Native teachers often tend to take their group's folkways for granted and find it very difficult to verbalize and present such essential background information. In fact, there is no native or non-native teacher who is *a priori* better equipped to do the job. The only teacher who can is one who is truly bicultural, in other words, familiar enough with the contrasts between the world of the learner and the target community to not presume that they can be ignored.

What should have emerged from above is that culture is not teaching who Churchill was nor is it merely explaining what April Fool's Day involves. Teachers do not have to directly refer to the concept *culture* at all when teaching. They must, however, be constantly working towards a heightened linguistic comprehension which cannot take place without a sensitivity for the underlying cultural presuppositions.

Cross-cultural awareness is by no means a difficult state to attain. It does not result from contact alone, nor even prolonged contact. "There must be a readiness to respect and accept, and a capacity to participate" (Hanvey 1979).

Sharing knowledge and a 'reality'

So language is a component of culture. One reason for teaching an L2 is because a language is a culture-preserving instrument. Cultural knowledge in non-literary communities is generally preserved in verbal forms such as proverbs, formulae, standardized prayer, folktales and genealogies while in literary communities it is stored in libraries.

Yet language is often taken as *representing* culture itself whereby the language of a so-called 'primitive' society is equally conceived of as 'primitive' by the unelucidated. Such notions are obviously ill-founded since language families vary independently of cultural type. If the formal aspects of the linguistic system are not significantly determined by cultural patterns, the meaning that issues from its structures is unquestioningly particularistic.

Moreover, this meaning is, by no means, always explicit. Linguistic communication involves many "cognitive economies" that rely on the speaker's and listener's presuppositions, i.e. on what is needed to know about a 'reality' to talk about it. An illustration of this natural principle has been effectively demonstrated by Krauss & Weinheimer (1964) who found that when subjects were asked to describe the reoccurrence of ambiguous figures so that these could be identified by a partner, a typical sequence would be for the first description of a figure to be highly explicit, e.g. "upside down Martini glass in a wire stand"; when the figure re-appeared, it might be re-described as an "inverted Martini glass in a wire stand", then as an "inverted Martini glass", then as "Martini glass", and finally as "Martini". Therefore, for this limited period of interaction Martini assumed a meaning which would have been only intelligible to those sharing the context that had been mutually built up.

What this experiment presents on a microcosmic scale is the process of the constitution of shared meaning over time and space and with many participants in cultural systems. But it is not necessary to prove this reductionist symbolization with experiments. One only has to remember the elliptical code of numerous partners in marriage (when they speak to each other) which can be unintelligible to outsiders who have not shared or learnt the routinization and stabilization of the forms they communicate to each other with.

In most cases, learning an L2 represents learning a new shorthand for cultural knowledge, This is because, as we have seen above, language reflects and integrates into itself features of the physical and ideational world in which it operates. With time both the external 'reality' and the language interpenetrate each other to such an extent that it becomes difficult "to make a complete divorce between objective reality and our linguistic symbols of reference to it" (Sapir 1974, p. 49).

The experiencing of a different version of sociocultural reality is an undeniably valuable and enriching process and most L2 teaching should offer the opportunity to gain entry into it by freeing students from ethnocentricism and sensitizing them to cross-cultural contrasts and similarities. Cultural assimilation is not automatic but requires effort of varying degrees, depending on how radically the culture of the target community differs from that of the learner. Furthermore, fluency in an L2 has been shown to be affected by the degree of ethnocentricism or cultural narrow-mindedness of the learner (Tucker & Lambert 1973). The effort to understand is vital. Without it the L2 user will be unable to discern and appreciate the complex of meanings symbolized and unable to signal his own appropriately and successfully. Teaching culture to L2 learners entails more than the familiarization with a differing social, political and religious Weltanschauung. It also involves the acquisition of communicative behaviour that is culture-specific. It is to this subject that I next turn.

4

Ways of meaning: communicative competence in a non-native language

The last chapter examined the relationship between language and culture and noted how the sharing of linguistic experience leads to a reduction in the explicitness of meaning and the possession of a specific version of meaning in terms of a sociocultural reality. The traditional study of language, on the other hand, has considered language solely as a formal system and not as a container and creator of meaning. This is because linguistics imitated the scientific movement toward mathematization and formalism. The result has been that linguists have not treated the way language is used in everyday life and instead limited their focus on its internal structuring without reference to its social framing. Metaphorically put, they have concentrated on the way the 'machine' is assembled without looking at how it works when people use it.

However, it is precisely because we want to participate in social activity that we learn (our first) language and it is mainly through linguistic experience that we learn how to live with others. Until very recently non-native language teaching followed the mathematical and purely formalistic perspective adhered to in linguistics but now it is beginning to consider language as a process of meaning, as communication.

From formalism to functionalism

Why has there been a turning away from formalism? To explain this, we have to go back into the recent history of linguistics and the work of a man who maintained the traditional linguistic rejection of all that was not directly connected to the form of language. This was Chomsky (1965) whose transformational grammar only considered language as an ideal, abstract phenomenon independently of socio-cultural factors. In this scientific vision a language was characterized as a kind of hidden knowledge about which forms could be strung together and which forms could not, as one homogeneous system shared by all speakers of a language, as a stock of fixed rules that could be described rather like computer processing methods. Whether our minds actually treat language like computers handle information or whether the analogy is only a useful descriptive device has never been properly established.

The inadequacy of the transformational approach to account for socially-constructed meaning provoked the reaction of the anthro-pologist, Hymes (1971), who pointed out that there was a lot more to linguistic activity than the production of grammatical sentences. If people operated language in the way transformational grammar postulates where any and all the grammatical sentences of a language are produced then they would be doubtlessly locked up as insane. Needless to say, it is only very recently that some language teachers have begun to teach something apart from grammaticality in their lessons.

For Hymes (1971).

> a normal child acquires knowledge of sentences, not only as gram-matical, but also as *appropriate*. He or she acquires competence as to when to speak, when not, and as to what to talk about with whom, when, where, in what manner. . . . This competence, moreover, is integral with attitudes, values, and motivations concerning language, its features and uses (pp. 277–278).

Here Hymes has provided a succinct definition of his concept of *communicative competence* which he developed in order to complement, if not counter, Chomsky's notions of a purely grammatical competence. Communicative competence is not simply what is 'done' with language; it also involves abstract knowledge but of a type that is much less systematizable and mathematizable than that proposed by Chomsky. It includes the sort of cultural knowledge that has already been alluded to in the preceding chapter: the organization of verbal means for socially defined purposes and the sensitivity of language for situations, relationships, intentions, etc.

The significance of Hymes' work for non-native language teaching has been in its profound replacement of formal linguistic knowledge by functional linguistic knowledge, in the shift it has caused from knowing how to produce a *correct* sentence to knowing how to produce an appropriate, socially acceptable and natural one.

Cultural and contextual ways

Unfortunately, many theorists and teachers have come to equate the concept of communicative competence with spontaneous self-expression, probably because they have taken the term absolutely literally as the ability to communicate. This interpretation is not only trite but also shows a grave lack of understanding of what is involved.

In order to transmit and decode meaning, we must do much more than arrange our sounds and words in a special order. One has to be aware of the diverse ways of constructing a message, of the guidelines which, rarely obvious and definable, constitute unquestioned principles of presenting the sound and word patterns together with other symbols. This code for verbal conduct is our communicative competence and it fulfills a multitude of social functions and is largely determined by the sociocultural system.

This code is not easy to describe since it includes many different dimensions and channels, some of which help to symbolize meaning and others of which serve as the framework for the transmission of the symbols. Furthermore, they all adapt to and evolve differently in each individual situation.

Consider some of these elements of communicative competence. To begin with, there are the symbols evoked by the vocal organs themselves; for example, huskiness and breathiness* suggesting femininity for English speakers. The range and change of pitch in the voice is also very meaningful, e.g. if one talks in English on a 'flat' voice without any high tones, boredom or great earnestness is often implied by the speaker. But we can only know which attitudinal

---

*Very aspirated speech involving a large volume of air passing through the vocal cords.

meaning the speaker intends by knowing the way he sits, looks and what he is talking about. The body and facial movements, of course, make up another meaning-channel that can sometimes be more important than human noise: how close we sit to each other, how much we look into each other's eyes, how we use our hands or place our feet, all these can carry meaning. Furthermore, this meaning is not the same in every cultural system.

When in conversation with others, people employ various means to indicate to their interlocutors when they have come to the end of their 'bit' and are ready to hand over the 'speaking rights' and let the other have a turn. When people talk, they also know how to relate an utterance to what came before it, in other words, they have learnt to coordinate and sequence discourse so that it should make sense. For example, when you phone an acquaintance up wanting to borrow something, you do not start the conversation immediately with "I wonder if you could lend me last month's *Gardening Monthly*" even though this is your sole intention in ringing. You are expected to greet, identify yourself, engage in a little chit-chat and so on before you can make your request. Of course, if the request was very urgent then it would be permissible to blurt it out immediately but a gardening magazine is clearly too trivial to warrant the violation of this usual but unconscious pattern for structuring interaction on the telephone.

The *paralinguistic* (facial and gestural), *proxemic* (spatial) and *language-organizational* patterns which are so essential for communicating are closely orchestrated with our speech. They are also carefully studied by those in communication with us in order to understand what we mean in a fuller and more accurate way, beyond the mere words we utter.

Certainly, *what* we say also signals a great deal of meaning. There is the grammar and vocabulary (Yeah, like I feel that's real smart/Oh yes, I consider that to be extremely ingenious), the topic we speak about (the weather or the reasons for one's nervous breakdown), the way we pronounce words (I expect so/'spec' so).

Again, this variation in language basically relates to the variety of social meaning such as how one presents oneself to others whether in a manner that is to be interpreted as 'trendy', 'sophisticated', role-conforming, distant or whatever. The reasons for such a self-presentation depend on many factors such as who one is with, where one is, what one is talking about.

Figure 3 shows the linguistic constituents of communicative competence resulting in the construction of meaning and some of their contextual determinants. In the diagram the meaning-carrying elements of communication are placed in a box-arrow representing the speaker's output. Of course, these constituents alter and adapt according to the context of interaction, i.e. are dynamic in nature. They are also influenced and constrained by social values and speaking conventions.

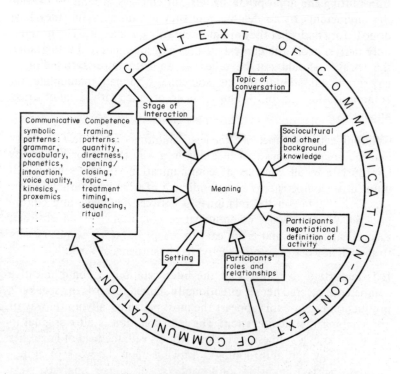

Fig. 3. The construction of contextual meaning: the sociolinguistic constituents of communicative competence and some of their contextual determinants producing meaning.

Communicative competence obviously involves much more than the traditionally taught areas of language: grammar, vocabulary and pronunciation. It entails knowing how to incorporate contextual determinants into linguistic constituents when producing meaning.

I would like to point out that only *some* of the contextual factors are presented. There are bound to be more but only the most general ones have been stated. Likewise, there are certainly many more framing or language-organizing patterns but these are the ones which sociolinguistic research has so far uncovered.

The diagram further shows that meaning is not the simple result of transmitting the appropriate signals but emerges in relation to what the interactants try to demonstrate they are doing, what they have done before and what they are momentarily engaged in. The meaning only derives from the context of ongoing interaction. Furthermore, the speaker should not be taken as an automaton responding to environmental stimuli but as someone who can manipulate the communication system for himself in accordance with social practices and needs.

Communicative competence then is, simultaneously, the *knowledge* and the *ability* to construct meaning in a way that is socioculturally appropriate in all contexts of communication. In this sense, communicative competence is an embodiment of what was outlined in the previous chapter on the relationship between language and culture (see pp. 35–42). Thus, communicative competence is an abstract, theoretical concept that is not easy to grasp. In fact, it is much easier to show it at work or, more exactly, its constituents at work.

It is important to realize that the interpretation of communicative competence offered here is intentionally slanted towards the speaker's production because this appears the most pedagogically useful way of approaching the phenomenon. The interpretation is also original in that it proposes a synthesis of various schools with the field of linguistics and sociology and anthropology, drawing upon the work of ethnomethodologists, linguistic philosophers, discourse analysts, text grammarians, semioticians, ethnographers of speaking, applied linguists and sociolinguists. Throughout the following discussion, however, no reference is made to these intellectual formations since it would only slow down and possibly confuse the analysis.

Before showing the constituents of communicative competence in action, it is necessary to distinguish between what I have called *symbolizing* and *framing* patterns. By symbolizing patterns I mean the various channels available for transmitting and gauging meaning which include LINGUISTIC FORMS (phonetic, grammatical, lexical) and NON-VERBAL FORMS such as gesture but also appearance (dress, body decoration, etc.). Framing patterns refer to the PRINCIPLES and CONVENTIONS which connect, compose and regulate communicative behaviour but which are not intrinsically symbolic although they are given meanings. Both framing and symbolizing patterns function in accordance with the social and cultural beliefs, values and practices of the community which employ them. They function in unison, helping to clarify sense, modifying each other and accommodating to the context. Their meaning only comes into being when they occur with and adapt to the contextual determinants shown in the diagram. Thus, their separation here is a totally artificial but useful theoretical construct.

We shall now study some of these symbolic and framing patterns more closely and see how they vary across cultural and linguistic communities. Unfortunately, very little research has so far been carried out in the field of cross-cultural and cross-lingual communication from a social perspective so that most of our data is restricted to the communicative competence of three principal communities: the Athabaskans in sub-arctic Canada with their Red Indian heritage, the Japanese and the Germans.

(i) *Framing patterns*

These refer to the 'machinery' for steering and managing one's self-presentation in communication according to social expectations and norms. Among the expressional norms, one finds that communities differ in their evaluation of the amount of speech necessary for appropriate and successful interaction. For example, it has been observed that the middle-aged men of the Puliya in Southern India investigated by Gardener (1966) seem to practically stop speaking altogether. In contrast, there is the Belizian speech community in South America which is extremely verbal:

> Each day of one's life is filled with words; the clever use of language is greatly appreciated; there is a highly developed metalanguage for types of speech acts and speech events; classification of an individual as to personality and character is based, in part, on the speech behaviour of that individual; and one's status depends partially on one's ability to perform verbally. . . . 'The window to one's soul' is not his eyes, but his mouth, and people who don't expose their souls are neither liked nor trusted. Though a person may say disagreeable things, at least his hearers feel that they know him. They may not like him, but they will feel more comfortable with him than with the man who says little or nothing (Kernan *et al.* 1977, p. 38).

On the other hand, North American Indians have frequently been noted for their taciturnity. This is apparently due to the avoidance of speech in situations where there is doubt about how one is to present oneself, talking only becoming acceptable where social relations are known and established. American English speakers, however, rely heavily on speech to develop social knowledge: "One talks to strangers to get to know them . . . [Red Indians] get to know someone in order to be able to speak" (Scollon & Scollon 1980b; p. 11). Where two community-interactional norms clash, the social consequences are rarely favourable. What tends to happen is that each group negatively stereotypes the other, e.g. in the above instance of interethnic communication, the Athabaskan Indians think that English speakers prate all the time while the English speakers see the Athabaskans as surly and withdrawn. The western emphasis on verbal expression derives from the Greek cultivation of public speaking into the art of rhetoric and it is by no means universally valid. As Kunihiro (1975, p. 97) states for the Japanese speech-community:

> language as an instrument of debate and argument is considered . . . disagreeable and is accordingly avoided. . . . It is only one possible means of communication, not *the* means of communication.

In fact, the articulation of thoughts and feelings in oral language is often taken by the Japanese as an unmistakable sign that the speaker is neither profound nor sincere. For them, the world is not verbalizable nor is it aesthetically pleasing to try. Many native proverbs support this view: "Mouths are to eat with, not to speak with" or "a hundred listenings do not equal one seeing" or "a man of many words has little refinement".

Thus, in their dealings with English speakers the Japanese are often regarded as "distant", "cool" and "cautious" and their conversations "endless and pointless" (Barnlund 1975).

Communicative differences in the treatment of specific topics can also be found. In Vietnam, the usual peasant response to a question by someone socially superior is "that must be so". If you ask "Is this the way to the station?", the invariable answer is that you are correct to avoid contradicting or ridiculing the superior who would generally use an intermediary to obtain information.

In the Middle East a refusal to come to the point and discuss the topic of a meeting can frequently signify an inability to agree with the interlocutor's terms and the avoidance of a blunt refusal. However, there is no feeling that the meeting should not take place, even though the topic is not discussed (Hall 1959).

In both cases the person unfamiliar with these interactional patterns and used to those requiring explicitness, tend to interpret them negatively as evasion or even deceit. In Madagascar, for example, there is a taboo on identifying individuals by name for fear that evil forces will be attracted and so that if "A asks B 'Where is your mother?' and B responds 'She is either in the house or at the market', B's utterance is not usually taken to imply that B is unable to provide more specific information needed by the hearer" (Keenan 1977). To come out directly with new and unpleasant information also violates Madagascar conventions and puts the giver in an uncomfortable position. Keenan and Ochs (1979) illustrate this with the example of someone travelling by car and not knowing which turning to take. When a passer-by is asked whether it is right or left, he responds with "Yes sir". As the driver starts to head left, a mildly excited cry can be heard: "There to the north perhaps" which means he should bear right. In this community, disagreement signifies confrontation and conflict and silence as a response implies that the speaker has not expressed himself appropriately. The situation just described where information has to be given quickly presents a particularly awkward case.

On the other hand, Athabaskans feel uncomfortable about presenting themselves in too favourable a light, resulting in their silence about personal accomplishments, abilities and plans because their direct reference could court bad luck (Scollon & Scollon 1980b).

I have already mentioned the negative attitudes towards verbalization held by the Japanese and this is also reflected in their feelings towards engaging in discussions about private experience which is generally avoided. In fact, explicit and ordered talk is considered definitely odd (Ogasawara 1972).

These examples have been presented here just to show that the highly cherished norm of linguistic precision in western culture cannot be taken for granted and is not universally sanctioned by society. The value is embodied in English in everyday expressions such as "Get to the point", "Out with it", "Don't beat around the bush" and "Let's get down to brass tacks".

But other cultures can often leave the heart of the matter unsaid and up to the listener/reader to put together. Thus, one characteristic structure of Japanese discourse (spoken and written) is the "dot-type" presentation of one item after the other in a highly anecdotal or episodic vein without articulating the conclusion. Westerners often react to this with "so what!", considering the presentation shallow. Furthermore, conversations (such as certain western ones) which are carried out as a logical game with continuous negative/positive judgements being made appears aggressive and offensive in Japanese speakers who prefer to stress mutuality and the emotive in social interaction. 'No' almost constitutes a term of abuse in Japanese and equivocation, exiting or even lying is preferred to its use.

Moreover, plain statements are fundamentally avoided by the Japanese speech-community who prefer to discuss matters indirectly and tentatively:

It isn't that we can't do it this way . . .
Of course, we couldn't deny that it would be impossible to say that it couldn't be done . . .

But unless we can say that it can't be done, it would be impossible not to admit that we couldn't avoid doing it.

Even grammatical notions can be limited to particular speech-communities. For instance, the Japanese conception of what constitutes a complete utterance or sentence differs considerably from the western. It is generally considered unrefined to clearly mark the end of one's utterance and so the ending is frequently left hanging with a word like "nevertheless".

Of course, the discussion of an entire cultural style is beyond the scope of this chapter but it is worth noting that different cultures differently evaluate the framing patterns of language. In Red Indian communities, for example, unlike many northern European-based ones, certain kinds of repetition and redundancy are not seen as signs of linguistic poverty but are appreciated and found to have rich subtlety (Toelken 1975).

The story-telling tradition of Athabaskans has similarly been regarded as 'degenerate', 'cryptic' and seriously eroded' by Anglo-Americans because the narrative performance shows no interest in embellishment. The storyteller's principle interest is in fleshing out his or her synthesis of the story in a special face-to-face relationship with the listener so that the latter can create their own synthesis (Scollon & Scollon 1979b). This linguistic patterning is closely tied to Athabaskan methods of individual learning through listening.

When we turn to the second type of framing patterns, the norms for organizing the business of language clearly vary interculturally. The conventions for routine communication are particularly interesting to examine. The English speaker who opens up a conversation with how awful or nice the weather is today tends to appear to Germans (who were informally asked about it) as somewhat mentally retarded (Clyne 1975). Although it might seem irrelevant as to who or how a conversation is started, it has been found that the person who speaks first also controls the topic of the conversation and assumes the role of a 'summoner' (Schegloff 1972).

Conversational openings are not meaningless mechanisms but generally bear a significant influence on the rest of the exchanges because one of their functions is to *set the relationship* between the participants; it is during the opening sequence that the partners evaluate each other and judge whether and in what way further interaction can be developed. L2 speakers can often be quite gauche in initiating interaction in a non-native language. Kasper (1979) gives various instances of Germans opening in English with a contextually inappropriate style, e.g. at a party: "Excuse me please may I ask you whether you are alone here?" *Excuse me* is an opening signal limited to contexts where addressing someone is linked to asking them to fulfill a request in English. Another 'mis-opening' observed to be carried out by Germans is to approach a stranger in a shop with "Well, hello erm . . ." since *well* is only used in openings between people who know each other as in "Well, fancy meeting you here". A further example of an inappropriate opening was the violation of the English conversational taboo on repeating something obviously redundant where, when asked if he was Mr. Bechstein, a German answered "Yeah, my name is Dirk Bechstein".

Moving away from this microlinguistic level to some communities who do not open channels until a certain relationship has been established, one finds that when Athabaskans and English speakers meet, the Athabaskans wait to see what will happen between them both before speaking while the English speaker starts speaking straight away—usually by asking questions to find out what will happen. The result is that Athabaskans feel that the English speakers are selfishly controlling their talk. In the Japanese speech-community the establishment of identity and status is a fundamental pre-requisite to interaction. Prolonged anonymous exchanges are difficult to maintain. Japanese speakers of English thus tend to transfer this pattern to their L2 behaviour, introducing themselves, for example, as "I belong to Mitsubishi bank" and immediately asking socially identificatory questions to their partners who can be offended due to their conversational sequencing, i.e. because they are asked at such an early phase of the interaction and not introduced 'surreptitiously' and 'casually' later on. The Japanese tend to see themselves as less self-contained and possessing overriding group-affiliations and so questions like "Where do you work" and "How old are you" are particularly relevant.

Certain cultural groups do not formally recognize someone who joins their gathering as I have noticed among young Germans. Similarly, on the island of Antigua in the West Indies when someone enters a casual group "no opening is necessarily made for him; nor is there any pause or other formal signal that he is being included. No one appears to pay any attention. When he feels ready he will simply begin speaking. He may be heard, he may not" (Reisman 1974). This is because Antiguans do not share the convention of one-party-at-a-time so that many Antiguan voices can sometimes be vying for an audience over considerable periods with conversations permissibly interrupted to communicate with passers-by.

This brings us to differences in the *timing of verbal exchanges* during conversations which are often a source of considerable frustration in cross-cultural communication. Some communities are used to immediate responses from interlocutors, others time their exchanges to leave pauses between each statement. "For Americans this silence is unsettling. To us it may mean that the person is shy, inattentive, bored or nervous. It causes us to repeat, paraphrase, talk louder, and 'correct' our speech to accommodate our partner" (Schnapper 1979, p. 137).

In Athabaskan interaction this chronemic variation, as the difference in verbal timing has been labelled, is not more than half a second longer than the English speaker's regular time length of a second or less. However, in cross-cultural exchanges the English speaker rarely waits, usually interpreting the pause as a sign for him to continue. The Athabaskan continues waiting his regular length of time but finds he is hardly given the opportunity to say his piece.

That for certain communities *silence* is distressful while for others it is normal and pleasant has already been mentioned. An example of the latter type of reaction is observable in Japan where silence is a virtue. Of course, well-meaning attempts to make a Japanese person 'speak up' in cross-cultural encounters often leads to resentment since from the Japanese point of view it is the non-Japanese interlocutor who is seen as the culprit and who should rather be taught how to shut up.

Additionally, Barkowski *et al.* (1976) have emphasized the problems experienced by Turks in their interaction with Germans in West Berlin. The former are used to long monologues without interruption together with considerably more narratives than the Germans expect. Thus, the Turks find it particularly difficult to function effectively in a society with short exchanges. They are not accustomed to interjecting nor do they take advantage of non-verbal cues for them to take their conversation 'turn'.

Further diversity in framing patterns exist in an area which has been appropriately referred to as *chunking* which relates to the strategies of conceptual organization expressed in language. European thinking and story making is often arranged in three parts while Athabaskan stories are organized in four. The effects of this difference, it seems, would be that those engaged in cross-cultural communication are always out of synchrony with each other:

> Each would feel the other was always responding at the wrong time. In longer units of talk such as stories it would give the English speaker the feelings that an Athabaskan story was always a little bit too long or had an irrelevant section. It would give the Athabaskan a feeling that an English story always left something out, the fourth part. This difference would also affect longstanding communication patterns by producing different memory structures of communicative events. An Athabaskan and an English speaker may well remember very different things to have happened in a conversation because of different themes of organization. In all cases the result would be a feeling that the other did not make sense in some profound way, so that one could just never figure out what interethnic communication had been about (Scollon & Scollon 1980b, pp. 33–34).

Now chunking, together with opening, distributing and even timing linguistic behaviour are all closely connected with a fundamental aspect of communication, namely *sequencing*. L2 teachers and most linguists have restricted their attention to the phonological and grammatical sequencing of words up to the level of the sentence. However, various contemporary studies have investigated structures beyond sentence limits and discovered supra-sentential sequencing rules. Some of these have been found in interaction and others in written communication.

All language is a linear representation and in order to ensure coherence we sequence language, repeat, substitute and delete, making it possible for it to simultaneously refer to what has gone before and anticipate what is to follow. These patterns of cross-referencing between sentences and utterances constitute the organization of discourse and occurs according to certain principles of purpose that belong to generally unconscious social knowledge. In order to make sense of acceptable paragraphs, essays, monologues, etc., the listener–interpreter has to make connections between the propositions in each statement. These connections are generally not expressed since the speaker–writer assumes that they are accessible. However, the connections are contextually and culturally determined. (They are related in part to the notion of *presupposition* discussed in the last chapter on p. 38.) Without these implicit, presupposed connections, the text or discourse would not be intelligible. Interestingly enough, children have problems with decontextualized language as embodied in the ideal essay. When five-year olds were given a statement and asked if a second statement logically related to the first was true, e.g. (1) John was hit by Mary, (2) Did Mary hit John?; their ability to answer depended on how much they knew about the characters and context mentioned in the sentences. If they did not know who John and Mary were or why the experimenter was asking the questions, they could not assign a meaning to the sentence. Unlike adults, young children seem to assign a speaker's meaning to a simple sentence only if it is contextually appropriate and directly relatable to prior knowledge (Olson 1977).

For instance, how do you make sense of the following:

> The reporting of Big Brother's Order for the Day in *The Times* of December 3rd, 1983 is extremely unsatisfactory and makes references to non-existent persons. Rewrite it in full and submit your draft to higher authority before filing.

Of course, if you have read the novel *Nineteen Eighty-Four* by George Orwell, you will probably have not puzzled over it for very long. However, you can only link the two sentences when you are familiar with the presuppositions that past news can be rewritten, that references to people who once existed but who have been officially disowned and liquidated cannot be made, that the journalist is conceived of as a tool of propaganda, that the sociocultural framework is totalitarian.

According to van Dijk (1980, 1981) every piece of discourse and text possesses a "superstructure", that is to say, a conventionally recognizable pattern for their particular arranging. Thus, a text such as an *essay* involves certain expectations about sequencing, argumentative structuring, proving of statements and so on which the superstructure of a *diary* does not have. Superstructures are contextually (and culturally defined) and their norms often institutionalized, determining what may or may not remain implicit. Furthermore, when producing texts we follow certain "microrules" which help us to assemble meaning into greater components and in order to reduce the information load we omit irrelevant information, select and generalize on what we think is important and integrate it to achieve global sense above the level of the individual utterance/sentence. If we did not employ these microrules we would have to keep asking after each set of statements "What are you talking about?" and "What do you mean by that?" Of course, we do this questioning already but usually as an exception and certainly not as a regular feature of communication. The following passage illustrates how the selection out of all the possible relevant information is socioculturally necessary:

> John came home at 6 o'clock. Walking to the main entrance of the flat he put his hand in his left coat pocket, searched for the key to the door, found it, took it out, put in into the lock, turned the lock, and pushed the door open; he walked in and closed the door behind him. . . . (van Dijk 1977, p. 110).

White (1974) has described the characteristic features of sequencing in scientific English with reference to L2 teaching: "anaphoric reference of determiners especially 'the'; use of sequence signals: and, then, as a result; lexical repetition . . . inclusion, e.g. '25 cm of the lower chloroform layer was removed and transferred to a bottle containing distilled water. The mixture was shaken . . .'", as well as certain superstructural features such as complete sentences providing self-contained units of discourse without need to disambiguate or expound, since feedback from the addressee is not possible as in spoken language, the absence of personal pronouns which maintains a distance between the user and addressee and, finally, the use of technical, specialist terms which indicate the sharing of a common fund of knowledge with professional peers.

Similarly, Widdowson (1979) argues for the devising of a "syllabus which is not a collection of (grammatical) structures or situations or notions but a sequence of relationships which build up into a structured paragraph, and subsequently into a series of paragraphs which approximate to the kind of reading material which the learner will ultimately have to handle" (p. 258). He suggests presenting learners with a set of propositions and asking them to find examples of them in a set of sentences. The learners then move on to combine the proposition with the examples and are asked to consider their combinations and select a sentence which can be used to restate the idea in the example that can be linked with it by means of markers such as "that is to say" or "in other words", thereby getting the learner to participate in developing a paragraph which has the following sequence: main statement—support—exemplification—clarification—conclusion.

Clyne (1981) offers some comments on the relationship between discourse structure and culture with particular reference to German norms and non-native language teaching. He notes how a German book in translation (English) was described as "chaotic" and criticized for its "lack of focus and cohesiveness", "haphazardness of presentation" and "desultory organization" but was hailed as a landmark in its field by Germans. Clyne suggests that this is due to culture-specific patterns of discourse organization. English requires linearity while German appears to favour digression and "parenthetical amplifications of subordinate elements". Drawing upon Kaplan's (1972) study of non-English discourse structure in the essays of foreign students in the USA, this can be diagrammatically illustrated in the following way:

An extreme example of typically German non-linear discourse for Clyne is the work of Schütze called *Sprache soziologisch gesehen* (1975–1977) in which "there are not only digressions, but also digressions from digressions. Even in the conclusion, there are digressions. Every time the author returns to the main line of argument, he has to recapitulate it up to the point before the last digression, resulting in much repetition. The structure may best be represented by cooked spaghetti" (p. 63).

When it comes to the use of non-natives of the divergent, culturally-specific sequencing norms, we find that L2-employing adults are expected to know these apparently 'universal' principles and when they do not conform to them they are classified as "illogical", or worse, "stupid" simply because the natives cannot so readily supply the propositions that are taken for granted.

In this connection it is interesting to observe how strangers can have difficulty in following the cohesiveness of L2 discourse structures, and yet native acquaintances of the L2 speaker can understand and serve as interpreters. Perhaps this is comparable with the case of a speaker suffering from severe anomic aphasia whose wife was able to interpret his utterances to some extent due to familiarity with and knowledge about the speaker (Sabsay & Bennett 1977).

Sequencing plays a major role in interaction as well as in written communication. The one or more utterances contained in each speaker's 'turn' at talking are basically supposed to make sense in terms of what has so far been said, in other words, they have to be interpreted as relevant by listeners. Kasper (1979) provides a typical example of sequential irrelevance in L2 speech:

Doctor: Oh, come in erm Miss er Hammerschmidt yes
Patient: Hello
Doctor: Well what can I do for you?
Patient: Hello, Dr Johnson, well erm you treated me for tonsilitis. . . .

Here the position of the address, "Hello, Dr Johnson" in the last turn of the L2 speaker–patient comes across as odd since it should have been produced with the first hello.

In fact, fixed sequences of specific linguistic elements have been found in telephone calling, joke telling and even casual conversation. We will only focus on the sequencing rules for casual conversation of the English speech-community as reported by Ventola (1979). The basic linguistic sequences discovered are (1) greeting; (2) addressing; (3) identifying; (4) approaching, e.g. 'How's life?' or 'Nice weather' which serves as conversation bridgers indicating a degree of readiness for further interaction; (5) centring (the broaching and the handling of a topic of concern to the interlocutors or relevant to the immediate situation); and (6) leave-taking. These often occur in this order for first encounters but in urgent situations (2) can precede (1) e.g. "John, hello, I wonder if . . ." and (5) is naturally only present in conversations whose function is more than the mere establishment and maintenance of a social relationship. Among friends (6) and (7) may be repeated more than twice as they become involved in new centring or continue previous centring. Ventola's work brings to light the existence of particular interactional sequences and their determination by the overall purpose of the encounter and the social distance between the actors involved. As Ventola (p. 286) perceptively states: "Casual conversation is part of our daily life. As interactants in our own culture we hardly need to consider how to start, maintain and end a casual conversation" but the question is how obvious is such sequencing to non-native speakers?

Related to this is the investigation by House (1979) who found that opening routines in German and English differed in that the response to the approach sequence ("how are you?") is followed by a similar question about the interlocutor's health with English speakers but not with Germans. Thus, in English one observes:

A: Hello Steve
B: Oh hello Joe. How are you doing, okay?
A: Yeah, I'm okay. What about you?

Germans do not reiterate the question. If Germans using English as an L2 employ their L1 sequence, they will most likely appear somewhat inconsiderate and selfish.

Closing encounters can be accomplished in various ways. In a Philippine community, it is perfectly good manners for two people to terminate a conversation on a public path by saying "you go now" (Frake 1975). Athabaskans, on the other hand, have no formal departure formulae while English speakers expect a routine closing marker such as "see you". For Athabaskans this phrase would set up explicit conditions for the future which could be unlucky. English speakers consider it essential to define the end of an encounter, cementing what has taken place so that it can be resumed at the next opportunity: "It's been nice talking to you", "I hope we meet again", "That was interesting". Athabaskans who fail to clearly indicate the termination of interaction are, at extreme, taken as signalling the complete rupture of the relationship with their English interlocutor because this is what the lack of a closing sequence usually signifies in a native English context.

Moreover, Schlegoff (1976) has pointed out that the meaning of all utterances can only be determined within the environment of their sequencing which provides both a device for implicitly ordering and interlocking social activity as well as a mechanism for making sense of it.

We have seen above how contrasts in framing patterns and the social values attached to the organization and presentation of language can result in special problems for cross-cultural contact. Framing patterns have been shown to carry meaning in that they are used to evaluate the personality, intelligence, readiness to communicate and so on of speakers and writers. Of course, native speakers can and often do frame their language inappropriately, especially children who have not yet penetrated its workings. But the non-application and non-observance of the framing rules is certainly less extensive among L1 adults than L2 adults, unless the former are schizophrenic. It is worth, in fact, comparing the characteristic features of schizophrenic speech with the performance of certain L2 speakers. Schizophrenics produce tangential responses, pursue irrelevant detail, omit transitional markers and offer disparate ideas (see Vetter 1975; Werner et al. 1975).

There is evidence that schizophrenics would like to communicate normally but are unable to do so. "Schizophrenic patients themselves often complain about the confusion in their talk and thinking, saying that everything seems mixed up, the words do not come out as they once did, thoughts rush in and are all jumbled" (Cameron & Margaret 1951, p. 511). Not only do L2 speakers tend to transfer their L1 framing patterns into their L2 discourse with sometimes negative consequences but they also seem to share some of the organizational problems of schizophrenic speakers.

(ii) *Symbolizing patterns*

Symbolizing patterns are, like framing patterns, employed without an awareness for their cultural specificity. This can also result in much unnecessary cross-cultural misunderstanding.

Let us start with the traditional domains of language which symbolize: grammar and vocabulary. If I asked the question "Why don't you read this book?" I am not requesting for an explanation about why you will not read a particular book but asking you to do so. This is what is technically known as an *indirect speech act* and refers to those phrases whose surface form and social function differ. Direct speech acts are a usual component of language teaching, e.g. the command "Read this please". Of course, to recognize the social function of indirect speech acts one has to be familiar with the contexts in which they are employed, i.e. their sociocultural embedding (Loveday 1981a). Moreover, many speech acts have been ritualized or institutionalized which frequently means that speakers do not take them literally, e.g. the natural response to "Oh, I don't have a pen" is to obey the implicit command and give the speaker a pen and not to remain inactive while the speaker fumbles around demonstratively.

But what about the less conventionally recognizable indirect speech acts such as the accusation detectable in "Have you started smoking again?" or the request for someone to be brought to the phone contained in "Is Peter there?" As Criper and Widdowson (1975) state:

> In foreign teaching the tendency is to assume an equation between linguistic form and communicative function. . . . Learners are commonly misled into thinking that commands are uniquely associated with imperative sentences and questions with interrogative sentences (p. 202).

To illustrate this point, here are some utterances which express commands in English:

You haven't eaten your spinach (statement)
You shall not mispronounce 'th' (future)
Do you want to come in now? (interrogative)
Why don't you come over? (negative interrogative)
You might close the door (superficially 'polite' model).

It goes without saying that the use of these and other indirect speech acts depend on a host of situational factors such as the roles, status of the interactants, the topic communicated about, in short, they depend on communicative competence. Although we have not yet fully stressed this point it is vital to realize that all the symbolic and framing patterns discussed here are very much subject to contextual and cultural constraints.

As for the cross-community comparison of speech act behaviour, House (1979) found that Germans persistently employed more explicit phraseology than English speakers in similar, separately simulated situations:

I   (student at a doctor's who has prescribed a too high dose of antibiotics)

Y: tonsilitis cleared up all right

X: yes but I've developed a rash . . . *I think well you told me to take* double the dosage that the leaflet given with the medicine prescribes you told me four spoonfuls and *it should only really be* two . . .

Y: wie gehts Ihnen denn (how are you)

X: ach überhaupt nicht gut . . . ich hab n fürchterlichen Ausschlag bekommen . . . und jetzt hab ich festgestellt daß die Dosis die Sie mir verschrieben haben also doppelt so hoch ist

   (oh *not at all well* . . . I have got a terrible rash . . . and Now I *have just discovered that the dosis you prescribed me is doubly high*)

II   (a student knocks at the door of a neighbour who is having a loud party)

Y: *how much longer is your party going on for*

X: oh a coupla hours maybe

Y: what I'm busy doing a bloody paper for tomorrow when I've got to do a presentation

X: na das find ich ja unheimlich unverschämt daß Ihr hier oben so einen Lärm macht . . . ich finds daß man doch mittlerweile den Lärm etwas abstellen könnte sonst hole ich irgendjemand vom Ordnungsamt rein

   (Well, *I find it absolutely impertinent that you* up here are making so much noise . . . *unless you turn the noise down* in the next minutes *I'll get someone in from the 'office for order'*). (pp. 83–84).

Here we see how the English speech-community favours indirect accusations and commands which is not the case in the German speech-community.

To further illustrate to what extent the interpretation of a speech act can be culturally and contextually sensitive, let us briefly look at the linguistic form of questions. Goody (1978) notes that among the Gonja questions asked by superiors are generally taken as rebukes and low status interactants avoid asking questions which are, in turn, interpreted as challenges. Hymes (1971) tells us that to Chilean Indians to repeat a question constitutes an insult while a direct answer to a first question among Brazilian Indians implies that the answerer has no time to talk, i.e. it is downright rude.

In fact, natural conversation is full of indirect speech acts which L2 speakers often seem to fail to recognize as such because of their lack of participation in and social experience of everyday L2 talk. In a study of German users of English conversing with native English speakers, Kasper (1979) found cases where the German took the propositional content of the utterance literally:

(The English speaker, E, comes home exhausted and drinks a beer with the L2 speaker, G.)
E: Uuh, I needed that, you know what the rush hour traffic is like
G: Oh tell me

Instead of responding with something like "Yes, it's terrible, isn't it", the L2 speaker takes up the referential meaning contained in the first utterance (rush hour traffic) and missed to acknowledge the partner's state of exhaustion with an appropriate sympathetic comment. Another example is when a landlady gives a German some sandwiches for a journey and says, "I hope it'll be enough" and receives the response, "Yes, of course, it will be enough" instead of a conventional indication of polite gratitude, e.g. "Oh yes, thanks that'll be just fine".

Actually, indirect speech acts are one of the most frequent components in *strategies of politeness,* especially in English. Ways of expressing politeness are, of course, a central area of concern in the learning and using of non-native communicative competence. The fundamental resources of verbal politeness are its 'softening devices' which Bublitz (1980) has conveniently summarized for English:

> the direct reference to the addressee(s), e.g. "Children, Mary, love" interjections and certain particles such as "oh", "well", "I say", "just"
> semantically restrictive elements which question and subjectify the utterance, e.g. "Do you think . . .", "as far as I'm concerned", "surely", tags such as "isn't it?", negation (I suppose Judy *won't* be here by Friday), modal verbs which suggest the speaker's assumptional approach, e.g. "the train *should* be here by now"
> the employment of indefinite pronouns and the passive, e.g. "Could *someone* give me a lift" and "I don't like *being shouted at*" and interestingly enough, insistent commanding forms such as *"Don't you* panic", "Do sit down"
> as well as the use of an in-language such as jargon, regional dialect and so on.

These softeners are undeniably essential for the establishment and maintenance of satisfactory social relations. Moreover, grammatical and phonetic errors are not considered as gravely as violations against appropriateness. As Bublitz writes, inappropriate linguistic behaviour is interpreted rather as personal weakness or even a personality defect (arrogance, coldness, tactlessness) and not as a lack in L2 mastery to which they are very often attributable. Since children start learning these softening devices at a very early age (it has been observed that already at three years old indirect speech acts are correctly constructed and appropriately employed because of their greater effectivity in achieving wants) it would make sense if they were also integrated into the early phases of the L2 teaching process and not simply 'grafted' on at an advanced level.

However, politeness strategies in culturally different communities have been shown to be based on universal principles by Brown & Levinson (1978) so that the divergent nature of cross-cultural communication is not in so much *what* is communicated as in *how* this is done. These investigators into comparative politeness do nevertheless point out that cultures select from universal possibilities certain preferred styles and strategies but the motivation for their selection tends to be obscure.

Now there are different conventions of offer and acceptance. In the Mediterranean and Middle Eastern areas an offer is generally never accepted the first time. In Greece, politeness may require at least four offers. Where such a pattern prevails, it is considered quite ill-mannered to accept immediately. If a Greek transfers such a pattern to an Anglo-American or British context it will probably result in him going without (Applegate 1975).

There are actually many cases where habitual verbal patterns which are satisfactorily employed in an L1 for dealing with recurrent situations will cause problems if transferred to an L2 context. This is particularly so with formulae. Every speech-community possesses a *stock of ritual routines* which may or may not include formulae for greeting, leave taking, apologizing, thanking, congratulating, stumbling (oops), cursing, toasting, introducing and so on. When speakers employ formulae, they draw upon the community's resources and demonstrate recognizable familiarity with and loyalty to the community's code and implicitly to its values since the petrified forms relate and refer to a special, historically given social framework. Adherence to this framework is expressed and partly achieved in the employment of formulae which in turn, contributes to an affirmation of the social order which is metaphorically alluded to in the uses of the formulae (Loveday 1981b). When L1 speakers do not possess formulistic competence they can be interpreted not only as lacking in politeness and sophistication but also as incompletely socialized. Formulae, of course, also define status and the situation, e.g. "hi" versus "Good morning". However, what interests us is their contrastive use in different communities and the ensuing cross-cultural 'interference' or negative application of L1 patterns in L2 contexts.

To illustrate this, let us return to the Japanese community where politeness is closely connected with the use of ceremonial-like formulae which are unhesitatingly used, without fear of sounding unoriginal. Japanese speakers tend to transfer these, resulting in inappropriate utterances. For example, on seeing an acquaintance who one has met at a party held by somebody else, it is quite acceptable to greet him with "Thank-you for Sunday". However, if this occurs in English, the native will probably be dumbfounded. The whens for apologies and thanks are considerably less in English than in Japanese so that the Japanese speaker of English must refrain from extensively employing these prefabricated routines. Similarly, Japanese speakers express gratitude more intensively by means of apologies:

> . . . during my early days in America—when a psychiatrist who was my superior did some kindness or other—I have forgotten exactly what, but it was something quite trivial. Either way, feeling the need to say something, I produced not "Thank-you" as one might expect, but "I'm sorry". "What are you sorry for?" he replied promptly, giving me an odd look. I was highly embarrassed. My difficulty in saying 'thank-you' arose, I imagine, from a feeling that it implied too great an equality with someone who was in fact my superior. . . . The reason, of course, was undoubtedly my deficiency in English at that time. But I had already begun to have an inkling that the difficulty I faced involved something more than the language barrier (Doi 1977, p. 12).

What the Japanese psychologist was facing here was a different cultural interpretation of what for him was a simple linguistic symbolization of gratitude. See Loveday (1982c) for a further discussion of Japanese inappropriate formulistic usage in English.

Another sphere related to communicative strategies of politeness are the varying rules for *addressing* persons which may also be inappropriately misused by non-natives. It is, for example, not uncommon to find Japanese users of English who call people Mr + First Name because in their speech-community the use of the first name alone is reserved for very intimate relationships or indicates extreme rudeness. In fact, names in the Japanese community are generally followed by suffixes which have various social meanings. It would, of course, be necessary for an L2 user of Japanese to be familiar with these in order to be able to communicate appropriately and effectively. Figure 4 presents a flowchart of the suffixes summarizing some of their contextual meanings and providing idealized competence for addressing in Japanese. The speaker enters at 'E' and chooses positively or negatively from the options. It is important to realize that the chart is only an abstract formalization of the social symbolization process. A speaker might well proceed to *san* in every context for suffix usage

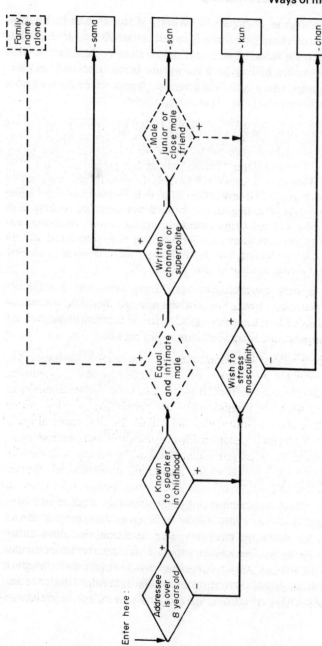

Fig. 4. How to use Japanese suffixes in addressing or referring to a person: an example of how language depends on sociocultural and contextual knowledge. (The dotted diamonds are only to be entered if the speaker is a male addressing another male.)

is, to a certain degree, idiosyncratic. What is discernible and interesting to note from the chart is that the linguistic symbols relate to grading or ranking on the basis of age, e.g. *kun* and *chan,* on the basis of superior/inferior status (*kun, san, sama*), on the basis of sex (*kun, san,* no suffix), all of which are fundamental themes of Japanese social organization.

Addressing in European language seems perhaps at first sight a lot less complicated. They are certainly less forms but are the rules for use simpler? In contemporary German, for instance, there is now a strong tendency for those who look (or want to look) under 35 to use a second person singular form DU instead of a plural SIE for most informal dealings. However, the appropriateness of the symbol depends on multiple factors such as setting, clothes, the drinking of alcohol and can also be limited to just one occasion with a speaker while on another occasion a different form might be used. This is obviously confusing for L2 learners—as well as sometimes L1 speakers. In an experiment reported by Schenker (1978) students in West Berlin went into department stores and asked saleswomen: "Du! kannst du mir sagen, wo es hier Tonbänder gibt" (literally: "You! Can you tell me where the tape recorders are" but in German this comes across as much less abrupt and not insolent but far too intimate). The reactions varied. The younger saleswomen did not mind; one older one asked the L2 speaker if he was foreign and explained that in German SIE is used to adults. Otherwise, the older saleswomen proved unhelpful and did not wish to speak to the students. This last reaction was obviously a kind of sanction for violating the norms but it also points to the variation between generations in the evaluation of DU in such contexts. Here the violation was part of an experiment but what about the situations where it is unintended?

We shall not dwell long on the subject of address since it has been widely discussed (Ervin-Tripp 1969). It is clearly an area of direct relevance to L2 teaching. However, one final example of a multilingual community deserves mentioning. These are the address rules among the Indonesian élite as reported by Tanner (1967) where a wide range of languages serve different social functions similar to the pronouns or suffixes of address described above. Thus, a variety of 'low', urban Indonesian (Djakarta slang) is the common code for parties, informal gatherings, excursions of bachelors, meetings in classes. (The linguistic behaviour is of the élite while studying in America.) When handling specific topics in conversation, however the language could switch, e.g. English for academic talk or Javanese for discussing religion or traditional Javanese culture. When it comes to working out which is the most suitable language for using in a particular relationship, the sociocultural calculating is far from straightforward for those multilinguals:

> . . . social distance—being a composite of so many potentially conflicting elements—was not always a clear guide to code choice for participants in an encounter. This had given rise to an increasingly common rule of thumb: "When in doubt use Indonesian." The following example serves to illustrate the point. When asked what language he usually spoke to his friend's Javanese wife, a young Javanese man answered, "It's a little unusual, with most of the other Javanese I speak *ngoko* (low Javanese, a symbol of easy-going familiarity among equals when used reciprocally). But with her I speak Indonesian. Perhaps she feels that we aren't so close yet!" In this case, the language repertoires of both are similar, although the man knows Dutch, can use Djakarta slang, and a little Sundanese, while the woman's repertoire is more limited. However, they both know low and high Javanese, standard and everyday Indonesian and English. They are both young adults of nearly the same age, good friends, neighbours, and are both university educated. In addition they are both sincere Moslems, quite religious by Javanese standards, and thus have an additional tie of 'closeness' (although the woman was considered to be 'more religious' than the man). Social distance is minimized in all these respects. However, they are of the opposite sex and both married, factors which tip the scales towards constraint, and more importantly, are of differing class backgrounds. The woman comes from a family that may be characterized as bourgeois while the man is a descendant of the old Javanese aristocracy. Use of *ngoko* (low Javanese) with him would plunge her into a degree of familiarity that would seem inappropriate to one reared to show respect to the nobility. Yet, use of *krama* (high Javanese) would seem incongruous to a friend and neighbour so similar in age, education and religious philosophy. (Tanner 1967, pp. 130–131.)

This passage highlights the problems of linguistic appropriacy which is one of the key-concepts in communicative competence. It also brings us to the important question of the diversity of synonymous forms. It seems to be that where multilingual communities use different languages for signalling social symbols, monolingual communities use different styles and dialects. Thus, the Indonesian case is really a culture-specific solution to a basic issue in social relations and behaviour in every speech community.

Fishman (1971) writes that a frequent comment about American travellers abroad is that they know, at most, only one variety of the language of the country they are visiting. As a result, they speak in the same way to a child, a professor, a shoe cleaner or a shopkeeper. This reveals not only their foreigness but also their ignorance of the appropriate ways of symbolizing a social relationship linguistically. The subject of linguistic varieties is discussed in the next chapter, but L2 speakers must be able to recognize and produce more than just the formal and usually written style and should be aware of the *internal variation* within language, whether it is based on social distance or on regional, class, age and ethnic differences. L2 learners should additionally be familiar with the so-called 'co-occurrence rules' which make sentences such as "How's it going, your Eminence? Centrifuging okay? Also, have you been analysin' whatch' unnertook t'achieve?" quite deviant (Ervin-Tripp 1971, p. 38).

Up to now we have restricted our attention to the contrasting interdependence between sociocultural system and grammar and vocabulary. Another domain which appears in the last example is the sound system or phonology. L2 learners are rarely taught about the significance of phonological reduction rules (slurring) in informal contexts. The consequence is that often their speech can redefine the context as formal which may be regarded unfavourably by native interlocutors. The phonological compression which symbolizes informality can be explained as a signal of 'less effort', although it might be even more complicated for the L2 learner than the usually limited type of sound system he has been exposed to in the classroom. An example from American English is in descending order of formality:

(1) What are you doing?
(2) Whaddya doin'?
(3) Whach doon? (Ervin-Tripp 1971, p. 43).

What has happened here is the loss of segments with weakest stress and the loss or assimilation of the semivowels. The American /r/ in postvocalic position is lost; /t/ has become /d/ and "are" reduced to a *y* sound. In (3) above, the /d/ has turned into a /t/ which combined with the /y/ sound results in a /ch/ sound.

In German, to give another instance, the middle section in *ich habe es gesagt* is reduced to *ich hab's gesagt* in casual speech (the sounds change from something like 'haabé es' to 'haps'. Those L2 speakers who fail to do this in appropriate circumstances sound 'stuffy' and 'pedantic'.

Segalowitz and Gatbonton (1977) carried out an experiment to find out how non-fluent users of an L2 handle a situation which requires a speech style outside their competence. English subjects with only an intermediate level of proficiency in French were asked to communicate twice in French with an unseen French partner and, for purposes of comparison, twice in English with an unseen English one. During each exchange with the partner implicit cues were given as to the formality or casualness of the communication. An exchange between the subject and intercolutor consisted of the interlocutor speaking first on an assigned topic and then the subject speaking on the same topic. There were no real interlocutors but only tape recordings. After the four exchanges, the subjects answered a questionnaire about how they felt while speaking and what general impressions they had gained of their partner and what impressions about themselves they believed to have conveyed to him. The subjects reported feeling most uncomfortable in the *casual* French exchange and attributed more negative personality characteristics to their interlocutor than they did in the careful speech situation whereas this reaction vanished when they used their L1, English. The subjects also believed they appeared less friendly when using their L2 in both exchanges than when using their L1; they felt they appeared significantly less intelligent and self-confident in the casual exchange than in the formal one. They found it easier to express themselves and claimed they were better understood in the casual L1 encounter than in the formal L1 encounter but the reverse when using French. The study shows how L2 learners lacking the competence to situationally adapt their language find casual interaction with native speakers a relatively negative experience. The investigators state that the learners may become discouraged from pursuing language practice with native speakers. Thus, the mastering of L2 basic vocabulary and syntax is not worthwhile without the skill to appropriately apply them.

This ability to adjust one's speech to contexts is related to another very important aspect of communicative competence which has been called speech accommodation (Giles *et al.* 1977). Giles has proposed that the extent to which individuals shift their speech style towards or away from the speech style of their interlocutors is a mechanism by which social approval or disapproval is communicated. When two people interact there is a tendency for them to become more alike in the way they sound, in how long and fast they speak and pause. Choice of linguistic form plays a significant role here—the more a socially and ethnically different interlocutor desires another's approval, the more he will make an effort to sound like the other person and, it seems, the more positively the reaction of the other person will be— although this is not always the case for the L2 speaker as we have noted in Chapter 2. Nevertheless, this strategy to sound like one's conversational partner, technically known as convergence, in many cases serves as a favourable symbol of attempted solidarity. Of course, when it does not occur speakers are seen as producing speech distinct from their interlocutors and the contextually created social distance increases. The negative consequences of convergence omission is exemplified in the case described by Gumperz (1976) where a black American student who was carrying out an academic survey did not respond appropriately to another black interviewee's opening: "So y're gonna check out ma ol lady, hah?" Instead of shifting his speech style accordingly to "Yea, I'm a git some info" which would have proved his familiarity with local verbal style, he responded with "Ah, no, I only came to get some information. They called from the office". The interviewee dropped the smile he had produced and disappeared without a word. the interviewer's standard English reply had been taken as a symbolization that he was not 'one of them' and could not be trusted. The student reported that the interview that followed was stiff and quite unsatisfactory. Being black himself, he knew that he had 'blown it' by failing to converge.

Naturally where L2 speakers lack the specific sociocultural and contextual linguistic knowledge, having only been taught and exposed to one L2 style or no style and only words as versions of a formal L1 style, they will most likely provoke a negative reaction in those circumstances where the style is grammatically, lexically and phonologically inappropriate.

Sometimes it is not just that sounds alter according to the context and are reduced but also that accompanying vocal noises also change. Corum (1975) has remarked that when speaking to a good friend, a child, or someone with whom you share a certain amount of solidarity, Basques will palatalize several consonants which are not otherwise palatalized. This contextually determined vocal variation is bound to exist in many other speech communities but it has only begun to be documented.

Up until the case of palatalization in informal contexts in Basque we have only dealt with the traditional areas of L2 teaching: grammar, vocabulary and the sound system. There exists, however, another highly significant symbolic code hardly ever touched upon in the L2 classroom known as *paralanguage,* that is to say, the vocal, kinesic (gestural) and proxemic (spatial) channels which accompany, interfuse and partly synchronize the traditionally recognized ones.

The first paralinguistic code we shall deal with is the *tone of voice.* One part of this is voice quality which refers to the special physical and habitual settings of an individual vocal tract such as nasalization. Impressionistically, different voices are often labelled as husky, gruff, adenoidal, bleating and so on by laymen. Voice quality provides different kinds of information: it helps give us a picture of a person's stature and physique, age and sex, medical condition and personality but it also carries social information. Often particular accents have a specially associated voice quality which gives clues to regional and social status, sometimes also occupation (an English clergyman, for example). Velarization* is typically associated in British English with the speech style of the Beatles and Liverpool; in Arabic it is a mark of masculinity. But voice quality also is interpreted as giving indices to personality, e.g. Scherer (1979) discovered that nasalization in English females was considered "unattractive, foolish, lethargic, and self-effacing" (p. 183). The implications of these findings are worth

---

*The articulation of a sound accompanied by raising the back of the tongue towards the soft membrane forming the roof of the mouth behind the hard palate.

considering for L2 speakers who come from communities where nasalization does not carry a negative association. For instance, in a Bolivian language, nasalization carries an honorific or a superpolite function whereby individuals of lower socioeconomic status address those of higher ranks with a prominence of nasalization for all vowels in the utterance; thus, a woman being polite to her husband or a man asking a favour nasalizes their speech (Crystal 1971).

Naturally, L2 voice quality can assume a value dimension that it does not possess in the original community. For instance, when Japanese speakers and especially Japanese women transfer their voice quality setting for politeness contexts which is composed of breathiness, openness, lowered volume and raised register into English, the L2 symbolization is not one of social distance (as in Japanese) but of extreme intimacy as in private male-female relations and of feminine baby-talk usually associated with a lack of intelligence (Cammack and Van Buren 1967).

Related to cross-linguistic differences in voice quality, I have observed how in situations of intimacy or commiseration, North Germans pucker and protrude their lips as in baby talk (e.g. when adults in English say kutshee kutshee koo) while they speak to symbolize sympathy or solidarity. In Tzeltal a creaky voice is used to express commiseration or complaint and a ritual sustained falsetto for inter-action with very high status interlocutors (Brown & Levinson 1978). However, in British English, creaky voice at the end of an utterance is a 'noise' which bears prestige and adds authority to the speaker's words; it is perhaps characterizable as a low-pitched, 'machine-gun' drawling.

In fact, pitch range, as glimpsed in the Tzeltal example, is a very significant aspect of voice quality. Its employment by Japanese speakers of English can lead to cross-cultural miscommunication (Loveday 1981c) for while standard English speakers of both sexes tend to converge on a relatively high pitch in the expression of politeness, Japanese males and females markedly diverge. The cause for this varying community use of pitch can be linked to different social expectations of sexual role: Japanese men are normatively required to take a low profile linguistically, understating and being terse while

Japanese women are expected to be dainty and delicate in their speech. In English, on the other hand, males use polite high pitch to metaphorically signal deference since high pitch is associated with the voice of children and women who traditionally have occupied less threatening and authoritative status positions. On top of this, the low pitch performance of the Japanese male speakers in polite English contexts tends to be interpreted as boredom, absence of involvement or rudeness.

Gumperz (1977) has also shown how interethnic misunderstanding can occur from differential use of pitch and volume. In a heated discussion in English between an Indian L2 speaker and an English college teacher about admittance to a course, it emerged that the former interpreted the teacher's high pitched tones as emotional and impolite. On the other hand, the teacher felt that the L2 speaker was shouting but this impression was caused by features of increased loudness and pitch register which are patterns symbolizing to the Indian a claim for speaking rights when interrupted. A native English speaker, on the other hand, will try to regain the floor by purely linguistic means such as by saying "I didn't finish".

Different speech communities have different norms of loudness for talking. Of course, these vary according to the contextual configuration of setting, participants, topic and so on while it has been noted that the British English take care to pitch their voices so as not to intrude on those around them, this may look conspiratorial to Americans whose normal volume appears, on the other hand, too low and sounds insincere to Arabs (Hall 1972).

From what we have presented so far it is evident that language is not solely built up with words but is enveloped in layers of richer vocal meaning. Sadly, studies into cross-cultural variation in the tone of voice are rare probably because few have ever questioned the relativity of their vocal symbols and also due to the lack of developed frameworks for dealing with the subject. However, one recent study on English *intonation in interaction* by Brazil, Coulthard & Johns (1980) is an encouraging sign that the pedagogic relevance of vocal symbolizing is at last being considered. As these investigators note in their preface:

The further one's interests move towards some notion of 'communicative competence' and away from the lesser ability to produce and understand grammatical sentences, the greater the pressure one feels to take proper account of how intonation contributes to the communicative value of an act of speech. One also begins to realize more and more that engagement with intonation is not merely a cosmetic exercise, concerned with the removal of residual and comparatively unimportant, marks of foreignness in the otherwise competent utterances of an advanced learner, but that in fact it leads one to a consideration of some quite fundamental aspects of the communicative process.

The investigators go on to discuss the function of intonation in the management of conversations, e.g. when participants take the floor.

Finally the *non-verbal channels* in the communication process are considered. These too are culturally relative to a degree but no one yet knows exactly how much. Obviously, L2 teachers should familiarize their students with basic aspects of the L2 gestural code and, in so doing, they will have to rely in many cases on their own observations since the study of community variation in this domain is still in its infancy. However, various researchers have pointed out that the maintenance of conversation crucially relies on the interactants' abilities to establish a rhythmic exchange of speakership and listener-ship signals through gaze direction, head nods, eye blinks and so forth.

A pioneering investigation into communication between different ethnic groups showed that the successful ability to establish and continue this rhythmic exchange depended on the shared ethnic background of the speakers (Erickson 1973).

The theoretical difficulty with the study of gestures or *kinesics* lies in the drawing of the boundary line between 'instinctual' movements, expressions and acts versus the numerous culture-based kinesic systems that have to be learned just like any arbitrarily evolved symbolizing pattern. In fact, it seems that man has very little of the species-specific in his motor acts. We cannot, of course, go into the entire description of culturally different non-verbal signs; not only would it be far too lengthy but it would not really serve our purpose here which is essentially to reveal the extent of the sociocultural determination of communicative behaviour and provide a justification for the learning of non-native symbolizing patterns.

Instead, the treatment is restricted to the ensuing confusion and irritation caused by the differential decoding of non-verbal symbols which, it must be noted, are here only 'bits' abstracted out from the complex flow of movement in communication.

Consider, as one tiny example, how the Chinese hate to be touched, slapped on the back, or even to shake hands; how easily an American could avoid offence by simply omitting "these intended gestures of friendliness" (La Barre 1974, p. 218).

While some communities regard an interlocutor as suspicious or shifty if he does not make a certain amount of eye contact with his partner when talking face to face, Japanese children are taught in school to "direct the gaze at the region of their superior's Adam's apple or tie knot" (Morsbach 1973, p. 269). Unlike the Latin or Middle Eastern or certain North European patterns, the Japanese consider being repeatedly looked at or intensively focused on with the eyes as unpleasant and even rude. Intent gazing at the person one is talking to does not signal respect. Rather, the tendency to look downwards is appreciated, especially among females, and this is thought well-mannered and elegant. Consequently, the Japanese desirous of an effective transaction with an American, for example, in a non-intimate context, need to understand the significance of eye contact as it works to signal turn-taking and provides feedback during social interaction (Argyle & Dean 1965).

Another aspect of non-verbal behaviour is facial expression. Self-control is highly valued in Japan and the ideal of an expressionless face in situations of great anxiety was strongly promoted by the Samurai ethos. Such expressionlessness occurring in communication with non-Japanese can be misinterpreted as coldness or lack of sensitivity. However, even if it is possible to train the L2 communicator in this subtle and complex sphere (one's way of expressing emotion non-verbally is normally acquired during childhood and adolescence) the L2 actor-speaker still needs to be able to recognize the basic meanings of facial gestures in the target community. That facial signalling movements are in no manner universally interpretable is well proven in an analysis of responses from American, Turkish and Japanese natives to sets of facial expressions (Cuceloglu 1967). However, it should be added that *natural* facial expressions are universally interpretable. The problem arises in decoding the manipulation, concealment and controlling of the movements.

Leaving interactional non-verbal symbolization, let us turn to gestural communication. In Japan the extension of the right-hand palm upwards and flapping the fingers up and down is a beckoning signal; Seward (1968) describes an amusing incident where it was miscoded:

> One day in Hakone, I was watching a Japanese girl-guide whose American tourist charges had become separated from her by a considerable distance and saw her use this gesture [described above] to try to gather her flock of about twenty, elderly, bewildered-looking souls about her. The diverse effects were amusing. Some thought they had been abandoned by their girl-guide and began to mill about like worried sheep. Others appeared to think that it was a signal for a drink and started to straggle back toward the bar of the hotel. Still others apparently interpreted it to mean that they were now on their own and began to disperse through the town (p. 42).

Similarly confusing was an incident I once observed. A Japanese acquaintance asked an English friend about her plans for the weekend upon which the latter tapped her nose with her index finger twice, making the English signal for mind your own business. This caused confusion. In Japan, one points to the nose to indicate me, oneself. In the west the stomach serves to signify one's person. This minor incident clearly illustrates community variation in non-verbal symbolizing patterns. From an English point of view, Germans seem to be moronically swotting invisible flies with their right hand in front of their face when they want to indicate the haziness arising from the fact that they or someone else is unable to follow something. The French shake a limp wrist to signal something difficult or arduous.

Although gestures and facial expressions are spontaneous, partly automized symbols this should not deter the L2 teacher from making the learner conscious of the differences in communicative systems nor from helping him/her to omit, adapt and adopt target body symbolism if native-hood is an objective.

Space between people also expresses meaning because humans define territorial boundaries around themselves. This is achieved in a variety of ways such as chair arrangements, standing positions, etc., but what is of interest is how different communities perceive the size of the bubble of personal space surrounding an individual. Pioneering investigations into this symbolizing pattern have been made by Hall (1972) who claims that American space judgements depend principally on the tactile (whether parts of the body come into contact during interaction) and visual senses, although body odour and heat as well as the oral–aural systems are also involved. There exist two commonly observed levels of American spatial proximity in contexts defined as 'casual-personal' and a 'social-consultative' which are four and twelve feet, respectively. These distances represent the extremes of closeness and remoteness. However, the distance are not culturally universal. Arabs, for instance, do not feel friendliness or solidarity unless they can detect the heat, moisture and smell of the breath which, in fact, leads to the violation of the American smell zone in cross-cultural encounters. The spatial distance between North Europeans and Latin Europeans has been widely observed to vary and L2 actors should certainly be familiar with community variation in *proxemics* (spatial symbolism) to avoid potentially giving and receiving offence.

Posture also plays a significant role in interpersonal communication and, although like most of the non-verbal symbols outlined above are part of unconscious knowledge, consciousness of its functions is particularly valuable for cross-cultural exchanges where a host of target community signals are not being fully transmitted. Scheflen (1972) estimates that there are less than thirty culturally standard postural configurations of shared communicative significance for Americans each occurring in a limited number of contexts and, of course, as with many symbolic patterns, there exist variations in style relating to personality, sex, age, status, occupation and health. The basic American postural indicators of social relationships are body orientation (how interlocutors arrange their body to focus on each other) and congruence (the extent to which they adopt similar body poses, e.g. outstretched legs or crossed arms). Postural congruence is a symbol of mutuality. Where congruence is absent, other evidence of non-association is often present: the posturally non-congruent interactant tends to be looking out of the window, not talking, appearing lost in thought and so on. Poyatos (1977) offers an interesting example of inappropriate performance of one's native community non-verbal signals, including postural behaviour, and how they can be misunderstood in a non-native context:

> Back in the days when I was a student in Madrid, I went to the railway station to meet an American boy who was going to be my roommate for some time . . . we went home and I introduced him to my landlady, who had to draw back her hand because Tom, the average Midwesterner, was not thinking of shaking a woman's hand. "Well, how was your trip?" she asked in Spanish and Tom, thinking of English *"Well—"* because it had not been good, answered "Bueno . . ." which actually means good, so she smiled and said "I'm glad". Well, after that Tom sat on a chair, began to talk with his hands crossed over his head using long hesitation vowels, "Uh—" quite often, and once he stretched as if . . . it was the most natural thing in the world to do.

The American value of a relaxed pose clashed here with the Spanish postural pattern appropriate for interacting with an elderly hostess.

Because discrepancy or conflict between verbal and non-verbal cues for interpersonal attitudes is often an emotionally disturbing experience, Schnapper (1979) has set down certain exercises to make Peace Corps volunteers conscious of non-verbal communication. He constructed situations which resulted in emotional responses and encouraged trainees to continue the practice of this behaviour until it became a natural and accepted part of their communicative repertoire. Part of the technique is to divide a group of trainees in half, give directions to one half so that when they are paired up with a member of the other half, the non-directed partner will have feelings of discomfort about his partner's 'strange' behaviour. Here is a description of an exercise on the use of space: the group leader directs the separated groups into discussions and then one group is told that when they rejoin the 'uninformed' group and are matched with a partner, they are to establish a distance of comfort and then decrease it by one inch. At each signal from the group leader, they are to come one inch closer to the partner. Eventually, when the distance has been shortened by six inches or more, the non-directed partners will experience discomfort and consciously or unconsciously will start moving back. Later, in discussing the experiment, the directed partners can be explained that they were imitating the comfortable positions of South Americans and that if the undirected partners were to behave in the same way with a Latin, the Latin would think them unfriendly and cold. Conversely, in Somalia, it would be the American who would be perceived as being too close for Somali comfort. In such a follow-up, visual material, e.g. photographs of face-to-face interaction can be effectively used to heighten the sensitivity for the prime question: how do I interpret and signal non-verbal meaning in a culturally different community?

This brief examination of framing and symbolizing patterns demonstrates the immense complexity of the communication process and its multiple channels. The patterns involved here have very diverse functions but the most immediate and relevant ones for the L2 speaker-actor are:

the establishing and maintaining of interpersonal relations;
the provision of feedback, e.g. agreement, apathy, rejection;
the signalling of the nature of a social relationship, e.g. as distant, informal or status-full.

As well as these basic indications, interactants also use the patterns to evaluate each other's personality. Thus, there is a constant monitoring of intended and uncontrolled verbal and non-verbal signs in order to make sense of what the other person means and is. This sense, however, only derives from a mutually shared and mutually created context. It is negotiated sense-making where patterns employed by the participants mediate and adapt to the construction of meaning.

Although it is wrong to exaggerate the differences in cross-community framing and symbolizing patterns, the L2 speaker-actor certainly needs to be sensitized to their cultural and contextual relativity. Human communication all over the world is undeniably based on many commonly-shared principles but communities select and build and institutionalize certain patterns in preference to others. Successful intercultural interaction depends on the extent to which participants correctly interpret each others' signals and the level of good will they attribute to each other. Of course, the framing and symbolizing patterns do not inherently present anything negative but research shows their non-occurrence or inappropriate or miscoded occurrence to produce unfavourable consequences: negative stereotyping often follows, confusion, discomfort and tension or even communication breakdown may ensue; subsequent interaction is avoided; suspicion and hostility can arise. It appears that native speakers are much more ready to excuse L2 deviancy in areas of grammar, vocabulary and pronunciation but when it comes to the deviant handling of framing and other symbolizing patterns, the native often perceives the L2 speaker-actor as impolite, uneducated, aggressive, indifferent or uncooperative. If this happens, then both interactants are responsible for the miscommunication resulting from a contrasting symbolic and organizational construction of contextual meaning. The gravity of such asymmetry is to be measured against the degree of its negative effect on the evolution of further interpersonal and intercultural relations. What is ideally required is a degree of mutual tolerance and willingness to make an effort to understand cross-cultural transactions. However, the L2 community is many cases possesses power and territoriality and superior group size so that they find it unnecessary to make concessions to the non-native individual. Thus, in these instances the non-native will have to conform to the L2 communicative system if he desires successful encounters and must be aided in the acquisition of the framing and symbolizing patterns of the target community or, in other terms, must learn L2 communicative competence.

Implementing communicative competence

(i) The new ideology

For some time now, applied linguists and language teachers have been fashionably proclaiming communicative competence as the path to enlightenment and salvation but very few have explicitly discussed how communicative competence can be attained in the classroom. An interpretation of the term as the operational knowledge of a culturally and contextually embedded meaning-system has been offered. This supports the argument in Chapter 3 that a necessary dimension to bilingualism is biculturalism. The significance of the interrelationship between language and culture has already been discussed and one is now faced with the question of how such competence should be imparted. Some maintain that one should not bother with the subject because it is too difficult to teach, impossible to test, not accessible via the written medium, imposes an alien personality on the learner, undermines the L2 learner's confidence in interaction by drawing attention to too many factors and can only be transmitted by natives (Williams 1979).

Admittedly, today there exists a conspicuous gap between theories of language and theories of language use. As often as not, the L2 speaker-actor is left to himself to discover, literally by trial and error at whatever personal cost, how framing and symbolizing patterns vary cross-culturally although it is doubtful if many learners ever penetrate their dynamics for, as it is vital to underline, most of us believe that our native community's patterns are the natural, normal and adequate expressions of self.

However, it is not being suggested that the teaching of L2 gram-maticality be replaced by a counterpart totalitarian communicative conformity. The reason that communicative competence should be a goal of L2 teaching is that without such knowledge and ability varying degrees of dissatisfaction and frustration in transactions for both native and non-native are bound to arise. The purpose of teaching communicative competence, then, is to avoid and overcome this potential dissatisfaction and frustration. This does not mean that perfect nativeness should be principally aimed for, unless so desired by the learner, but rather, more subtley, that those aspects of non-nativeness which disturb and rupture communication and which can lead to negative stereotyping concerning personality and intelligence should be avoided. Communicative patterns that promote inter-actional synchrony and aid cooperation in L2 exchanges should be learnt and applied.

This is, of course, not at all a simple and straightforward goal to attain. For most of us, L1 communicative competence takes place at a subliminal level. We have built up our repertoire of patterns mainly through socialization but also by observing, selecting, imitating and elaborating on particular models in our sociocultural environment. The fundamental problem is that our communicative behavior is really a flexible system of norms which vary and correlate with a number of stable factors such as generation, sex, urbanity/ruralness and contextual factors such as interpersonal relationship, status, role and many more. Somehow we know, although we may not know that we do, how to produce and interpret these patterns appropriately in order to achieve particular ends and satisfy particular needs. The task of L2 teaching then is to focus on those patterns which are most relevant to a particular type of learner and to bring him to a point where he can satisfactorily achieve his ends through communicating in a variety of contexts without provoking negative reactions or evaluations, although not necessarily like a perfect native.

This brings us back to the question of *functionalism* with which this chapter opened. We have seen that in order to function in L2 communication, learners need to realize the crucial nature of the *how, when and where* something is said rather than, as has been the classroom situation up to now, just concentrating on the *what*. It follows from this that L2 teachers must also alter their view of language in the classroom and come to the realization that it constitutes a means as well as an end itself. This goal of effective communication in real life contexts is far from novel—in the Middle Ages monks tried to develop it by introducing the compulsory use of Latin in daily monastic routines and later pupils made the grand tour accompanied by native tutors to attain it.

In contrast, the nineteenth and twentieth centuries moved away from functionalism because of its intellectual fascination with the mathematization of thought and the parallel formalization of the vehicle of thought itself, language. As Tyler (1978) observes:

> the movement of formalism triumphant is at once the moment of its decline, for nowhere is the intellectual poverty of formalism more clearly revealed than in the empty formalizations of language . . . for . . . language is neither an objective form nor a formal object, but is instead a rhetorical instrument which makes use of objective forms and formal objects only in the interest of getting the work of the world done, and not in the interest of abstract science (p. xi).

Even though functionalism has been the ultimate purpose of traditional L2 study, its realization has been placed somewhere on the distant horizon, that is to say, at a comfortably (utopian?) distance from what goes on in the classroom. Thus, L2 teachers have tended to presume without any basis that once the forms were correctly acquired, their use would naturally follow (Criper & Widdowson 1975).

However, too many examples in the real world are known that prove otherwise; for instance, Roulet's (1978) comments on students who obtain good results in tests but are incapable of holding a conversation in the L2. If the principal aim of L2 study as the adequate and appropriate expression of self is generally shared by learners and teachers alike the fundamental problem lies in the methodology chosen to accomplish it. After all, the techniques of behavioural drilling and audio-visual courses were a conscious attempt in this direction. They were not successful because they restricted language in the classroom to referential meaning, leaving out its equally important social, cultural and expressive dimensions and were traditionally orientated to a conservative, written norm fascinated by the linguistic rules of sentences in isolation. They totally ignored the rules-for-use above and beyond the sentence level and their variation across communities and contexts.

A further aspect which is perhaps less easy to accept for some is the L2 teacher's new role in a classroom aiming at communicative competence. A shift away from the limited, one-way communication track from teacher to students has to take place towards a multi-track group-dynamic situation where the teacher is still in control but in a far more advisory and organizational capacity than before.

In fact, all classroom inflow ultimately rests with the teacher. Even when students demonstrate initiative, they still look to the teacher for the responsible maintenance of the mutually accomplished enterprise of the lesson. Communicative competence obviously does not mean necessarily the wholesale rejection of traditional materials. There is nothing to prevent communicatively-based materials from being subjected to grammar-translation treatment just as there may be nothing to prevent a teacher with only an old grammar-translation book at his disposal from teaching communicatively (Littlewood 1980).

The crux of the matter is the teacher's conception of what learning a second language is and how it should take place. The basic principle involved is an orientation towards collective participation in a process of use and discovery achieved by cooperation between students together as well as between teacher and students.

Three stages of learner-centred communicative teaching can be delineated: a first minimal level for interpreting and producing basically stereotypic linguistic behaviour in the most essential areas of the target community experience which is based on satisfying primary needs, e.g. asking for information in public contexts such as in the street or at the railway station; a middle level of competence where the L2 speaker-actor can creatively apply and vary the patterns and secondary needs can be satisfied, e.g. expression of self in dialogue or text; and a maximal ideal level which corresponds to the concept described by the Council of Europe (1973) as near-nativeness in the mastery of the language as regards pronunciation; intonation, non-verbal behaviour, absence of error and the acquisition of an active vocabulary equal to an educated native speaker together with a familiarity with stylistic and dialectal varieties likely to be encountered, on top of the awareness of the sociocultural background shared by average educated natives.

(ii) *Methodological magic*

If the majority of L2 learners together with textbook writers and language school directors view L2 teaching as a form of witchcraft (Antier 1977), let us now examine exactly what kind of classroom sorcery can be conjured up to impart communicative competence.

As stated above, there has been considerable discussion on the application of communicative competence in the L2 classroom which has restricted itself to the sketching of course contents and the correspondence between learner's needs and the linguistic resources required to satisfy them (see Munby 1978; Widdowson 1978; Brumfit & Johnson 1979). Very few have seriously considered the many other aspects of communicative teaching: the culturally specific construction of meaning, the entire symbolic dimension of non-verbal behaviour and voice quality, the problems arising from contrasting communicative patterns and the techniques to be employed by the L2 teacher to transmit communicative competence.

Since all of these have been dealt with, except the last aspect, the rest of this chapter is devoted to the teaching of communicative knowledge-for-use.

A useful starting point for teachers is to critically examine textbook material, asking the question: do written dialogues about Mrs Brown shopping at her friendly neighbourhood grocer's constitute communicative competence? A recent German investigation found that less than 14% of all English material in German grammar schools was conceived of from the perspective of the communicative strategies required by a German speaker of English (Piepho 1977).

Fitzgerald (1980) notes that although in recent years there have been attempts to make courses and course books more communicative, there have been few alterations in methodology. Only a small portion of the lesson is devoted to oral pair work which often undermines the whole purpose of its introduction, for example:

Talk about the football players. Choose any player you like. For example:

	Question	Answer
(1)	How old is Jim?	He is 25.
(2)	Is he married?	Yes, he is.
(3)	What's his wife's name?	Her name's Sandra. (p. x).

These examples show that the statement and question can be manipulated but in reality the natural answer to (1) and (3) would simply be the last word. The teacher, however, often corrects the student who fails to produce the whole sentence. What is obviously needed here are the ground rules for authentic communication with a challenging kind of activity where effort must be expended in order to stimulate motivation and interest.

One way of providing a challenge is to work with a problem, e.g. students have a map and ask each other for directions or a student is sent out to the front to draw something on the blackboard on the basis of instructions given by other students who have been given material by the teacher for this purpose.

Kettering (1974, p. 76) provides more culturally contextualized problems:

Dinner at an American Home
Read the following problem individually. Consider the possible solutions. You may add your own solution if you think you can improve on the ones given. Decide on the solution that you think is the best one and be able to justify your solution.

Then discuss your solutions in your group, giving your choices and discussing the advantages and disadvantages of each. You must decide together on one solution (that means that you may have to give up your own solution) and be able to justify it.

Meet as a class and discuss group decisions. REMEMBER: There is no one single right answer.

Time limit: approx. 20–30 minutes.

Problem
An American family asks you for dinner. They pick you up and take you to their home. They are very nice and try hard to make you forget how nervous and afraid you are about your English and the new customs. The wife has made a special dinner for you and has used her best dishes and tablecloth. She serves the food and you take a lot of the main dish to make her feel happy. You taste it and you *hate* it! It has liver in it and you never eat liver. She is waiting to see if you like the food. What do you do?
a) Excuse yourself and tell her you suddenly feel very ill.
b) Explain to her that you just don't like liver.
c) Try to eat the liver and pretend you like it.
d) Don't say anything and just don't eat it but eat a lot of the other food.
e) Tell her your doctor told you never to eat liver because it makes you sick.
f) . . .
g) . . . .

Wherever possible, native speakers should be sought out to participate in truly authentic communicative situations as Selekman (1973) developed for learners of Hebrew in Israel and found extremely effective:

1. Each student is given a phone number of a participating monolingual native speaker.
2. The student must call this number, introduce himself and indicate why he is calling—all of this in Hebrew, of course.

3. The student must find out a task that has already been planned for him to do and that the native speaker is ready to give to the student; for example in coordination with the "have to do something" structure my students were working with, one task was, "You have to bring a prayer book to Hebrew school tomorrow".

4. It is the student's problem to arrive at some understanding of the task if he does not immediately grasp what the native speaker is communicating.

5. The student should thank the native speaker, and make the proper farewell.

6. The student should go through with the task assigned, and be prepared to tell in class in Hebrew a summary of the phone conversation and the resulting activity.

Furthermore, L2 learning has been shown to be aided by the presentation of the language in contexts of communication which, after all, is the way it is naturally acquired as in the case of an L1, Oller & Obrecht (1968), for instance, discovered that mechanical manipulation of structures could be best assimilated in a context in which the language performed a clearly communicative function. They also found that sentences were more easily learned when they were placed in a meaningful sequence. Another experiment conducted by Savignon (1972) investigated the teaching of French to three groups of university students where a control group used classic audio-aural teaching methods with a language laboratory, the second used materials consisting essentially of conversational exercises on French culture and civilization and the third used materials employed based on the carrying out of specific communicative acts. What is interesting is that with this last group the researchers particularly aimed at enabling students to use French in spoken contexts from the first week of the course without paying much attention to the linguistic accuracy of what was said. The results were significant:

> To summarize, all students had received similar instruction in linguistic skills, and there was no evidence that one group knew more French than the other in terms of the level of linguistic competence attained. However, those students who had been given the opportunity to use their linguistic knowledge for real communication were able to speak French. The others were not (p. 160).

These findings bring us to the use of drama and, more specifically, the use of spontaneous improvisations in the form of role play in L2 teaching. A great deal of literature on this subject already exists (Bedford 1972; The British Council 1977; Maley & Duff 1978). Littlewood (1975, 1978, 1979); Butzkamm & Dodson (1980) directly refer to the application of drama to the teaching of communicative competence.

First of all, it should be pointed out that role play, like all interaction activities does not *automatically* lend itself to developing communicative competence but can easily be slanted that way.

For instance, Roberts (1980) describes a technique of practising the influence of context on language production in a role play exercise. Students are handed cue cards giving details of the speaker's intention, attitudes to each other, relative age, status and possibly location too which must be incorporated into their linguistic enactment of the situation, e.g.:

A: You are an MA student at a British university. Tomorrow you are going to Leeds University to have an interview connected with an MPhil you want to do. You want B to take lecture notes for you. You like B and you often play squash together.

B: You are an MA student at a British university. Tomorrow you have to go to the Home Office in London to sort out a problem with your visa. A is on your course and you often play squash together.

Before this, students have discussed how to ask someone a favour such as what they would do as a favour for a colleague or relative. The students then act out the situation on the cards. They are presented with a skeleton of the stages of the encounter on the blackboard beforehand and have to suggest possible ways of expressing the abstract speech acts with the teacher. They are asked to adhere to the skeleton framework during the role play:

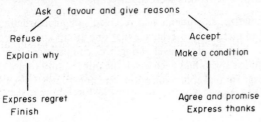

There are three basic ways of staging role play exercises: (1) the students assume a role in a contextualized dialogue, the structure and vocabulary of which have been presented in advance; (2) role play involving more creativity and initiative from students who have to perform interviews or playlets in small groups based on certain situations or themes with the possibility of being prepared in written form; and (3) the students are presented with specific roles to adopt in the solving of a given problem. This is often called a *simulation* exercise.

Here is an analysis of the third type of activity described above carried out by intermediate L2 speakers of English. The students were provided with a map of an island (showing the position of swamp, desert, cannibals, crocodiles, surrounding reefs and a missionary) and an information sheet explaining their situation (that they had been shipwrecked and were without food and water but possessed a radio transmitter and a compass and had to decide collectively on a plan for survival). Additionally, each student received a role card which they had to base their performance on. For example: "You are Professor Johnson, a university professor and think yourself very, very clever. You want to work this problem out with your brain and mathematical formulae. You can't stand emotional people—especially Miss Jones who is always moaning—you tell her that she's a silly girl. You point out that 1. there's not enough food for everyone; 2. there's only one day's water and two bottles are left; 3. it is dangerous to split up because of the cannibals and you've only got one compass. Say once: 'We must be logical about this' and 'First, we have to . . .'."

While bearing in mind the details of their role cards, the general information given to the group and the map as well as the linguistic information prepared in class (here the speech acts of suggesting, persuading, agreeing and disagreeing) and stimulated by pictures of islands which they have talked about, the students set about solving the problem. Exactly what form the input will take depends on the group's level of communicative competence and imaginative abilities. The class could also have been offered a description or story about tropical islands. It is important to realize that students are rarely able to incorporate L2 structures and words which have just been presented to them immediately into such an exercise. Of course, in classes where group cooperation has not been worked at, shyness, resistance, silence and insecurity during the performance will have to be overcome. This can be achieved by warm up games or even by first producing written materials, although these should not be used at the improvisation stage.

Anyway, there now follows a transcription of a group of adolescent students of English as a second language carrying out this simulation activity. Normally, the students converse in Gujarati and this is the very first time that they have performed such an exercise. There are four boys (referred to as 1, 2, 3 and 4 for convenience) and two girls (5 and 6) seated in a circle on one side of the classroom. The rest of the class are sitting at their desks turned towards them. I was situated at the opposite end of the room trying not to intrude or be called upon during the enactment.

Transcription of simulation activity (first part)

1: Where do you come from?

3: Maidstone, the posher part of London. I come from Maidstone.

1: How about you, then?

5: Oh, I'm Miss Jones.

1: Are you married?

5: No, but I've got a boyfriend.

(class response: oooh!)

4: Where do you come from?

5: I come from England.

4: England . . . whereabouts?

5: Um . . . Liverpool.

4: Oh, Liverpool.

1: How about you?

6: I'm Mrs. Bagstone, your wife.

(roar of laughter from class)

1: Oh, I didn't know that.

3: Come on, OK.

1: Who are you?

2: I'm Professor Johnson.

1: Professor . . . Joh—. . . .

4: Where do you come from?

2: From England.

1: England?

2: Yeah.

1: Which university did you go to?

(suggestion from audience: Oxford)

2: Oxford. I come from . . . you know, Cornwall, down there in south-west England. . . .

1: My son was there three years ago.

4: Yeah, *I* was there.

2: Which uni— . . . university is he learning?

1: In Oxford University.

2: But you know, there are too many children, I can't remember his name.

3: We are here. Something to do. We must . . . we must. . . .

2: We must do something.

4: Is that all?

1: One, two, three, four . . . five, six of us.

3: Yeah, where is the another one? What's his name?

(someone in audience: your son. Laughter)

1: He's in England now.

3: He's not my son. He's my nephew, you know that, my nephew.

1: Who?

3: David . . . David. All right come on. . . .

4: Yeah.

3: There's doctor, professor and . . . we've got enough people.

1: (Slowly) There's a professor, there's a doctor, there's a doctor. . . .

2: I think . . . I think . . . er.

3: What's your opinion?

1: In the map it says here's a mission down here.

3: Doctor, did you see that?

4: Yes, I see.

1: And we are right in the bottom.

2: Can I see?

(calls from audience: you've got the map)

1: You've got a map, you know.

3: Are you geography professor?

2: History professor.

4: History . . . oh, can you tell us the history of this island?

2: Also I can teach maths . . . biological maths, you know?

(laughter)

simultaneous talking

3: You know what's time two times two?

2: Pardon?

3: What's time two times two?

2: Twenty-two.

1: Well, I think that . . . we've got to think of getting at this mission and don't argue please. We've still got plenty to do.

2: First thing, we have . . . must find some food.

5: I'm frightened.

6: I'm hungry, aren't you?

general murmuring

3: I'm allright . . . food.

2: Yeah, we must er find food and er after er we have to look er see er what kind of desert is this island?

1: Well, it says on this there's a jungle. We might find some red berries there.

4: What about the 'cannibulls' just down there?

1: It's quite a long way. . . .

3: Yeah!

4: We need food, don't we?

3: Yeah . . . let's. . . .

4: What plan can you think of?

5: I'm frightened!

3: She's always frightened.

1: Without her boy it's very difficult.

(audience laughter)

5: Oh, shut up! Can't get rid of you!

simultaneous talking

2: Because er you know, in our boat, the leak, we must make a boat and go, you know, you'll find er coconut trees.

3: You know, that's very hard work to do.

1: You get sharks in there.

simultaneous talking

5: We're all going to die.

4: Yeah!

3: No.

2: You are silly girl!

1: Don't worry, I'll get you out of all this trouble if you come with me. My great grandfather was an explorer.

(laughter)

3: Allright, cool it, cool it. I got transmitter, you know that?

2: Have you?

3: Yeah!

1: Oh come on, let's get it out that. . . .

3: The problem is I must go in high place, something like that high hill so that I can contact with the British people in England. But maybe is possible.

2: Where did you get that . . . er transmitter from?

3: From the sea.

1: Let's forget about the transmitter. Let's look for something to eat.

2: Yeah! We must find food first.

3: Allright, allright, who's hungry?

6: I am and (she continues but is suppressed by louder voices)

1: Everybody's hungry.

5: I'm hungry!

2: Allright. You go and I'll stay here er make fire, first thing.

1: I'm very, very hungry. I'm always eating, you know.

6: Go get some food then!

1: Where shall I go?

6: In the jungle.

4: Yeah!

(continues). . . .

To construct cultural and contextual meaning in the classroom is by no means an easy task; the very nature of the classroom imposes special restrictions on the natural use of the L2. However, this kind of simulation activity aims at getting the students to employ the L2 as a social tool and to establish their own situationally defined meaning, thereby coming close to the way language is used in the real world outside the classroom. Moreover, by trying out structures and phrases triggered by the context the learners feel for them is strengthened. Of course, the more contexts in which they encounter and employ the L2 items, the greater their meaningfullness will become.

I shall not deal here with the diagnostic function of the simulation, i.e. how it can be used to discover students' consistent errors and general difficulties. What this transcription demonstrates above all is the developed sense of cooperation between the participants; comments made by previous speakers are taken up, evaluated and reinterpreted; classroom comments are integrated. There are many signals which affirm the interaction (*come on, OK, allright, don't worry, yeah*). The participants direct their ideas to others and do not merely state: "What plan can you think of? What about the 'cannibulls'?" The conversational rule of one-speaker-at-a-time is always adhered to. The opening shows the students' important handling of establishing identity and introducing themselves before being able to solve the problem. Another interesting feature is the dominance of speaker no. 1. He makes the least errors and seems to be the linguistically most able of the students. However, speaker no. 3 is also very verbal but among the least accurate. He is not intimidated by the others' proficiency nor the classroom situation and uses his limited but resourceful L2 stock to satisfy immediate ends; the question of the L2 learner's deviancy will be discussed in the next chapter.

Moreover, the cultural dimensions of the students' efforts deserves consideration. The relative taciturnity of the female participants (5 and 6) should not go unnoticed. The prominence of geographical names at the beginning is significant. It seems to be linked to a concretization of L2 nativeness. Status factors hinted at in the role cards are also made explicit, e.g. "the posher part of London", "which university did he go to? . . . Oxford". As for the generation of meaning within a particular reference frame, it is evident that once the introductions are over, an intensive focusing on the situation occurs: the map is referred to and hunger is expressed. This growing awareness of the fictive reality (it appears for the students imaginatively real at the moment of enactment) results in very simple structures, i.e. utterances of suggestion and persuasion: "We must find food", "We've still got plenty to do", "We need . . . don't we".

Although this is not always the case with simulation work, many of its positive aspects are illustrated in this transcription: the mutual, active creation of contextual meaningfullness where L2 symbols are employed with a more intensive commitment to them than in the usual artificial class exchanges. In this connection Hakuta (1975) has clearly demonstrated that the development of natural bilingualism (outside the classroom) crucially depends on the speaker's perceived necessity to satisfy expressive and integrative needs.

Role play undeniably motivates and extends L2 acquisition but it also can bring some problems which need to be sensitively treated by the teacher. I have already mentioned some techniques for overcoming anxiety. Competitiveness between performing groups resulting from a self-imposed obligation to entertain the class can be partly resolved by asking groups to perform simultaneously. What is ultimately required is the students' realization of the true purpose of the activity. Resistance can also take place if a monolingual class starts questioning the common sense of communicating with each other in an L2, i.e. where the artificiality of using the medium becomes too conscious. This can be partly due to the teacher's own attitudes (to what extent he/she speaks the L2 in the lesson for organizing and explaining) as well as the actual linguistic level of the students. The latter must be linguistically able to do what is required of them; the roles must be relevant and familiar. Thus, Black & Butzkamm (1977) carefully and successfully centred their subjects for role play on themes which corresponded to the reality of their pupils' world: the planning of lessons, homework, marking, teacher's expectations, criticisms of the teacher, problems of self-expression in an L2, etc., instead of declaring duty at the customs.

Moskowitz (1978) provides an extensive description of humanistic techniques for the foreign language classroom which aim at the learner's self-actualization by concentrating on the expression of his/her personal feelings, opinions, attitudes and so on. Moskowitz found that self-awareness exercises enhance students' wishes to communicate in the target language as well as furthering their personal growth which is a legitimate educational goal in itself. The result is inevitably increased proficiency although an atmosphere of tolerance and trust must first of all be established.

With all these kinds of communicative exercises, discussion of the L2 framing and symbolizing patterns should be carried out in a value-free manner so that neither community's system is presented as 'superior' but simply as different. Furthermore, role play should be conceived as only *one* very intensive component in the promotion of communicative competence. It goes without saying that it involves varying degrees of tolerance on the teacher's part towards the naturally deviant language of his learners, their code switching and introduction of L1 vocabulary. The implications of such tolerance are discussed in the following chapter.

In order to effectively participate in role play and real-life L2 situations, the L2 user must have recourse to the interactional mechanisms which he already operates in his L1 but generally tends to ignore or forget to apply in his L2 behaviour. These are now briefly sketched out below.

(iii) *The art of conversation*

The possible reason for the absence of native conversational framing patterns in L2 interaction could be that learners are usually taught the target language in the form of complete sentences. Conversation, however, when examined as it naturally occurs turns out to be degenerate from a purely sentence-grammatical viewpoint, full of asides, interruptions, false starts, imprecision, repetition, hesitation, incompleteness, ungrammaticality among others. All of these features are perfectly natural and normal and, in some contexts, even necessary.

Furthermore, research has indicated how these 'adulterations' actually follow basic rules and principles. As earlier stated, it is quite wrong to equate communicative competence simply with the ability to handle conversations since this is *only* one component of communicative competence, although certainly a crucial one for the L2 speaker.

Hymes (1971, p. 272) has wisely observed that "if one uses one's intuitions as to speech, as well as to grammar, one can see that what to grammar is imperfect, or unaccounted for, may be the artful accomplishment of a social act". We have already explored some of the ways conversations are opened and sequenced across culturally different communities in the discussion of framing and symbolizing patterns above. Now we turn to how such knowledge can help the L2 speaker-actor.

One of the most obvious deficits of even advanced L2 users is their inability to manage conversational partnership, to play the appropriate speaker/hearer roles properly. The signalling of these roles is essential because it provides the supporting framework for talk and carries meaning in so far that its absence can be taken as indicating lack of interest, coldness, arrogance, etc. As we shall see, the signals are structurally quite simple and there is no reason why they should not be taught from the early phases of L2 acquisition. Their learning at a later date when the speaker has never utilized them in his L2 behaviour does not come easy (Crystal & Davy 1975, p. 6).

Keller (1981) develops the supraconcept of "gambits" which is used to cover the whole range of 'conversational strategy signals' with which speakers structure their presentation of topics, their taking of turns in the conversation, indicating their state of consciousness in regard to information, opinion, knowledge, emotion or planned action and to check whether communication is being passed onto the listener. The choice of a gambit depends on two aspects: *appropriateness,* under-lying social and psychological information together with the perceived real-world such as the degree of politeness holding between the speakers. We have already discussed certain gambits above but cannot adopt this conceptual framework here because it is obviously too gross. It seems to refer to almost every conversational strategy and thereby runs the risk of theoretical emptiness. Instead let us examine those routinized features of communication which are especially important for managing conversation and are of direct, practical relevance to the L2 learner.

It appears that one principle of conversation is the ensuring of under-standing that goes far beyond the clarity of form. The need for cooperation between participants is an essential factor. Every speaker wants to know if his message has been received and, if so, whether it has been properly understood; while the listener has to show that he has received it and correctly followed its sense (Goffman 1975). One of the basic ways this mutual focusing is achieved is through little phrases—others include looking at the speaker, holding one's body in a certain posture. These little phrases also serve other purposes which we will discuss below but they are also frequently employed to achieve this conversational cooperation and overcome potential difficulties (unwillingness to listen, incoherence, disagreement and so on). Thus, speakers use tags such as *isn't it* to make sure their listener is keeping up with them and enlist their support as well as *you see, see what I mean, mind you, well, you know* among others. These are also used to soften the potential harshness of naked statements and to bring the listener into the talk, to let him share his feelings, if not motivate him to adopt them.

On the other hand, the listener is also expected to provide feedback such as *ah-ah, sure, oh, mm, I know, I see, yes, yeah, really, right, fine, okay, gosh, wow, lovely, fancy that, but* and a more active device is to simultaneously say something as the speaker comes to the end of his piece or offer a verbatim repetition of the contents. These hearer cues not only testify to the listener's ongoing interest and affirm the speaker in his role but they also point to the level of agreement and comprehension as well as revealing the listener's emotional involvement. Some of these can be paraphrased as 'now I understand', 'I've half-understood what you mean but I'm still trying', 'that's obvious', 'that's right', 'well, I'm not sure', 'I didn't know that', 'I'm listening, go on', 'don't worry, I'm with you' (Walmhoff & Wenzel 1979). Needless to say, smiles, gazes, nods, posture shifts also signal some of these.

The art of conversational partnership also entails sharing the floor and regulating whose turn it is to speak. A number of turn rules have been found to operate. They contribute to a smooth interactive flow by determining when exactly each person is allowed to play speaker or listener. Poyatos (1980) has provided an extensive summary of some of these turn-regulating mechanisms and has come up with ten types. We have already touched upon certain of these above, so let us just concentrate on turn (i) claiming, (ii) yielding, (iii) taking, (iv) holding, and (v) suppressing. In English (i) can be signalled by, for example, *but—, I—, one minute,* raised eyebrows or posture shift and obviously indicates that the listener wants to, or must, say something or that the speaker has held the floor long enough; (ii) occurs when the speaker feels he has gone on long enough, when his listener looks bored or ignorant of the subject, when the listener has claimed or briefly taken the floor and can be signalled by phrases such as *yes, go ahead,* or a self-interrupted sentence, a long drawn out final syllable, a nod, an offering hand palm, upwards, crossing one's arms or sitting back; (iii) takes place when the listener takes the floor after the speaker shows his willingness to relinquish his turn, or when his turn claiming has failed and he just decides to take it and linguistically marks this with *No, I was going to say that—, Yeah—, Well—, Uh—,* a thankful nod, a posture shift; (iv) is an attempt to suppress a turn claim with, for instance, something like *Wait, Let me finish,* or increased volume to overpower the listener; (v) is related to the last case but it can be instigated by any of those present and not simply the speaker, e.g. *let him finish, wait, listen,* gestures symbolizing *stop* or holding the claimer's arm.

Poyatos (1980) notes that these last two mentioned types, claim suppressing and turn holding, vary according to personality and cultural norms. He believes that attitudes towards simultaneous turns are one of the causes of intercultural conflict between Anglo-Saxons and Latins/Arabs because the latter share a stronger tendency to simultaneous floor-holding behaviour. Although this pattern, of course, cannot last too long, its duration and intensity differs across cultures: Anglo-Saxons avoid simultaneous taking turns (*sorry, no, go ahead*).

Apart from these ways of dealing with our turns to talk, we also need to employ other strategies for (a) justifying talking for some time on a topic or (b) when we want to digress from the topic or (c) to indicate that it has been sufficiently talked about:

(a) you know what/I've got something to tell you/I've got a question/ Well, now anyway it's like this;

(b) something really strange happened today/that reminds me/by the way/talking of . . ./incidentally

(c) that's about it/right, shall we . . ./well then/so. . . .

All the communicative strategies described so far do not really inform in the traditional sense. They mark stages in the mutual accomplishing of talk and simultaneously strengthen the social links between the participants during talk as well as helping to make interaction run smoothly. Some of them furthermore belong to the politeness strategies mentioned above.

How essential these devices are in conversation and how inadequately they seem to be handled by L2 learners is well revealed in the study of three German students who had studied English for nine years in their free conversation in English with a native American university assistant (Götz 1977). They used embarrassed laughs at the end of their utterances to signal turn-yielding; they never introduced their topics with phrases such as *well, you know, I mean, it's like this* and when they discussed their topics it was without any approximating words such as *sort of, kind of, so to say, in a way* which would have made them sound less definitive and abrupt. Additionally, they hardly provided any listener role signals (*I see, ah-ah, oh*) and seemed to pounce on any idea at any moment in the conversation that they knew they could say something about, thereby rudely interrupting the speaker and becoming totally irrelevant. When their interruptions were valid (i.e. they had to go back to a lecture, and needed to know the time) they failed to prepare them with apologetic formulae. They reacted to the gambits for elaboration simply as yes/no questions turning the conversation into an interview. The results of such poor conversational management included, of course, giving an unfavourable impression of boredom, curtness and making the interaction jolty and jagged. More importantly, is the fact that native speakers will only attempt to understand L2 speakers if a friendly relationship and a sharing of interests are conversationally established. The performance of the German speakers fulfilled neither of these demands. Götz points out that the consequences of such behaviour in an everyday setting would be social rejection because the conversation would not be considered worth carrying out or continuing. The native speaker would give up searching for explanations for the gaucherie of his interlocutor and give up making strenuous attempts to maintain conversation. It is therefore up to the L2 speaker to make his native conversant want to attempt to interact and not the other way round!

Without doubt, the learning and practising of the art of conversation signifies a transformation of traditional communicative patterns in the L2 classroom. The students will have to engage in exchanges with each other and the teacher adopt the role of animateur. In fact, Jones (1977) has already provided exercises aiding the development of some discourse skills in his English textbook for L2 learners *Functions of English*, cf. conversational opening (pp. 6–8); turn claiming, turn yielding (pp. 27–30) and topic preparing and story telling (pp. 77–80).

Another exercise practising the hearer role would be for a student to say something for a short period while another provides feedback signals. In this connection certain 'tricks of the conversational trade' should be mentioned which natives employ to repair their speech when they cannot find the word they are looking for or want to correct their grammar or want to make something they have communicated clearer to their listener.

Although these first seem not directly sociolinguistic, they are to the extent that they correspond to certain cultural attitudes towards pauses and hesitation in speech which can make communication distressful and may lead to negative evaluations of the speaker. Shimanoff & Brunak (1977) have found that there are special ways of signalling that a 'repair' is coming: there can be a slight pause or this can be filled with *you know, and, well, but, okay, so* or, of course, *uh, um, er.* Another way of repairing what has just been said (perhaps because it does not sound sufficiently relevant or precise) is to use *you know, I mean, anyway, in other words, that is,* e.g. "It's incredible when you can't do that. *I mean* when every little step if painful". Speakers may also cut off their utterances before completion sometimes in order to repair it by substituting another item. This substitution can help to repair or it might also be a sophisticated way of filling in the pause until one can go on.

> "when I felt pain in my leg, I thought that was *that gave me* the first thought that I was alive"
> "and the driver of the car—wha's sort of interesting is—*he was*—*um*— he had like some accessories in the car—".

Acquisition of these repair strategies may be assisted by paraphrase exercises which can first take place in the L1 so that the learners understand the technique. Another possibility is for someone in the class to ask a question involving a general idea, e.g. "What do you think of when I say violence on TV?" and then the other students having to draw up associations such as fighting, bodies, shouts, fights (Beneke 1979).

An eroded catch-all?

When Hymes launched his attack against the inadequacies of the transformationalist approach in linguistics, little could he have foreseen how the term he coined to cover all those aspects of linguistic behaviour that were not included in the production of grammatical sentences would become the spearhead of a movement that would radically alter the field of language study.

Not only did the Hymesian notion of communicative competence inspire anthropologists and linguists, it also stimulated sociologists and psychologists and, ultimately, the language teaching profession. Today, however, it must be admitted that the concept has assumed a certain vacuousness. It has grown into a catch-all phrase for practically every aspect of communication outside the traditionally considered areas of phonetics, grammar and the lexicon.

As was pointed out at the start of this chapter, the term has been sadly taken to denote no more than its superficial meaning as the ability to communicate. In L2 teaching it has been and still is mistaken as comprising solely one of the following: etiquette, speech acts, routine, situational language, discourse machinery, see Widdowson (1979, p. 257):

> Let us then assume that a specification of needs indicates that the appropriate teaching approach is one which concentrates on the development of communicative competence, and that this is defined as *the ability to cope with the interactive structuring of discourse*.

Although each of these obviously forms a vital component of the concept of communicative competence, one of the most fundamental points of Hymes' argument has been ignored and that is the sociocultural framework in which all linguistic behaviour is embedded.

The cultural sterility of many discussions on L2 communicative competence may well be due to the fact that many of the L2 theorists involved are or were in the business of English teaching. Now English is increasingly recognized as approaching the status of a world lingua franca and because of this fact there are many involved in its teaching who seek and support its de-ethnicization and de-culturalization. Whatever the outcome of this particular debate will be, L2 teaching should not blindly follow the extreme utilitarianism of the Zeitgeist and reduce communicative competence to the mere acquisition of skills. Perhaps this is all that is needed for English as an international medium but I doubt it because the cultural background of the L2 speakers of English will still be present in their communicative activity if this consists of more than booking into an hotel or answering business letters or writing scientific reports and even these will involve specific cultural presuppositions.

It should be patent that learners of second languages apart from English cannot afford to disregard the cultural reality of the target community and its culturally relative ways of constructing meaning. For, as was observed, these patterns vary across communities and are open to divergent, even conflicting interpretations. However, this does not mean that the teaching of L2 grammar is to be replaced with that of absolute conformity to the L2 community norms. What is vital is a value-free presentation of the contrasting ways of communicating carried out in the same fashion as proposed in the preceding chapter on the community's cultural world. In an extreme sense this will entail a kind of re-socialization of the L2 learner and must therefore be tackled with sensitivity and tact.

This cultural dimension has yet to be integrated into current work on the teaching of communicative competence. But this is not the defective area. Butzkamm & Dodson (1980) list a host of methodological mistakes in the classroom implementation of communicative competence such as the use of communicative exercises as 'sugar on the bitter pill' of language learning (as relaxation and amusement), the attempt to achieve communicative competence without any underlying knowledge of the linguistic structure and the lack of sociopsychological fusion of L2 forms with reality because they are learnt only as memorised texts, even in role play. The result is the learners' failure to identify and associate the L2 with true self-expression even though the material precisely is designed to achieve this objective.

This last point, of course, relates to traditional attitudes and learning styles in the foreign language classroom which underlines the most important argument of this chapter: communicative competence is an *active process of cultural symbolization*. It involves the *construction* of meaning and not reproduction that results in meaninglessness. This raises many questions regarding the conceptions of the contents and methods of teaching a non-native language which I examine in the concluding chapter.

5

The confection and demise of the institutional norms for learning a non-native language

In the preceding chapter we learnt that communicating in a non-native language means much more than the ability to produce grammatical sentences. The L2 user must also adopt sometimes radically diverging patterns for organizing, presenting and expressing himself. Thus, successful communication in an L2 entails not merely performing meaning in a different way but also conforming to different constructions of meaning in order to be comprehended and accepted.

At least, this is the usual legitimization for much of what goes on in the non-native language classroom. Yet the question of conformity is not without its contradictions and complexities. For instance, a target community is rarely homogeneous so that the model of the L2 presented to the learner is essentially a social decision to conform to the speech style of one particular group within the target community. Moreover, the question arises as to what degree the patterns of this chosen group are established and to what extent the learners should be judged according to its standards.

These are fundamental issues that have to be considered by institutional L2 teachers who, as we shall see, can become so obsessed with norms that they paralyse their own efforts. But before examining this paradoxical situation, we first have to examine the way humans treat language and unravel the confusion between *norm* and *convention*.

Language is, above all, a social product. It works on socially agreed upon principles or conventions that make it somewhat systematic and somewhat stable, although, of course, it is neither. As with other conventions, linguistic ones help us to know how to behave with each other and this brings security with it. The sharing of conventions also reinforces a sense of identity. Furthermore, the conventions are rarely conscious or explicit because:

> if their man-made origins were not hidden, they would be stripped of some of their authority. Therefore, the conventions are not merely tacit, but extremely inaccessible to investigate (Douglas 1973, p. 15).

Norms are also conventions but I would like to distinguish them here from the latter by suggesting that they are much more than mere custom and usage. They represent ideals and provide criteria for evaluation. The difference between norms and conventions is probably clearer when one considers the difference between 'normative' and 'normal'. Norms generally declare themselves to be *the* system instead of recognizing themselves as simply a possible system. Additionally, the nature of linguistic norms greatly depends on the social inter-pretation of a particular activity, and are closely connected with how individuals relate to each other and what they hope to accomplish with each other.

Of course, conventions are necessary to guide and promote human behaviour. If there was no basic agreement on the meanings of words and their associated sounds, for example, language would fail utterly as a means of communication. Norms can also be beneficial in that they may contain experience which we are saved from having to find out ourselves, thereby reducing the complexity of our environment. However, not every single norm fulfils all these functions and many are relics that have been held over from a time when they were once valuable.

Ideally, norms should be able to justify their observance in functional terms but this seldom happens. What is interesting, however, is the fact that both norms and conventions only last as long as they are legitimized and valued by their use and presence in society. Norms are upheld out of a genuine fear of punishment for their violation. Linguistic norms cannot remain frozen for language, as a 'social product', is forever in flux and can never constitute a timelessly sealed system.

The variable and dynamic nature of language has given both linguists and language teachers headaches. Even though general linguistics in this century did not wish to appear as a normative authority but as a descriptive and explanatory science, it turned out that by establishing what language is and how it operates, linguists were taken (and some took themselves) as constituting an authority for providing and defending norms; needless to say, the data for their research consistently derived from one section of society, the élite, so that the connection between the linguistic conventions of this dominant social group and the power inherently associated with them contributed to an age-old conception of the discipline linguistics as norm keeper and arbiter.

Sociolinguistics, on the other hand, has in its short span of existence already partially succeeded in divesting the norms of the social élite of their mysticism and mythology. The basic sociolinguistic rejection of idealized data, its concern with imputedly aberrant systems such as pidgins, creoles, black English as well as the 'impurities' of bilingual speech have led to a scientific upgrading of these language types. They have, in fact, been found to contain conventions not unlike their legitimate cousins with the difference that these conventions have not been enshrined as norms. Thus, from the sociolinguistic perspective it becomes obvious that linguistic norms do not lead to more effective communication—as they ideally should—but primarily serve to emphasize social differences.

Furthermore, within the camp of non-hyphenated linguistics there have also been some theory-shaking discoveries showing that the perfection and regularity of abstract data can no longer be justified. There exists what has been called "fuzzy grammar" (Lakoff 1973) where forms cannot be absolutely categorized but seem to 'squish'. Another recent insight is "rule variability" that is not necessarily socially determined, e.g. I didn't dare to answer/I didn't dare answer/I dared not answer.

Not only is there a greater concern in linguistics for the real way people talk, but in educational research a noticeable shift has taken place away from the hunt for sociopsychological variables such as motivation, family background, intelligence and so forth which were supposed to lead to a better control of students' achievements towards a more learner-centred approach where the systematics of the learning process itself and the teacher–pupil relationship are the object of investigation. These general trends together with many other factors to be discussed have led to a questioning of the traditional norms of non-native language teaching and forms the basis of this chapter's argument.

We shall start by looking at the operation of pedagogic norms in the L2 classroom and their harmful consequences on the learning process. Then we will consider the case for upgrading the status of the language of the learner, i.e. the establishment of a new linguistic norm for the L2 user and finally the institutional requirement for a particular L2 social dialect as a normative model to present students with.

Lessons in conformity

All speech communities create and follow a set of beliefs and attitudes about their language. One aspect of these folk notions, especially prevalent in literate communities, is the development of linguistic orthodoxy. In fact, this conservatism can go far beyond an ecological need for stability and security in communication. It can assume the proportions of an ideology which prescribes and attempts to enforce in an absolute manner norms for the treatment and employment of language. Among such prescriptive norms one finds postulates such as

linguistic purity where the mixing of sounds and forms from other languages or dialects constitutes 'pollution';

linguistic perfection where one particular set of linguistic conventions represents the most aesthetic, beautiful, supreme, etc.;

linguistic immutability which expresses itself in hostility towards language change;

the primacy of written norms over speech so that talk is regarded as a degenerated version of the written language; we should aim at a precise, de-contextualized talking in sentences (however, writing and grammar are first based on speech conventions but with time the former bear weight on the latter);

the autonomy and homogeneity of a standard language, e.g. that there is a definable standard form of the language which is historically established and treated as if it was not the medium of the dominant social group but existed somehow independently of it.

This normative ideology is, of course, maintained through community consensus. It is supported by varying sanctions ranging from social ridicule and discrimination to rejection. It is also upheld by institutional guardians such as the Academie Française, the Language Academy of Israel, the Japanese Ministry of Education or published works such as dictionaries in the English world. However, the latter have since renounced their role of lexical father figures in line with the new *descriptive* doctrine of linguistics. The refusal by linguistics and dictionary-makers is probably the reason for the feelings of betrayal that have been voiced by those desirous for absolutes on a planet of linguistic relativity and diversity (Wells 1973). In fact, most of the normative ideology described above can be summarized as social snobbery since consideration of the enshrined postulates shows them to be propagated by the social élite who presents its own dialect as the primary norm.

However, this normativism is not found in every speech community. The Mayan language, Jacaltec, in Guatemala, for instance, has no standard form and there are as many variations of the language as there are settlements of its speakers. When one of its speakers was recently taught how to read and write it, she refused to transcribe and translate texts recorded by other people, feeling that this would betray them and that she would not be able to guarantee that what she heard and understood would be what they really meant to say (Craig 1979). Moreover, the informant had no notion of right and wrong in the language but just of personal differences. Speech was perceived as a personal property and the expression of free will, for which an interpretation could be found although this interpretation was not necessarily the intended one:

> Her hesitation and scruples in dealing with more than her own speech and her attitude toward language in general stemmed from both the status of her language as an unwritten language and her lack of formal education (p. 53).

In other words, writing and education foster linguistic intolerance.

When one examines L2 teaching, it becomes apparent that the normative ideology of the target community constitutes the foundations for most pedagogic practice: teachers attempt to eradicate language-mixing, they exclusively concern themselves with standards of perfection in terms of correctness, they usually impart an embalmed (non-contemporary) version of the L2 strongly orientated towards the written language so that speech is a form of 'oral prose' and they usually present students with only one social dialect as supreme model.

However, it must be admitted that in many cases this ideology corresponds exactly to many of the learner's expectations because of the supposed inherent virtues of prescriptivism. Thus, some learners make persistent demands for the holy writ: the codified rules, the good grammar, the 'best' and most correct way and sometimes even the logicality of the language due to the belief that language represents some philosophical or mathematical proposition. This last notion is closely connected with the ideology of linguistic perfection mentioned above. But not all learners yearn for this absolutist conformity. Today, there is a widely-noted tendency, particularly in younger learners, to abandon L2 courses because they are seen as a hindrance to freedom, self-discovery and natural creativity (Hester 1970) and many of which even have become one of the most unpopular parts of the school curriculum (Rée 1972).

To demonstrate the extent of the similarity between the normative ideology of speech communities and that held by L2 educationalists, let us look at what L1 teachers say about the language of their students. Doughty & Doughty (1974, p. 62) tell of an English teacher in North Kent who was very worried by the 'laziness' of pupils who were too careless to speak 'properly':

> . . . all she wanted these pupils to do was to speak clearly and grammatically, in sentences, articulating each word precisely, and thus to give up their dreadful slovenliness. . . . She argued forcefully that if pupils could not perform the simple task of "speaking properly" then their intelligence was such that she could not be expected to teach them English.

These observations are not unlike those reported by Shuy, Wolfram & Riley (1967) on the attitudes of teachers in a survey of Detroit black speech, 80% of whom felt that their students had a limited vocabulary, were ignorant of the sounds and grammar of the language, used monosyllables and incomplete sentences which merely reflected the incomplete nature of their thoughts.

Although these teachers are talking about native speakers of *their* language, do they not remarkably resemble the criticisms of L2 teachers about their students? Is there not the same dangerously false asssociation between conformity to norms and intelligence?

If one considers most institutional non-native language teaching, it becomes evident that the method of evaluation is based on the principle of conformity to the norms of the non-native language. Success is measured in terms of proven assimilation of, in most cases, grammatical norms. When these are violated they are taken as the most significant indications of failure. The cultural and contextual construction of meaning plays a minor role. This tradition is certainly connected with a conception of education as an instrument of socialization and it is also linked to the questionable criterion of assessing achievement in terms of formalistic conformity. Of course, it is related to the normative ideology in speech communities which has been transmitted and sustained by professional linguists over the last 2000 years:

> Linguistics, as grammar, came into existence to dissect and teach . . . [one] language variety that embodied valued cultural tradition (Homeric Greek, the Sanskrit of the Vedas, the Chinese of the Confucian classics), not just any language . . . indeed, not any other language at all. The grammar, like the language, was an *instrument of hegemony* (Hymes 1974b, p. 433).

It can often be observed how grammatical norms are employed in schools as an instrument of teacher hegemony.

The concentration on one linguisitic norm can actually be traced right up to contemporary work on transformational grammar where the linguist ascribes to himself the role of ideal speaker and holds his feelings for grammaticality as insights into some ordered, predictable, logical knowledge of language called *competence* which results in a mathematical justification for prescriptivism (see Chomsky 1957, p. 13). "The fundamental aim in the linguistical analysis of a language

L is to separate the grammatical sequences which are the sentences of L from the ungrammatical sequences which are not sentences of L and to study the structure of the grammatical sequences''.

Applied linguistics which is often understood as the application of linguistics to language teaching recently turned away from what Fishman (1968) has called the witch-hunting of corrupt forms in bilinguals' speech. From its ouset applied linguistics was dominated by a theory known as contrastive analysis which was concerned with the *errors* produced by learners transferring L1 norms and patterns to the L2 (Lado 1957).

Of course, since L2 educationalists have always turned to the discipline linguistics for guidance (just as you are probably doing now), their normative ideology has until quite recently always been affirmed and encouraged. It follows from this that in the traditional L2 classroom language has rarely been taken for what it really is—a social way of meaning—but has tended to be regarded as an ideal product consisting of prescribed norms to which the teacher had to get students to adhere. Thus, the whole enterprise of institutional non-native language teaching could be described as recurring lessons in conformity to norms of grammar, secondarily norms of pronunciation and very infrequently norms of culturally appropriate meaningfulness. Exactly what the results of this and other educational conceptions have been for the classroom of L2 instruction is the question we shall now turn to.

The court of correction

Today, there exists a growing body of research specifically devoted to the nature of the communication process in the classroom (Barnes 1974; Sinclair & Coulthard 1975; Coulthard 1977; Griffin & Mehan 1981). This work owes its origins to the field of discourse analysis (see Chapter 1) which has an interest in the abstract structure of interaction. The primary purpose here, however, is in the social significance of interaction and the sociolinguistic consequences of the way teachers structure their classroom language to teach language.

Language is probably the most fundamental component in western institutional learning. What is special about its use in schools is that it is both the subject and goal and means of learning. Actually, teachers are less conscious of this last point, although it is they who primarily manipulate it as a tool for 'accomplishing' learning. This they do in accordance with the expectations of the classroom context concerning roles and their corresponding patterns of behaviour. Thus, teacher talk can be functionally characterized as giving orders, advice, reasons, explaining, controlling pupils' attention, warning, stating intentions, making suggestions and, of particular concern here, questioning and handling pupils' responses (Heaton 1980).

In fact, classroom talk works on a quite different logical basis from that observed in daily conversation. One example of this is the way teachers ask for information they already know the answers to and where the repetition of a question carries the meaning that the answer offered is incorrect. The patterns of classroom conduct are founded on the special norms of the context: the class must cooperatively deal with institutionally set tasks and the teacher must transmit and judge the relative abilities of the students so that most verbal activity develops out of its relevance to ideas about school, lessons and the learning of information (Mehan 1979).

Teacher–pupil interaction typically follows a triple sequence: the teacher asks a question with an answer in mind and designates a pupil as the next speaker who answers the question which is then evaluated by the teacher (with a nod of the head, a partial repetition of the response, a comment such as 'good' or even simply by going on to the next subject). For example:

> Teacher: What is the last thing in the top row, Lisa?
> 1st pupil: Um, a duck.
> Teacher: What is the first thing in the second row, Joseph?
> 2nd pupil: A bird. (Streeck 1979, p. 244.)

Usually, a new question is not asked or the topic is not changed until the answer has been found. These interactional norms do not, of course, correspond to those observed in everyday extra-institutional life. What is their social meaning?

The teacher's evaluative response implicitly legitimizes an utterance as a piece of information which from then on assumes official authority as knowledge for the class. This ratification is a part of a process of categorizing utterances as knowledge or non-knowledge. The teacher is obviously not interested in the propositional content of the pupils' answer but in testing his ability to answer. Classroom communication, consequently, reveals itself to be a trial where learners submit themselves for judgement. Their performance during the trial is contextually taken as evidence of their learning ability. This verbal ordeal is *per se* competitive and requires students to present themselves strategically, e.g. by remaining silent or shouting out.

With regard to the general preference of adults and children not to speak a language whose rules and meanings they can only imperfectly handle, Gary (1978) argues that if L2 learners are not required to speak immediately, though allowed to if they wish, they make more significant gains in reading, writing and speaking and listening comprehension than students required to speak right away. This approach seems to be one way of reducing stress and embarrassment and the ensuing reduction in the concentration and success of the learner.

Up to now I have only described the nature of communication in western education in a broad fashion and it is by no means universal, see Scollon & Scollon for an account of how Red Indian culture teaches on a peer basis via observation and verbal 'abstracting'. As stated above, the institutional patterns of classroom interaction in western education are based on unquestioned notions of what teacher and student are supposed to be doing in class. When it comes to L2 teaching, the matter is difficult to unravel because the linguistic display of knowledge that the student has to offer for judgement is, of course, itself language. In other words, students' verbal contributions are taken as proof of learned information which is composed of L2 norms.

In the last chapter I attempted to demonstrate that humans normally employ language to actively symbolize their intentions. According to such a view, language should and cannot be regarded as an object but only as a medium. But as has been seen above, teachers do not handle the performance of their students in this way. The absurdity of handling talk in a non-native language as the exhibition of acquired

norms is painfully shown in the following excerpt of an authentic
teacher–pupil exchange in a German school:

1st Student: I have a question. Why does the postman rings the bell, when
                does Miss Maxwell deaf?
Teacher: Now again, that sentence. Why . . .
1st Student: Why . . .
Teacher: does . . .
1st Student: . . . does Miss Maxwell . . .
Teacher: . . . the postman . . .
1st Student: . . . the postman ring the bell.
Teacher: Why does he ring the bell? Miss Maxwell is deaf.
1st Student: Yes, she can't hear him . . . him.
Teacher: She can't hear the bell. She can't hear the bell. What do you
                think? Miss Maxwell is deaf. She can't hear the bell?
2nd Student: (asks if he can say it in German) Herr Butzkamm, kann
                ich's jetzt wohl mal auf deutsch sagen?
Teacher: Oh no, you can say it in English. Or not? Can you say it in
                English?
2nd Student: Yes, I think the postman thinks she is deaf. (Black &
                Butzkamm 1977, p. 119.)

This example illustrates a host of norms operating in the L2 classroom.
First of all, we can recognize the teacher's treatment of students' speech
in terms of a formal product for evaluation (quality control) rather
than in terms of its propositional content. The student here is trying
her utmost to communicate her genuine surprise at the incongruous
fact that a postman should ring the bell of a house inhabited by an
old lady he knows to be deaf. The teacher, however, refuses to
respond on this meaning-level and interprets the utterance as a deviant
production of the target language norms. This product-orientation is
underlined by the fact that the student is refused access to the meaning-
level which he sees as only available in the native language of both
teacher and student. In fact, this only serves to heighten the artificiality
of the L2 medium which is reduced to the mere proof of students'
linguistic assimilation. It also undermines the reality of communication
since it is perfectly natural that when interactants know that they are
both familiar with two language systems and find that something is
more conveniently expressed in one of these, they will resort to the

other code for as long as necessary. This question of classroom disapprobation of code-switching is further related to the taboo on code-mixing mentioned above. It can, of course, be interpreted as a well-meaning attempt on the teacher's part to get the students to *produce* rather than to *transmit sense* in the L2.

To return to code-mixing, it is worth noting that American teachers of English as an L2 to Spanish natives, describe the linguistic performance of their students as follows: "They can't speak English and they can't speak Spanish either. . . . They take one word from here and another from there and think it makes sense. You know, they don't speak any language at all" (Hatch 1976, p. 201). This capacity of bilinguals to switch rapidly and fluently from one language to another in the middle of conversation or in the middle of a sentence is, of course, generally held in contempt by non-bilinguals when it occurs as an on-the-spot linguistic phenomenon. However, in a fossilized state code-mixing as it exists in modern English (Germanic and Latinate) where its normativeness has been sanctified by history and the emergence of a standard it is rarely perceived. In fact, it has been frequently observed that bilinguals have two separate languages—one for monolinguals and a mixed language among themselves. This natural pooling of communicative resources and an inevitable outcome of interbilingual communication is despised in the classroom, which adds to an atmosphere of artificiality.

A further aspect revealed in the teacher–pupil exchange cited above is the stress on the formation of complete sentences. The effects of this are not always simply the slowing up of the communication but can lead to totally redundant and inappropriate speech:

> Teacher: What do you see in the picture?
> Student: There are some tables and a teacher.
> Teacher: Say it in a sentence.
> Student: I see some tables and a teacher in the picture. (Rehbein 1978, p. 20).

If natives orally answered any questions in complete sentences they would be certainly considered very odd, at the very least. Of course, what has happened here is the transference of written norms into spoken practice. Furthermore, the forced repeating of utterances which have been properly understood dismembers them from the interactional process and increases their fictivity.

The effects of teacher correction can be much more than the suspension and throttling of potentially genuine teacher–pupil interaction. It can also serve to block and silence students in their 'production display':

Teacher: But why did Johnny leave the garage?
Student: Johnny leaves the garage
Teacher: Johnny?
Student: left the garage because he could not welcome them
Teacher: at the garage
Student: at the garage
Teacher: any more
Student: any more
Teacher: Yes.
(class laughter). (Rehbein 1978, p. 33.)

From this real example we can see how the student grows less independent and shifts from production to imitation. This yielding up of communicative autonomy and the student's apparent confusion are reflected in the laughter of the class.

There is much too little room for student initiative in institutional L2 learning discourse and this fact is amply illustrated by the findings of Hüllen & Lörscher (1979) in their investigation of English lessons in West German schools. The researchers note that students are not allowed to deviate from the fixed subject which in every case seems to be the contents of a text. Moreover, teachers accept students' utterances on the basis of their grammatical correctness even if they are sometimes propositionally wrong. There is also marked asymmetry in the distribution of speaking rights: the teacher who verbally contributed the least among those studied still provided 65% of the utterances in the entire lesson and the teacher with the highest amount 75%. Thus, in both cases more than half the lesson was monopolized by one individual whose conscious aim was, paradoxically, to increase the fluency of all the participants but himself. Another aspect observed by the researchers is a preoccupation with correctness. This is hardly surprising as we have seen that the objective of lesson talk turns out to be the testing of the degree to which students can prove their acquisition of instructed knowledge. In two of the three classes investigated by Hüllen and Lörscher, the teachers corrected or commented on nearly every mistake, demonstrating their conceptualization of their task as getting the learners to conform.

Such correction behaviour clearly results from the view that learners' errors are signs of deficient learning and lack of norm adherence. Related to this is Chaudron's (1978) claim that error correction fulfils a positive function in the L2 classroom such as providing incentive, reinforcement and information leading to reform. Although research into the effects of correction is sparse, Brown & Hanlon (1970) maintain that in the acquisition of a first language, explicit correction as well as non-correction has equally negative consequences for the learning of the language.

There are, in fact, many illuminating insights to be obtained from studies on mother–child corrective interaction. Ramge (1980) remarks on the fact that children's grammatical mistakes are hardly ever corrected at all by their parents. This is not because the latter are uniquely interested in the propositional content of their children's utterances but because the relationship that has grown up between parent and child allows for a great degree of error tolerance. When parents do correct, it is generally by indirect and implicit means so that it does not sever ongoing communication. Moreover, whether explicit or implicit in nature parental correction always directly relates to the interests and needs of the child who adopts the forms to get what he/she wants. In contrast, classroom learners frequently offer their L2 utterances to demonstrate that they are willing to please the teacher and satisfy institutional needs. The social interpretation of corrective procedures here can only be that the teacher knows better, stressing his superior control function. The act of correcting can, of course, be understood in various ways depending on the context: instructing, clarifying or scolding (Ramge 1980).

In naturally occurring adult conversation there is a definite preference for *self-correction* as opposed to corrective intervention from interlocutors (Schegloff 1977) and this also has been shown to hold for the correction patterns between natives and L2 speakers in *natural,* non-classroom environments. Thus, Gaskill (1977) found that when the native corrects, he displays uncertainty, i.e. the correction is not asserted but proffered for acceptance or rejection. It seems that some corrections of deviant forms are presented in the form of restatements which appear as affirmations suggesting agreement with what the L2 speaker has just said rather than overt correction. However, where overt correction is made, they either occurred in a special context which almost asks for the correction or, most significantly, where there was major disagreement with the L2 speaker on the part of the native.

Unfortunately, the level of corrective intervention is much more frequent in the institutional context, where the distribution of knowledge and roles is traditionally imbalanced. The result of work on natural L1 acquisition has led some to suggest that teachers should just hint at the correct form or supply it indirectly as parents do for children (Corder 1967) or to allow the students to present their version instead of requiring imitation (George 1972). We shall explore some possible scientific justifications for this in our next section but it should be remembered that as yet there exists no educationally established criterion for deciding on what constitutes an error nor about how to deal with it. Generally, it seems left to the prejudices and intuitions of the teachers involved. Interestingly enough, learners appear to be more doctrinaire about norm conformity than their instructors. In surveying the attitudes of American college students towards error correction at all levels of learning an L2, Cathcart & Olsen (1976) discovered that not only did all the students want their grammar and pronunciation to be corrected but many also expressed the wish to be corrected more than teachers feel they should be. However, these students ranked grammar slightly lower than pronunciation which reflects the belief in the higher value of a better accent than a flawless syntax and partly seems to correlate with certain social attitudes of the L2 community towards accent convergence referred to earlier. Nevertheless, just because these college students desire an increase in corrective activity, it does not mean that it would necessarily be beneficial for their learning nor do they represent all L2 learners. George (1972), for instance, notes that if the errors are considered as minor or redundant by the learner, teacher correction only annoys the learner and wastes class time.

One of the principal reasons for the widely-registered failure of so much L2 learning must partly lie in this obsessively prescriptive treatment of the L2 as an artifact to be continually scrutinized instead of as an instrument to signal meaning. It is this norm of teaching that has not ended with the coming of the so-called "communicative approach". For example, Dodson & Butzkamm (1980) comment with disdain on the continued conception of teachers to view learners' attempts to mean as display. In this connection it is worth quoting the definition of a *natural communication task* by Burt & Dulay (1980) as:

> one where the focus of the student is anywhere but on the language forms themselves—on communicating an idea or opinion to someone, exchanging information, telling a story, relating past events, offering one's view on relevant matters, expressing one's feelings, emotions or beliefs.

In fact, the demand by L2 teachers for the conscious execution of norms really has much less to do with learning and speaking a language and much more with a particular type of operation usually activated by mathematical problems, memorization and methods of analysis in natural science. Felix (1977) calls this *reproductive competence* and sees little difference in the mental learning involved in mathematics and chemistry and traditional L2 courses; in all cases students are expected to mentally grasp the material presented and recognize structural limits in order to be able to solve the tasks. Once again, it must be said that the L2 tasks to be solved traditionally entail the ability to operate a set of linguistic norms.

The question being asked here is to what degree is the view warranted that reduces an L2 to an object embodied by norms and exalting their structural manipulation to the supreme level of conformist meaninglessness? Apparently, teachers still lack a clear understanding of the nature of communication even though they follow its conventions outside the classroom. There seems to be a naive confusion that lesson activity which is oral corresponds to real interaction. However, everyday interaction is rarely based on the persistent, one-sided demonstration of acquired knowledge for purposes of ratification from a superior. Its fundamental dynamics involve the mutual construction of meaning and this is what has ultimately to be accomplished in the L2 classroom.

Furthermore, recent studies of the way students go about implementing what they have demonstrated as 'learnt' in class, seriously challenge the premises of much institutional theory and practice. Schumann (1975a), for instance, focusing on the acquisition of English by a 33-year-old Spanish speaker who followed a seven month intensive course especially devoted to the 'knowledge' needed to handle negatives, discovered that in a subsequent test on negatives the student obtained 80% but in a free interview after the test he only used the negation structures learned seven months previously. L2 students can, therefore, consciously display the 'knowledge-product' when it is demanded by teachers but do not necessarily apply it to their real communication. There is no reason to suppose that the patterns and noises produced in lessons for their own sake can be internalized and identified with the expression of the learner's intentions and emotions outside the classroom. What is vitally needed then is a classroom environment where there exists a genuine opportunity for learners to express and develop *their* messages and a genuine interest to receive them as such.

This means that educators will have to rethink their norms of teaching for learning a non-native language. Teachers will have to relinquish their roles as deficiency experts and learners have to adjust their role expectations of being led through the learning process by teacher correction. The argument for such an approach is affirmed by the revealing fact that when non-native L2 teachers step out of their evaluating role and communicate with L2 students such as in the role of an adult or respected partner, they switch to the native L1; compare this with the misguided remarks of Hardin (1979, p. 3):

> there is much more in language learning than playing at communication (incidentally, let me emphasize the fact that when I want to communicate with my students [of English] I do so in French . . .).

However, this need for more intensive and less asymmetrical L2 classroom interaction does not signify an end in teacher monitoring nor, for that matter, in teacher input. The teacher will still have a tremendous amount to do in helping the learning process by, above all, getting the learners to cooperate with each other, ·iltering, selecting and planning the language to be learnt, facilitating the sorting-out process by using pointers, explanation, exercises and with reinforcement and re-exposure activities, aiding memory, instigating and running learning activities in which learners experiment with language in communication and providing added feedback to them on their progress (Rossner 1980). But the teacher's feedback should be based on observation rather than direct questions and the students' contributions should not be degraded to symbols of conformity. This perspective undeniably raises many far-reaching topics that are outside the scope of this book such as the pressure to perform normatively in examinations, the training of teachers in interactive skills among others. There will also be a conflict between the goals of high communicative ability and high grammatical precision, between a stress on adequate communication in the present and faultless performances in the distant future. The court of correction cannot solve this dilemma but perhaps attitudes towards the notion of deviancy can.

Reappraising deviancy

The fact that L2 teachers see their principal task as the eradication of error is a clear reflection of institutional concern for the upholding of linguistic norms which we know are socially determined. What is more, the implementation and recognition of the norms are closely tied to social relationships such as the presence of notions such as distance, status and face in interaction. The decision as to what constitutes a linguistic violation is fundamentally a social one.

An insightful illustration of the link between norms and social power is the case of the élite in a Senegal community who are obliged to make minor grammatical mistakes in their speech because "correctness would be considered an emphasis on fluency of performance, or on performance for its own sake, that is not appropriate to the highest of nobles" (Hymes 1974b, p. 442).

It has, of course, been widely observed that taken against the linguistic ability of adults, the speech of small children appears quite 'deviant' and similarly, measured against normative grammar, the speech of adults appears 'defective' (Ramge 1980). Yet few members of the speech community choose to see the matter in these terms. Moreover, when it comes to the non-institutional, natural acquisition of both first and second languages the attitudes of adults and natives have been particularly noted for their indifference, tolerance, considerateness and helpfulness towards error (Raabe 1980). As Kolde (1980) has perceptively stated, the incorrectness of a linguistic item is not a property intrinsic to the item but something that is attributed to it by the hearer/reader. In other words, native child and adult linguistic deviancy is tolerated simply because it is in no way socially regarded as corrupt: the children are excused because they are on the long road to acquiring *their* language while the adults are, after all, speaking *theirs* and, therefore, cannot be deforming it but simply not following the one socially honoured, ideal model. When it comes to L2 speakers the matter is generally treated quite differently: the imperfections of L2 speakers are tolerated far less, above all by teachers it would seem. Could this then be because it is only the native speaker with a legitimate ethnicity who has the right to be deviant in his speech?

Andresen (1976) has remarked that the more asymmetric the social relations are, the more the deviancy in speech can be focused on. The Senegal example above supports this in that it demonstrates that only the powerful can afford to flout the norms. Most L2 learners today, unless having attained an extremely advanced level of proficiency and in a position of authority, rarely enjoy egalitarian status in their interaction with natives. It can easily be seen how native speakers are believed to hold the right to set themselves up as authorities of judgement on the L2 speaker. This supposed right is appropriated usually by the teacher, whether native or not. The acceptance and understanding of what the non-native says, however, is a social act and this is what makes the L2 user vulnerable.

A personal experience while in hospital in Germany can perhaps reveal how the social choice to understand or not to understand is available to the native in communication with the L2 user. I was among a group of patients making jokes at the breakfast table about each other's food. One of the patients, a boy whose nose and upper lip had medical tape over it, he was not very intelligible, said something which I could not make out and when I asked whether he had said "horns" (in German), he paused for a second and said in a German pidginized style of talking to foreigners: *"Nicht verstehen"* (literally, not understand). I persisted once with further attempts for clarification but he repeated *"wie"* (what?) several times. When I proposed that he might be deaf and in need of an ear operation, he asked another German at the table if he could understand me, i.e. a social support for his act of non-comprehension. This boy was trying to be humorous and did not intend to taunt. Two days earlier when he told me about the broadcasting of a traditional festivity on TV (Karneval comic speeches) and I responded with "Oh yes, I'd like to watch that—it's interesting to see how Germans celebrate", he answered with "That sounds really funny. You don't sound like a foreigner. Yes, you're a foreigner but you sound German or like someone who's lived here a long time." The reason for mentioning his evaluation of my German is not for egocentric reasons but to show the fact that my level of fluency had already been positively evaluated and that the table response was supposed to be interpreted as a joke. When one analyses wherein the humour lies one comes to recognize the social authority of nativeness and ethnicity. My requests for clarification had triggered an awareness of his power to take them not as indications of his faulty performance but mine—my non-native handicap. He was clearly aware of the existence of the conscious option to understand a person or not. Such a reaction is, without doubt, not limited to non-natives; speakers of non-standard varieties or with speech defects may also suffer in this way. What is particularly significant here was that up until that moment I had felt that my foreign status in speaking the L2 has been purposely ignored and never referred to overtly. The joke also knocked down this taboo that had been socially constructed by the native German patients together. The boy's response also included the connotation of social inferiority due to the special socioeconomic situation of immigrant workers in West Germany who are stereotypically seen by Germans as being incomprehensible and requiring a broken language back as signalled in *"nicht verstehen"*.

In connection with the potential, in-built inequality of encounters between non-natives and natives resulting from the purely linguistic handicap of the former, it can frequently be noticed how natives consciously exploit their linguistic superiority in small-talk situations. Thus, superiority is present in many native–non-native encounters and is accompanied by the native consciousness of his right to comment on the deviancy. Native tolerance will be greatest when the interaction with L2 speakers satisfies a specific goal. This context of cooperation may result in the native's temporary condoning of a different treatment of his language or even modifying his own verbal behaviour and adopting some of the learner's language. An example of this is provided by Shapira (1978) who, although a fluent speaker of English, responds in the following manner to an L2 learner in conversation:

L2 learner: Do you think is ready.
Shapira: I think is ready.
L2 learner: Why she's very upset for me?
Shapira: S. is upset for you?
L2 learner: Yeah, is. (p. 247.)

Nemser (1971) also notes that some L2 teachers may not only concur in the use of a "learner pidgin" but even participate as users and cites an exchange he observed (p. 118):

Arabic-English speaker: Same? (i.e. Are the two words pronounced in the same way).
L2 Teacher: Same.

However, the use of deviant utterances by natives does not always function to foster cooperation with L2 speakers. It can also serve as a means to keep non-natives at arms' length, cf. the broken language of the German boy in the situation described above illustrating the inherent power of nativeness and the choice to understand or not. Valdman (1977a), for instance, argues that a markedly simplified French has connotations of condescension and racial discrimination and erects a psychosocial barrier between the native and the L2 speaker who is treated as an inferior. Of course, this *foreigner talk,* as the pidginized language of natives has been called, does not really correspond to the authentic nature of L2 speech but more to folk notions of how foreigners are expected to speak.

Apart from signalling distance in stereotypic form or solidarity by adopting non-native patterns, the native violation of linguistic norms serve a variety of other strategic purposes which in interaction, all seem closely connected to the liberation of individuals from social pressures. For example, someone who is regarded as a leader of a group and who is intentionally casual and slightly deviant in his speech is taken as indicating to the rest of the group that they can relax and cease aiming at the norm of talking-like-writing (Sittal 1980). Related to this, it must not be forgotten that the linguistic non-orthodoxy of artists (poets, novelists and song-writers) as well as advertisers has long been licensed and praised for its creativity and originality.

Whatever the treatment of norm infringements has been for L1 and naturally acquired L2 speakers, the institutional and classroom reaction has been wholly negative if not openly hostile. After the Second World War, most L2 materials were specifically designed to ensure that, as far as possible, learners performed without error. This tabooing of error gained support from Skinner's view that if an error occurs the probability of its recurrence cannot be permanently reduced by punishment and that all the teachers' efforts should go into rewarding correct responses (Clark 1975).

As we have seen in the previous section, this behaviouristic procedure obviously still characterizes current teaching methodology. The thesis was certainly taken up by audiolingualism in the 1960s when in the manifesto of that decade's teaching profession, *Language and Learning Language,* Nelson Brooks (1960, p. 58) declared:

> Like sin, error is to be avoided and its influence overcome, but its presence is to be expected . . . the principal method of avoiding error in language learning is to observe and practice the right model a sufficient number of times; the principal way of overcoming it is to shorten the time lapse between the incorrect response and the presentation once more of the correct model.

Lately, however, linguists from various fields have come to question this traditional postulate and begun to investigate the sociolinguistic dimensions of error. 'Comprehensibility' and 'conformity' both make up the most fundamental objective of L2 learning but the two are often in conflict with each other. For instance, Johansson (1973) suggests that if the goal of L2 education is comprehensibility then errors cannot be evaluated irrespective of their communicative effect. Moreover, nearly all teaching material has been based on a supposition that has never been empirically proven, namely that grammaticality was an essential feature of communication. Thus, Johannson argues that conformity is a misguided goal for most learners of foreign languages, most of whom do not aspire to become full-fledged members of the foreign language community but simply want to communicate with its members. Therefore, it is reasonable to regard comprehensibility or the ability to communicate as the primary goal for foreign language teaching. L2 errors should be studied to find out to see how they interfere with the decoding of the L2 message by the native and to discover what social reactions they evoke.

In fact, there now exists a steadily growing number of investigations into the social evaluation of L2 error. Ervin (1977), for example, examined how proficient speakers of Russian would accept and comprehend the verbal narrations of picture stories by American learners of the language. What was interesting was the way each group of judges differed in their ranking of the students' performance. Native Russians who were not teachers most readily accepted the narrations of the intermediate and advanced students in contrast to teachers of Russian who were native English speakers and who were most accepting of the narrations of low proficiency students. Native Russian teachers were the least accepting of narrations overall. That teachers react more negatively than non-teachers to L2 deviancy is a finding that reappears in many other similar studies. When Galloway (1980) presented videotapes of American responses in Spanish to general questions to four different groups (native Spaniards in Spain, native Spaniards in America, native Spaniard high school teachers and non-native Spanish high school teachers) it was found that the non-teaching natives established rapport with students who demonstrated sincere difficulty and made an exerted effort to express themselves while non-native teachers proved the least tolerant of the students' errors. "Most [of the latter group] held their heads down, paying little attention to the visual portion. In many cases, they completed the scoring sheet before the student had finished speaking" (p. 430). Moreover, none of the different errors in grammar and pronunciation seriously impeded overall communication and the group in Spain had a relatively easy time understanding a student who practically resorted to pidginization. Interestingly enough, Galloway clearly states that native speakers seemed mostly concerned with the content of the students' presentation while the non-native teachers appeared to be focusing more on grammatical accuracy. The use of gesture elicited a particularly favourable reaction with natives and was seen as decreasing the distance between students and judges; those students who did not employ body language were considered cold and aloof. Non-native teachers, however, expressed severe annoyance with the students' use of gesture demonstrating the divergence between native and non-native evaluation in the matter. Galloway concludes that an L2 speaker's lack of grammatical accuracy does not produce negative reactions as long as the desire and urgency to communicate are evident. Significantly, natives did become critical of those students who communicated with apparent ease and grammatical accuracy. Galloway does not offer any explanation for this but there are a number of possibilities:

native expectations of norm adherence increases with perceived L2 fluency;

natives become more critical as L2 speakers become linguistically closer to their own productive abilities;

L2 fluency makes speakers appear 'cooler' and did not put the judges in the position of sociolinguistic superiors as could have been the case in the less sophisticated performance;

or, as Valdman (1975, p. 245) has claimed: "while sensitivity to grammatical deviance varies from community to community, native speakers do seem to expect a high level of correctness from learners who have acquired a language by formal training".

Beneke's (1979) study of an international team in a business company communicating in English further substantiates the findings of the research mentioned above. Breaks in speech are judged neutrally as "excusable sins" and many violations of grammatical, lexical, stylistic and linguistically aesthetic norms are confidentially nullified by the participants to achieve communication. However, it must be remembered that these norms are suspended in a context of predominantly non-native speakers. Furthermore, the L2 speakers are using English rather as a tool in order to get a job done, as it has been defined by the company, rather than for intimate or self-expressive purposes. Additionally, the participants enjoy an institutionally derived equality of status—although, of course, some of them hold hierarchic- ally differentiated tasks, the social premises for the interethnic and interlingual communication were fundamentally egalitarian in that any of the L2 speakers could potentially be in the position of superior. Although it was not the case in his study, Beneke believes that deviant intonation and stress are usually (unconsciously) taken by natives as signals of intelligence and personality and that it is the non-observation of socioculturally linked norms which provokes interpretations such as aggression and arrogance. The natives in this context, however, were used to non-native varieties of their language and rarely applied their L1 community norms. For Beneke the most essential elements of L2 communication does not exist in the mastery of grammar but in the ability to establish speaker-hearer relations, the management of the "phatic" functions of language, i.e. the apparently empty but socially significant routines such as "What horrible weather we're having", and flexibility in the use of pitch and stress.

Some investigations have restricted their attention mainly to the effects of grammatical errors on the communicative process itself. Guntermann (1978), for instance, played recordings of Americans' grammatically deviant Spanish to native speakers unfamiliar with English whose task it was to restate what the Americans had said. Only 20% out of the 2000 native interpretations were wrong which was surprising because no context for the utterances was supplied. Guntermann concludes that grammatical errors do not constitute serious impediments and agrees with Olsson (1972) in the obvious finding that mistakes in meaning such as wrong word selection or misuse of a word or unclarity of expression block understanding more than anything else. But Guntermann does note that native listeners react more negatively to certain errors than others and find some more humorous than others: "Indeed, the informants laughed spontaneously 43% of the time at sentences that contained errors in agreement" (p. 252). Exactly which are socially interpreted as the most grave, stigmatized or ridiculous errors should be the subject of intensive future research in order to concentrate on overcoming these first of all.

In a similar kind of investigation, Politzer (1978) examined the importance attached to errors by West German teenagers. Sixty deviant sentences were read out in German with a slight American accent and presented to three different school types. The errors included faulty pronunciation, wrong case endings, verb morphology, genders, word order and vocabulary. No conclusive patterns of evaluation emerged but deviant pronunciation was generally seen as less serious than mistakes in vocabulary and word order but counted more than error in redundant grammatical features such as gender error. Once again, it was vocabulary errors that were considered the most serious type of error:

> Not unexpectedly, speakers of German seem to know quite intuitively that using the right words is the most important aspect of language use. Correct pronunciation and the use of correct case endings—especially after prepositions, where the case endings are redundant—are of relatively lower priority (p. 258).

Politzer also discovered that error evaluation varied according to school-type. He observes that the judges were not naive in that they had been exposed to foreign language pedagogy at school. Thus, children attending the least academically orientated school (Hauptschule) rated vocabulary errors much more seriously than any other type, clearly reflecting the unindoctrinated (natural?) perspective that 'correct' grammar plays an insignificant role in the communicative process.

Native reactions to errors produced by Swedish learners of English were the object of investigation for Johansson (1978). In two experiments native speakers were asked to interpret or rank passages containing specific types of lexical and grammatical errors produced by Swedish learners of English. The experiments showed that the native speakers had greater problems in interpreting lexical than grammatical errors and also judged the former to be more serious than the latter:

> It is suggested that the principle . . . which assigns a higher degree of gravity to grammatical than to lexical errors, may often have been given too much weight at the expense of the communicative principle (p. 126).

Furthermore, in another experiment Johansson found that natives attached more importance to errors in prosody (intonation and stress) than to errors in individual sounds. When the reaction of a group of Swedish teachers of English or prospective teachers of English was compared with the native one in the same experiment, a consistent difference was discovered which showed the native to be more tolerant in their assessment of deviant individual sounds than non-native teachers but less so in the assessment of deviant prosody.

Chastain's study (1980) is yet a further substantiation of the unnecessary overemphasis on grammaticality in L2 teaching. Here errors observed by teachers of Spanish as an L2 to Americans were collected and incorporated into written sentences that were given to native Spaniards for judging in three ways: (1) comprehensible and acceptable, (2) comprehensible but unacceptable, and (3) incomprehensible. The results were that even in the absence of an adequate 'world' to relate the isolated sentence to, 90% of the native speakers were able to comprehend 83% of the errors in the sample. Only half of them were felt to be unacceptable while 38% were described as acceptable. Again, it was the employment of wrong words or the additional omission of words which severely limited comprehension. It seems natives can easily supply the correct forms but cannot so readily supply the "correct meanings". Chastain writes that the evaluation of errors as comprehensible and acceptable depends upon native speaker linguistic tolerance, insight, interest and patience and this comment closely corroborates with what we stated earlier about the noticing and censuring of error as an essentially social act.

All these contemporary studies forcefully indicate that grammatical precision does not lead to intelligibility, let alone successful communication. Even though intelligibility is the avowed goal of L2 education, we have witnessed how it concentrates most of its energy on grammaticality. If a certain level of grammatical deviancy is tolerated and even expected by a community, then why is L2 teaching devoting so much of its time to the superfluous features of grammar? When no sanctions for norm violations are applied, the norms are generally viewed as defunct.

It is worth noting, as Beneke (1979) does, that L2 users are sometimes and, especially in situations where the L2 is merely an *instrument* to achieve something else, free from sanctions for violating the norms.

That the classroom teacher should represent the target community and presume the latter to apply normative judgements on the L2 speaker as the teacher has partly been proven unfounded in the investigations above. For many L2 speakers it is not the deficiency of their language but its effectiveness that constitutes the most important criterion. Fluent communication does not depend on precise and complicated syntax. Therefore, should not learners be prepared to communicate adequately at any moment in the L2 learning process rather than postponing this event to some hypothetical time never approached in the classroom?

This sociolinguistic questioning of traditional L2 teaching practice together with an explosion of research on the learning and communicative strategies of L2 users have resulted in the emancipation of non-conforming, non-native language from the disrepute of aberration to the status of a distinctive dialect or variety.

This view which may seem extreme or even preposterous to some is typically represented in the following statement by Klein (1974):

> . . . the language which a Turkish worker speaks after three years in Germany is just as much a variety of German as the language of an Upper Bavarian farrier, of a dentist from Iserlohn or of (the philosopher) Adorno. Genuine distinctions can be made here according to functionality and aesthetics. But that is a separate problem (p. 12).

How and why has this reappraisal of linguistic deviancy come about? The answer, of course, lies in the effects of sociolinguistic theories and research. First of all, work on non-standard dialects of English have shown the internal systematicity and grammaticality of these language types such as black English (Dillard 1972). In fact, many of the linguistic features of these non-standard language systems surprisingly correspond to those produced by L2 speakers, e.g. absence of person inflection (*John run*), absence of temporal inflection (*he go yesterday*), zero copula (*my brother sick*), multiple negation (*I didn't have no dinner*), regularization (*I seed; hisself* on the basis of *myself*), unmarked plurality (*a hundred pound*), double comparatives (*more rougher*) to name but a few. That deviancy can be strategically used is shown by Mitchell-Kernan (1972) who observes how black Americans will employ forms that are never part of natural usage but which emphasize the contrast between white and black English such as *I is*. Here the phonological component is also exaggerated and it is clear to the hearer that this deviancy is not the ordinary speech style of the speaker.

For Trudgill & Giles (1976) such forms are regarded as 'corrupt' because of their speakers' low social status:

> This low status leads to the belief that these forms are 'bad' and they are therefore judged to be 'wrong'. Evaluations of this type are therefore clearly social judgements about the status of speakers who use particular forms, rather than objective linguistic judgements about the correctness of the forms (p. 3).

These sociolinguists plead for greater tolerance of native dialects since speakers are often made to hate their own speech and can even become inarticulate and reluctant to express themselves. The two investigators reject all conceptions of the inherent superiority of a particular variety on scientific linguistic grounds although they admit the socio-economic advantages which accrue from the employment of a normative model. To prove that the standard language is an imposed aesthetic norm they carried out experiments first using different varieties of Greek which was played to British subjects with no knowledge of the language with the result that the non-educated Cretan variety was rated as slightly more pleasant than the Athenian. To further refute the counter-argument that foreigners are incompetent judges, the experimenters presented ten British varieties to American, Canadian, English and Scots listeners. A number of Americans gave responses such as "Spanish", "Mexican" or "Norwegian" in a number of cases and were much worse than the English at recognizing the varieties. However, the main result of the experiment was that none of the listening groups agreed on the aesthetic evaluations of the ten accents and this is because the social connotation of the different accents either vary for different listeners or were not known. Even when an accent was generally recognized, as with the London one, it was rated tenth by both the English and the Scots, third by the Canadians and eastern Americans. Thus, the question of linguistic aesthetics and correctness turns out to be one of social differences and prejudices.

As far back as 1955, Hall demonstrated that pidgins, language systems which draw on a dominant group's vocabulary but retain their own syntax and phonology using few tense, gender and plural markers, were capable of handling refined thought and possessed their own unique grammar. Pidgins are not spoken as an L1 but generally develop out of some generally socioeconomic need for communication. They bear a close resemblance to the early stages of L2 development. Since Hall many have gone on to show the effectiveness, structural logic and sociopolitical importance of pidgins. It is worth noting Valdman's (1977a) statement regarding the absence of linguistic elaboration and its association in Western society with a reduction in intellectual capacity. Valdman believes that this folk interpretation is clearly present in the correlation between the degree of social and ethnic distance separating natives from non-natives and the extent of their deviancy in simplified language. I would also like to raise the question whether the knowledge of the stereotypic, historical, linguistic interaction between the White Man and indigenous peoples who spoke a 'broken' L2 and held low status as portrayed in media, cf. as early as the eighteenth century when Daniel Defoe described the language learning of Man Friday in *Robinson Crusoe,* does not also reinforce attitudes of contempt towards the employment of simplified and supposedly "elementary" forms of communication by non-natives.

Here is a typical statement of the 19th century racist-linguistic view that perhaps still lingers in the unconscious:

> It is clear that people used to expressing themselves with a rather simple language cannot easily elevate their intelligence to the genius of a European language. When they were in contact with the Portuguese and forced to communicate with them, speaking the same language, it was necessary that the varied expressions acquired during so many centuries of civilization dropped their perfection, to adapt to ideas being born and to barbarous forms of language of half-savage people" (Bertrand-Bocandé 1849, p. 73).

Bertrand's theory was grounded on the tenets that there was a direct correlation between the level of civilization and the complexity of language and that European languages were too rich in morphological distinctions and syntactic categories for "simple black souls, so that the languages have to be stripped of these in order to be usable by

Africans" (Meijer & Muysken 1977, p. 22). Such deluded conceptions still live and and can even be found as partially adopted by non-standard speakers. Thus, Escure (1979, p. 114) quotes a user of Creole and standard English in Belize as saying "the darker the skin, the worse the Creole. . . . You still close to the African". But Belize Creole can also be prestigious for young people who see in it a symbol against the establishment since their parents and teacher have insisted that the use of standard English is the door to social success.

For Bickerton (1977a) the difference between arriving at a pidgin and arriving at a reasonably accurate version of a standard language depends principally on two social factors: the availability of target models and the amount of interaction with speakers of the target standard. He sees pidgins generally as an ongoing uncontrolled process that allows them to freely expand in their means of expression or to become expressively more rigid and restricted. The stunning similarities in the features of pidgins all over the world are explicable in terms of universal principles of simplification that can be found in all situations of 'handicapped' non-native language learning.

A creole is a second-generation pidgin which emerges to satisfy the communication needs of the children of pidgin speakers. It can arise whether the ancestral languages of their pidgin-speaking parents do or do not constitute adequate and feasible means of communication for them. It usually involves an increase in the vocabulary and a fixing of the grammatical system. The next stage is decreolization when the creole comes to resemble more and more closely one of its parent languages but a creole can even replace a previously dominant parent language, e.g. Middle English resulting from the interaction of speakers of Anglo-Saxon, Norman French and the Scandinavian languages spoken in Northern England (Lester 1978).

Recently, a standard language has been officially developed from a pidgin in New Guinea but this new language system called Neo-Melanesian has now become a creole. The fact that languages are not absolute entities is especially evident when one tries to establish the division between pidgins, creoles and standard varieties in a community where they all exist alongside each other.

Ferguson & DeBose (1977) consider pidginization as the natural outcome of L2 speakers' broken language and the "simplified registers" of native communities such as baby and foreigner talk. (The latter refers to the production of deviant forms by natives which are stereotypically supposed to represent the way foreigners speak 'badly', e.g. "Me hungry".) Foreigner talk is another demonstration of the fact that natives do not always wish to produce grammatical speech and, in specific circumstances, wholeheartedly participate in the 'debasement' of their language. Moreover, it is now well established that native speakers often fail to live up to their normative standards, even though they often will assert the contrary. Much of everyday speech is naturally and normally 'defective' from a prescriptive perspective and it is precisely for this very reason that general linguistics has refused to deal with the spoken medium for so long.

The current focus on the linguistic development of children has additionally revealed that children do not simply offer a garbled version of the language around them but that the mistakes they make are rule-governed and an essential part of the language learning process, helping to provide indications of the state of their development. Thus children are found to produce forms they could never have heard before, e.g. *goed* which throw light on their creation of systematicity and their hypotheses-testing.

In fact, many insights into the nature of error derived from these studies on child language have been applied to the linguistic 'deviancy' of the L2 learner and various sources of error discovered such as overgeneralization where the learner creates an incorrect structure on the basis of his experience of other structures in the L2 such as *maked* for made. Other errors have been found to arise from inadequate application of rules, ignorance of rule restrictions, e.g. *the man who I saw him,* and falsely hypothesized concepts. Psychophysical factors such as tiredness, alcoholic influence, etc., also lead to error as well as purely psychological factors such as stress, excitement, indecision and so on. Then there is the idiosyncratic hardening of an incorrect pattern through habitual use (called fossilization), false analogy, e.g. *that lasts shorter* on the basis of *that lasts longer,* redundancy and the negative transference of linguistic features and information from the learner's first language into his second, see the collection of articles in Richards (1974).

If the deviant language of native speakers when casual or dialectal or sub-standard or childish or in imitation of foreigners is systematic and correct in its own terms and sanctioned by linguistics, then can the same language when produced by non-native speakers be rated any differently?

At least, this is the question that is posed by an ever expanding body of work on second language acquisition which sets out to demonstrate the regularity and the active, evolutionary productivity of the language of L2 users.

As with pidgins and their nativized linguistic descendants, creoles, as well as non-standard dialects, the language of the L2 speaker varies not only from individual to individual but also in the individual himself, i.e. he can decrease or increase the non-standardness of his speech which can only be accounted for in terms of a continuum. Many terms vie with each other to describe the nature of a second language. Nemser (1971) calls second languages which have not reached the stage of absolute nativeness *approximative systems* and claims they exhibit true internal coherence. The uniqueness in these systems is that they primarily select external norms—in the form of the native speaker at which they aim and not the linguistic norms of the social group to which they belong or learn in, although, of course, the latter's usage may reinforce the features of the learner's language and he may find it more easy to communicate with other approximative system speakers rather than natives.

On the other hand, Corder (1971) describes the learner's language as an *idiosyncratic dialect* which can provide rich insights into the dynamics of learning. For Corder, well-formed utterances do not provide any information on the state of learning but are only imitations of heard utterances. By differentiating between errors which are systematic, those which are non-systematic (such as breaks in sentence structure, slips of the tongue which Corder calls *lapses*) and stylistic violations (classified as *social gaffes*), Corder maintains that the systematic errors should find a place in institutional teaching since they are necessary to the development of full competence. He also declares that the sentences generated by his system cannot be deviant by definition. Words such as 'error', 'deviancy' and 'ill-formedness' cannot be applied to L2 learners' utterances since

> whatever the surface form or apparent appropriateness of learners' utterances, none are utterances in the target language . . . he is not speaking the target language at any time, but a language of his own, a unique dialect . . . every utterance of the learner must be regarded as an acceptable utterance in his transitional dialect (Corder 1971, p. 61).

In a similar vein to Nemser, Corder stresses the systematic uniqueness of this language type that is neither the dialect of a social group nor the ideolect of an individual but contains the conventional rules of both.

A further term which has been misleadingly applied to very diverse phenomena is *interlanguage* used by Richards (1972) and Selinker (1972) to refer to such distinct and separate systems as a Nigerian pidgin and Indian English. Richards views the ideal L2 learner as one "who will *not* 'succeed' (in the absolute sense)''. In other words, the concept of interlanguage contains the in-built perspective of deficiency in that it tends towards seeing the learner as held back from approaching the norm by a number of learning strategies: language transfer, transfer of training, strategies of L2 learning, strategies of L2 communication and overgeneralization of target language features.

These three terms which, for the first time in linguistic history make an attempt to explain the 'deviancy' of L2 systems, represent a significant contribution to the acceptance of that 'deviancy', although this has not yet been sufficiently realized. Of course, this little 'revolution' has not been enthusiastically welcomed by all, Zydatiß (1974, p. 234) writes:

> calling obvious deviations perfectly 'grammatical' sentences in terms of the learner's 'transitional competence' or 'dialect' would be of no help to the student.

Corder (1978) notes that it is by taking the risk out of making mistakes in the L2 that interlanguage can progress and develop so that learners should be encouraged not to avoid risk-taking strategies "even at the expense of committing errors" and "to accept error as a sign of motivation for learning, or indeed a strategy of learning, and not something to be deprecated, let alone penalized" (p. 84).

However, the main thrust of this theory has been to de-stigmatize L2 'deviancy'. Current research on the non-institutional acquisition of an L2 further substantiates the arguments that learning an L2 is a creative process where the learner builds up for himself the rules of a new grammar. As Burt & Dulay (1980) point out, almost every recent study on L2 learning by children and adults shows that there is a definite developmental progression. This implies that certain structures cannot be acquired before others and that mistakes are an inevitable part of the acquisition order.

The pedagogic application of research on the sequential acquisition of French interrogatives by American students led Valdman (1974) to teach question forms at the beginning of a course which were "a sociolinguistically stigmatized construction which many educated speakers consider downright ungrammatical" (p. 24). In this, Valdman takes up Nickel's (1973) controversial proposal that language teaching materials should reflect the learners' acquisition order and teach 'incorrect' forms.

Of course, we cannot enter into the psychological dimension of learning an L2 here but it is patent from what has so far been said about research that their findings are steadily pressurizing institutional teaching to reconsider L2 errors and forcing educationalists and syllabus designers to acknowledge the L2 learners' natural strategies for coping with the strain of another linguistic system. Heuer (1978), for instance, proposes that textbooks should be conceived to match the learner's language in terms of complexity, vocabulary and pro-ductivity, e.g. third-year learners aged 12/13 years have been found to produce the maximum of five-syllable sentences and this should be reflected in the controlled sentence lengths of textbook dialogues.

The findings of investigations into the development of L2 learners in relation to their communicative needs in a non-institutional, natural setting are of special relevance for understanding L2 'deviancy'. In his analysis of children learning English as an L2 in a natural setting, Fathman (1977) finds that the structures the learners produce are influenced by their need for effective communication. Learners will produce correct forms if they consider them to be important for getting across their meaning. Moreover, these structures which are used correctly are not necessarily the simplest linguistically but often those needed for basic self-expression. Fathman's findings support the theory that the early stages of language learning are characterized by simplified and reduced forms which expand as the learner progessses, reflecting changes in his needs for expression.

What emerges from the similarities in the errors of learners of different L1 backgrounds and ages is that it is not what is taught of the L2 but *how* this proceeds which affects the learner's correct use of the target language: the establishment of a meaningful learning environment is probably the most important key to successful language teaching.

Related to these conclusions is Meisel's (1977) study of immigrant workers in Germany, few of whom attend language classes and who face social stigmatization from L2 characteristic features such as, (1) the enlargement of the sense of German words, e.g. *nix geld* for 'no money' when an adjectival negative *kein* meaning 'no' should be used instead of *nix*, a dialectal form for *nicht*, (2) the replacement of formal address *Sie* by the familiar *Du*, (3) the preference for lexical material which is very general such as *machen* 'to do', (4) missing elements such as articles, prepositions, copula, auxiliaries, personal pronouns, inflection and, (5) non-native word order. Meisel proposes this to be the result of the intention to *use* language adequately by means of strategies of simplification. Two of his informants share the same grammatical competence and yet one can communicate much more efficiently than the other. Yet Meisel categorizes them as belonging in the same 'subgroup' because of the state of their linguistic systems. He distinguishes between two types of immigrant worker speech that corresponds to two different kinds of communicative needs. In one group there are those who want to go back to their home country as soon as possible and those who do not know how long they will stay but who live in their own ethnic community which is itself not integrated into German society. He calls these "cultural outsiders" and maintains that their speech, due to this social situation, is limited to an exclusively functional information:

"The predominant if not only social information is that the speaker is a foreigner" (p. 107). In contrast, those workers who wish to stay for a considerably longer period or indefinitely, tending more to aim at integration into German society but without necessarily abandoning their own native culture learn harder and reach a higher level of L2 fluency.

In a similar fashion, Shapira (1978) describes the case of a 25-year-old Guatemalan women, a native speaker of Spanish, who came to the USA at 22 and who on arrival built up negative feelings about her life in the USA, about the USA and all things American. Once she had attained the basic objective of getting across her message, albeit without conforming to the conventions of English—she aspired no further even though her negative feelings had since dissipated because she had developed enough fluency in the L2 to enable her to under-stand all she was interested in and to make herself understood. Her daily interaction with natives constantly reinforced her feeling that her English was good enough since it was accepted, i.e. understood. Most, if not all, native speakers she comes into contact with are sympathetic and tolerant of her language problems. This L2 learner candidly reveals her linguistic strategy for communication:

Learner:	I never . . . I never listen, you know the . . . the words little, uh, small words for continue my conversation.
Interviewer:	What, like what?
Learner:	The /fras/, you know frase?
Interviewer:	Sentence.
Learner:	The sentence, sentence. In the sentence I never using this little, little words.
Interviewer:	Like what?
Learner:	Ah, 'and', and 'that', /ʌm/ /ipidit/ You know? If /bin/ /it/ Sometimes. . . . Well, maybe because I no study . . . never, and only hear the people and . . . and talking.
Interviewer:	Yeah, but people talk with these words.
Learner:	Yeah, pero /əs, əh/, I'm . . . hear and put more attention the big words. You know and . . . something 'house'. I know 'house' is the casa for me. And (əsəs) and little words is no too important for me (p. 254).

Although this learner sometimes uses "little words" she takes as redundant, she consciously restricts her speech to the essential and the most meaningful in order to achieve communication. Her deviancy is a successful strategy for effective transmission.

Another L2 learner's deviancy is explained by Schumann (1978b) as a refusal to integrate and thereby has much in common with the conclusions of Fathman and Meisel described above. This refusal is due to a psychological distance from the target community. Even though the learner claimed to be motivated and have a positive attitude towards language learning to the L2 group, his life-style contradicted with this: he made very little effort to get to know English-speaking people and stuck in a Spanish-speaking clique; he did not own a television and expressed disinterest in it because he could not understand English, purchasing an expensive stereo set and tape deck on which he played mostly Spanish music. He chose to work at night (as well as in the day) rather than attend English classes which were available. Schumann sees the persistence of a simplified L2 system initially resulting from cognitive constraints and resembling a pidgin but its subsequent non-expansion and non-elaboration as being closely tied to the learner's unwillingness to assimilate the L2 culture and identify with the community. From this perspective, L2 deviancy turns out to be the consequence of a conscious act of non-integration.

Another strand of research on the interactional dynamics of natural L2 acquisition (Hatch 1978a) shows that learners' grammatical development depends on their conversational abilities, cf. Seliger (1977) who has pointed out that the L2 learner who manages many contacts with native speakers outside the classroom are the best ones. Hatch (1978b) also claims that the most successful L2 speakers are those who do not give up but make it clear to their native interlocutors that they are really trying with head nodding, apologies (*excuse me, I don't understand*), second tries, while learners who just say "What" or "Yes" and show little work in their attempts to keep conversations going are 'hung up on'.

In natural L2 acquisition, the L2 child learner is contextually given an immense amount of practice which allows him to repeat models of the the native speaker:

Learner: thin broken
Native: broken

Learner: broken this əz broken. broken
Native: upside down
Learner: upside down. this broken. upside down. broken. (Data from Itoh 1973.).

In interaction with the native child, the L2 child does not need to tightly control his vocabulary—made up words are frequent. The L2 child learner often appears content to join in on repetition of vocabulary even though he cannot know what it means. Native adults, on the other hand, ask for elaboration and clarification of information on topics from L2 children which results in an extremely controlled set of question–answer routines based on objects present in the environment of ongoing interaction.

Hatch sees L2 children learners as getting the best of both worlds in that they are provided with language learning opportunities with a controlled input from adults where the vocabulary is made clear from the context and also the chance to practise, sometimes up to 15 times in a row, when playing with native children while throughout this interaction the language remains syntactically simple. Much of the latter type of interchange is language-play where the learner attends to rhythm, rhyme, intonation and phonology:

Learner:	Native speaker playmate:
	drring! drring! (like bells)
Oooh! Ooh! (like a siren)	drring! A fire mill, a fire mill! Ooh, look at how much
Ooh! Ooh!	we've done—'far no good.
Look at all—(sings low) Far, so good.—good—good (talks fast) good, good, good, good.	
[gʌ gʌ gʌ gʌ]	I can't do it. I just can't do it. Do what? Do this. Do this— do what,
Do that.	D what, do that, do what, D'—d'—d'—d'—d'—
(singing) My Daddy's in Mexico. (Hatch 1980, p. 180.)	d'—umm D'a—D'a—D'a—D'a.

Hatch (1980) wonders how older L2 learners can receive either the simple input or the kind of language-play practice as above. Another very significant aspect which relates to the argument about comprehension constituting a social act is the statement by native peers of L2 child learners that they know and understand the latter's language completely. This the native children also seem to sincerely believe. Thus, when a five-year-old Iranian learning English produced strings of nonsensical English such as "It's a do something airplane something do do rock not do rock do do takhta. Something do this [swish noises]. It's a going and do that airplane. I may do that do do the my Mark", his playmate, Mark, was highly supportive of such speech and claimed he understood everything his friend said. In other words, deviancy and incomprehensibility are sometimes socially ratified in the natural environment of L2 acquisition so that there is little threatening to the L2 learner in his interaction with natives.

In this connection, Wong-Fillmore's (1976) study of five Spanish-speaking children in their L2 acquisition in their contexts of play with school friends found that all the children first employ a "speak now, learn later" strategy of communication and two out of five then went on to the next stage which he calls the "concern for correctness" stage. According to Wong-Fillmore, the good learner joins a group and acts as if he understands even if he does not, giving the impression with a few well-chosen words that he can speak the language and counts on his friends. (Here once again the native peers were highly supportive of the learners and convinced that they could and did speak English.) Among the set of maxims followed by the learners for communicating and coping in the L2 environment discovered by Wong-Fillmore are

get some expressions you understand and start to talk;
make the most of what you've got;
string the formulas you've first learned as chunks together and add new lexical items as you can;
work on big things first and save details until later (morphology can wait).

This work on the natural learning of a non-native language helps to throw light on why, in comparison, classroom learning produces such miserable results. What we find in the non-institutional setting and which is lacking in the classroom is direct, meaningful interaction proceeding on the basis of a simple, context-orientated linguistic input where the learner's deviancy does not threaten their face but is, in fact, highly tolerated. On top of this, there is, for L2 children, ample provision for repetition and creativity. Could this be part of the explanation for the widespread evidence that children are more successful at learning a non-native language than adults?

When we look at all the research that has been carried out on deviant language whether produced by natives as a special way of talking to foreigners or seen by those communicating merely as a tool for dealing with a problem, whether as part of natural and interactional strategies for learning and using a not yet fully known system or as a rejection of personal integration in the L2 community, one can clearly recognize that hostile attitudes towards non-normative L2 speech styles are justifiably in need of reappraisal. One also realizes that it is fluency and not accuracy that counts in daily interaction and many errors that are seriously treated by teachers are ignored by many ordinary members of the target community. The findings in this area demonstrate that the obsession for immediate perfection and overcorrection is unfounded and can inhibit both learning and communication. The expectations of many L2 courses today, therefore, where students are supposed to internalize new grammatical rules after one or two lessons are not only unrealistic but unfair. Learners need a lot of time, incentive and support—all social givers—if they are to come to employ the L2 system like natives. If the goal of L2 learning is essentially to understand and be understood, then much effort is wasted in class on trying to make the learner into a 'chameleon' who has to pass for a native when this level of perfection is not at all required nor sometimes even desired.

The task that lies ahead is to distinguish the sociolinguistic expectations of natives and the realistic ways L2 users can satisfy these in communication. The body of research which challenges the normative premises of traditional L2 pedagogy is rapidly growing and is bound to eventually influence institutional policies. Much of this research regards the 'deviancy' of L2 users as contextually coherent, communicatively effective, necessarily developmental and formally creative. The resulting positive evaluation of L2 'deviancy' will undoubtedly take some time to take root in educational circles but when it does arrive, as it must, the result will be a much more beneficial and natural social environment for L2 learning to take place in.

Finally, in this section we should remember that speech styles that were long held in contempt such as non-standard dialects and mixed language types such as creoles and pidgins have all had their status upgraded as a *variety* of the language(s) to which they are related thanks to sociolinguistic argumentation. The next question that poses itself is whether an L2 speech style is not also just another variety of the native tongue, i.e. a different but equally valid, independent system to be accepted in its own right. This perspective has been made especially defensible through the emergence of English as a world lingua franca and in many countries as an internal national language. Thus, Esser (1979) wishes German-accented English to be considered simply as a variety of international English. The myth of language as one monolith and the recognition of the wide diversity existing in what is called *a* language has led to a questioning of the holiness of an élitist native model for teaching, an issue which I take up in the last section below.

Modelling with variety

As stated at the outset of this chapter, the discipline linguistics has only very lately begun to focus on the individual and social differences in a language, and then under the banner of sociolinguistics. For centuries linguistics attempted to transcend what was seen as annoying variation and to establish a pure grammar. Needless to say, this grammar derived from the speech of the élite of the linguist's society, of which he was usually also a member. This tradition remained unbroken right up to Chomsky's principle of the ideal speaker. Linguistics provided the scientific defence for the élite's strengthening of their own position by propagating its dialect or variety. By concentrating on the rules of a prestigious dialect or, more precisely, sociolect, linguistics contributed to the creation and maintenance of a set of norms which were derived from the rules of the sociolect. Of course, the grammars were originally founded on speech but over time came to override speech in authority. Dictionaries and grammars devoted to one sociolect worked towards making one variety of the language supreme, autonomous and homogeneous. In this matter linguistics approached the state of an ideology and concocted the fiction of only one correct speech style. This has been the story of European languages since the Renaissance: what were once vernaculars have been deliberately and successfully standardized into a prescriptive norm. L2 teaching has closely adhered to this doctrine and unquestioningly took the enshrined standard as pedagogic model. This was usually the rather archaic speech style of the metropolitan upper class whose language was considered more 'sophisticated' and 'expressive' than that of the 'vulgar' lower classes. Modernisms were not admitted since they lacked respectability and linguistic reality was smugly dismissed, e.g. for decades in French as an L2 the prescribed question forms have been *est-ce que tu viens* (are you coming?) instead of *viens-tu?* or *Tu viens?* while a sociolinguistic study has shown that this first form is the least frequent and that the institutionally stigmatized *tu viens* to be the most normal oral form at all social levels (Kleineidam 1975). Related to this artificially imposed "standard", L2 teaching has tended to impart a highly formal, if not stilted, style which has not been appropriate for every context of communication.

Sociolinguistics, however, has denounced the traditional approach of idealized linguistics and in its central concern with linguistic variation has brought indispensable insights into the heterogeneity of linguistic reality which L2 pedagogy cannot afford to ignore. It is thanks to sociolinguistics that we now have for the first time a socially neutral term for referring to a type of language as a *variety*.

Linguistic variation can be considered from three angles: regional, social and functional. In the last chapter I mentioned the importance to the L2 user of being able to shift his speech style to correspond to the needs of a socially defined context, to be able to encode and decode the social signs on multiple linguistic levels: phonetic, phonological, syntactic and lexical. Every native speaker has access to a bundle of socially differentiated ways of speaking, although his active command of these obviously is more limited than his passive understanding. Moreover, many sociolinguists seriously question the definability of a standard for a language, cf. Meyers (1977) on American English who sees the cosmetic norm as "a non-existing dialect . . . a useful fiction" (p. 223). No speech style can be neutral; it will always carry social meaning for some particular group in society deriving from the usually unconscious association with the social status of the users of the forms.

L2 learners unquestionably need to be presented with a consistent model in their early stages of learning and this will inevitably involve a social choice on the part of educators. The present-day linguistic variation of English, a result of its diffusion over such vast territories, presents a serious problem to the advanced L2 learner according to Tottie (1977) who sees a pedagogic need for "some kind of mono-lectal grammar, a variety of English that is at the same time coherent, widespread, socially desirable and suitable for eventual dissemination by future graduates to learners in schools" (p. 203).

Corder (1973) argues that L2 pedagogic models be chosen on the basis of, firstly, politicosocial factors, i.e. the attitudes and preference of the learners towards the L2 and by the native L2 community and, secondly, the communicative potential of the selected L2 (to what extent it satisfies the needs of the learner, for example). It is obvious that if the standard language is the only speech style treated in the L2 classroom that communities will expect non-natives to acquire this sociolect. But this is not necessarily the most appropriate variety. For instance, when Gannon (1980), expecting to be welcomed as a fluent L2 speaker of French, spoke mainland French in Montreal he was met with hostility because his French accent was not local and was advised instead to use English. Corder notes that when non-natives speak a variety of the L2 that is not standard such as waiters, sailors, immi-grants and so on, natives wonder where this has been *naturally 'picked up'*. It would appear that attitudes to non-standard L2 varieties are very divergent. Corder claims that if a foreigner speaks a non-standard dialect as an L2 in Britain it is socially acceptable and no attempt will be made to correct him/her while, in contrast, in Sweden he personally experienced regular correction for using non-standard Swedish forms which he had 'picked up'. Nevertheless, Corder maintains that the standard is the best variety for teaching purposes since it covers various sociolinguistic domains such as government, administration, the law, science, trade and journalism; the writing system is related to it (actually the standard is based on the writing system) and it is the most described and analysed variety of the language.

Yet there are languages for which the standard is very difficult to establish, especially for L2 teaching. Rabin (1977) describes the situation in Israel today where a normative tradition is developing prescriptive and proscriptive rules actually in conflict with general, contemporary Hebrew usage. Linguists are at the forefront of this movement, claiming that colloquial Hebrew is "unscientific" and "does not exist". In the sixties Welsh linguists were faced with a similar problem as the Israelis when they had to decide on a pedagogic model for bilingual programmes (Thomas 1978). There was no single, generally accepted prestigious spoken form of Welsh. There existed an "oratorical variety" which was associated with many religious institutions and which had since lost much of its status with the decline of the institutions it served. Thus, the linguists looked to the regional varieties of Welsh and regarded all dialectal variants as of equal status. The model they advocated was not only multidialectal but also a dialectal hybrid because in certain cases it was possible to select forms idiosyncratically from one dialect or another, making the pedagogic model socially unreal. Here we can see the artificiality of the normative tradition in L2 education being fabricated.

The effects on the L2 learner of an idealized approach where forms have been denied any recognition are described in Hughes & Trudgill (1979): on arrival in the British speech community and perceiving the linguistic variation, the institutionally taught L2 speaker may believe that the natives cannot speak English (and some might even agree with him!) or that he has not learned real English. Rather, his reaction should be, "Oh yes, Scottish", for example.

The problem highlighted above is the need for an L2 model that is not taught as an absolute norm but as one *possible* system. In other words, the social relativity of the model should be made clear to its learners from the earliest stages. This can be achieved by exposing the learners to the other varieties of the L2 which is an easy task today with the availability of recordings for classroom listening. If the goal of L2 teaching, especially where the L2 is taught as a foreign language and does not function as an internal, national lingua franca among a group of L2 users, is to approximate nativeness then, as Coulmas (1981) points out, a slight regional accent is much more authentically native than a synthetic standard one.

The contemporary state of the teaching of English provides an illuminating example of the thorny question of a normative model. Until the 1970s Received Pronunciation (RP), folk linguistically also referred to as the Oxford accent, BBC or the Queen's English, served as the only suitable blue-print for L2 learners in countries affiliated with Britain. This is essentially a class dialect whose historical origins go back to the sixteenth and seventeenth century recommendations that a norm should be constructed for English following the 'educated' pronunciation of the Court and the capital. The renowned phonetician at London University at the beginning of this century, Daniel Jones, provided descriptions of this speech style based on his own pronunication (Gimson 1977). The term RP remains ambiguous. It can refer either to the sociolect of a tiny (male) minority who attend public schools and go on to the universities of Oxford or Cambridge, or a slightly regional, more middle-class pronunciation (Widdowson 1978). For Atkinson (1975, p. 70):

> There is no logical reason whatever, taken on a world wide basis why a foreigner learning English should learn RP and not for instance Australian, Welsh or Scottish (the latter's vowel sounds presenting fewer difficulties than those of RP).

Atkinson tells of the case in West Germany where an American teacher was informed by school authorities that she would not get a post as an English teacher because she was American. This supports what we observed at the opening of this chapter, namely that L2 educationalists adopt and maintain the normative ideology of the target community. Atkinson argues that the historical significance of RP in English society as a standard should be kept distinct from English spoken elsewhere. He describes his own unsuccessful attempts at Newcastle University to find a regionally accentless RP speaker among the speech style of all the lecturers who clearly represent speakers of the 'educated' variety.

For Tottie (1977) the suitable choice of a variety of English for Swedish university students poses a serious challenge:

> The choice is one involving several dimensions—British or American English, different styles of discourse and linguistic variants used by different social strata of the population, to mention the most obvious ones. Obviously, at university level, one does not normally have to face the naive learner who demands to be taught what is 'right' or 'wrong' in English (p. 203).

However, my own experience at a West German university has proven the contrary. Here students really did ask what was more correct and showed irritation when told that certain forms held parallel status. These same students often revealed inconsistency in their L2 variety, mixing American pronunciations of certain words or marked American slang terms with RP, sometimes together with non-standard glottal stops in imitation of Cockney. Whatever variety is spoken by the L2 learner it should, at the very least, aim at internal social consistency and credibility.

If regional and social varieties of a language can no longer be regarded as defective but merely as different, can the same be said of L2 varieties? With their political emancipation, ex-European colonies are now seeking and gaining emancipation for their local versions of the formally imperialist languages; sociolinguistically of course, these local versions have always been regarded as deviant. But now, Nigerian and Singapore Englishes, for example, are being gradually considered by linguists and some L2 educationalists too as separate and unique systems in themselves. This has led to a controversial debate that is still unresolved as to whether these L2 local varieties can form the pedagogic model; see Lawton (1980) with reference to the refusal of officials to accept the existence of Jamaican English Creole for educational purposes.

Strevens (1978) notes that L1 local varieties, e.g. Cockney, never constitute an educational target but many Third World nations have completely different attitudes towards the L2 local variety and consider it part of their corporate cultural identity. A typical example of this is the statement made by the broadcasting authorities in Ghana who wanted its announcers to sound authentically Ghanaian in speaking

English and that of a head of an English department in a large secondary school who stated his hope that his students would speak English *like Ghanaians* (Norrish 1978).

If an L2 local variety exists and is felt by the learners to be desirable, then it should be institutionally adopted. The problem that arises is that the model here is *per se* a continuum, rather similar to that found existing between the pidgin-creole-standard spectrum. The L2 local variety includes speakers who come very close to a native speaker model but retain their distinctive accent amidst others whose supra-intelligibility is much more limited. Lester (1978) raises the question whether L2 local varieties can only be permitted on the spoken level with the native speaker written forms acting as a powerful normative influence. Norrish (1978) also expresses concern about how local "deviances" are to be assessed by examiners.

Prator (1968) polemically calls the slowly developing sociolinguistic autonomy of L2 local varieties "a pernicious heresy" that will result in "progressive deviation" since very few speakers limit their "aberrancies" to a shared set of features. He is convinced that the intelligibility of these L2 varieties will suffer from their emancipation. However, there are numerous L1 varieties that are not particularly intelligible in terms of the standard but are nevertheless accepted because of the ethnicity of their speakers. Prator draws support for his arguments from the special situation in South Africa where apparently non-white teachers of English as an L2 are institutionally prevented from acquiring standard South African (white) English or British English because this provokes "unpleasant" social connotations and are made to preserve a recognizably black African English. The L2 local variety is supported as a marker of social (here distant and inferior) identity. But for many other peoples, the L2 local variety serves as a symbol of ethnic uniqueness and pride. The children do not desire to imitate their parents' masters. This is poignantly revealed in the response of a Maori child who prefers to follow the conventions of his own group's English variety rather than standard New Zealand English: "Maories say 'Who's your name' so that's what I say" (Benton 1967, p. 93).

Kachru (1976) a vanguard of Indian English, observes how American

English was first ridiculed by the British (they still have not quite got over it) and sees similarities in the contemporary fate of what he calls "coloured" varieties of English. For Kachru, the L2 local variety is primarily a limited medium for the maintenance of indigenous patterns of life and culture, to provide links in a culturally and linguistically pluralistic society and to maintain a continuity and uniformity in administration, education and the legal system: "One wonders how sensible it is to present a speaker of RP as a model of spoken English to a class full of Black students in America, or a Midwestern speaker in a junior college in a village in India?" (p. 228).

Today, L2 local varieties are gaining increasing social recognition within the L2 profession. However, it is wrong to believe the claim of this group to be liberalizing their attitudes; they are just admitting sociolinguistic reality.

If local L2 varieties are legitimate, is it not justifiable to view other L2 speech also in terms of a variety? One frequently can identify a foreign accent and relate the L2 speaker to his/her native community and does this not support its status as a variety? Lester (1978) views the learner as creating a hybridized variety of an L2 which is his own private contact language which shares many features with other L2 speakers from his group since they all draw in part on the rule system developed in their native tongue. Kirstein (1978), on the other hand, believes individuality and originality in an L1 as acceptable but not in an L2 because the deviations in the latter are generally not intended so that anything short of the standard norm is ridiculous and not genuine. Kirstein maintains that natives are only willing to tolerate L2 deviancy if they perceive the speaker to be aiming at the standard norm. Corder's observations cited above about the positive attitude towards non-standard L2 speaking non-natives prove otherwise.

In connection with the autonomy of the learner's L2 speech style Jorden (1980) expresses traditional, institutional disapproval of the Japanese tolerance for American Japanese as a distinct variety of the language. It appears that native born teachers of Japanese as an L2 consider the non-native linguistic deviations of American Japanese as "automatic" and "natural". Jorden attributes this to the negative reaction towards fluent speakers of the L2 who come too close for comfort but this is not the sole reason. The Japanese teachers seem to view the L2 learning process quite realistically—perhaps too realistically if goals are to be set and achieved—and tolerate American Japanese as a "foreigner dialect", as Jorden writes.

The unresolved matter of the status of the learner's language is the cardinal question for L2 pedagogy today. At the moment the arguments for its receiving some recognition are steadily building up. This is certainly problematic since acceptance also seems to imply an authorization for disobeying the norms of the standard variety. However, nativeness is for many an utterly utopian goal that results in psychological defeatism.

L2 models in the future will have to take account of *native L2 variation* as revealed by sociolinguistics to exist regionally (dialects), socially (on the basis of age, sex, group membership and situation) and functionally (specialist languages of science or law). Furthermore, it is no longer self-evident that the upper middle class constitute the desirable model; attitudinal changes in modern society militate against this. L2 pedagogy must also come to terms with *non-native L2 variation,* as presented above.

The sole justification for any model today is its effectiveness: to what extent does it satisfy the learner's needs? Already a completely new branch of L2 teaching for special purposes has burgeoned as a response to coping with a real L2 world, specializing in transmitting the socio-linguistic competence required of doctors, technologists, diplomats and so forth without normative emphasis.

What the L2 profession has to confront is the linguistic pluralism that has existed outside the classroom for centuries but which it has stubbornly and arrogantly refused to incorporate into its teaching. Now it must renounce its normative inheritance and begin the honest and important task of modelling with variety.

Meaningful versus normative

In this final chapter I have examined the sociolinguistic reasons for the necessary relaxation of various traditional norms in L2 teaching:

classroom learning as relentless corrective interaction, the damaging effects of hostile attitudes towards natural and 'creative' error and the socially unrealistic maintenance of an absolutist and artificial standard variety.

This re-evaluation has come about because of the contemporary value on spoken skills and the need of many learners to communicate immediately and successfully rather than flawlessly. The movement has also coincided with the emancipation of previously despised speakers and their 'bastardized' speech styles. It is at last being realized that the transmission of meaning is a higher goal than adherence to form. The unresolved dilemma for L2 teachers and learners is to discover to what extent conformity is necessary to achieve effective communication. Further research on the native community's evaluation of L2 error should offer more reliable guidelines than those currently prescribed by those bred in an authoritarian tradition. Grammatical accuracy fulfils certain aesthetic functions and allows for subtlety in expression in some cases but, as such, is only available to advanced users of the system and then generally restricted to the written medium by native users. Grammaticality is itself a normative conception and can and has often been employed as a means of oppression. Norms like conventions should serve their followers and not hinder them. L2 teaching must finally admit that its traditionally normative approach has been cruelly self-defeating:

> In no other subject is the objective so uncompromising: anything short of
> [grammatical] perfection is stigmatized; and in no other subject is failure
> to reach the objective so obviously and continuously displayed before
> teacher and learner alike, so that it is no cause for surprise if foreign
> languages constitute one of the most unpopular parts of the school
> curriculum. A language class can seem an unrelieved post-mortem or an
> inquisition of grammatical sins (Littlewood 1974, p. 35).

6

Summary: the sociolinguistics of non-native language learning

This book has been an attempt to explain, relate and interpret socio-linguistic research and theories simply and concisely for the profit of those acquiring, using and teaching a non-native language. To my knowledge, no other extensive exploration of the sociolinguistic dimensions of learning a second or foreign language is available. Some of the reasons for this pedagogic and academic lack of concern for sociolinguistics have been given in the preceding chapters. It is principally due to the dogma of a purist linguistics separating language from its contexts of use and restricting the function of language to something narrowly referential which has exercised an adverse influence on non-native language teaching for far too long. Only very recently have the inadequacies of such a short-sighted approach begun to be admitted.

Language teachers must move away from viewing the non-native language as if it operated in a social void. It is vital to realize the essential fact that language is, above all, a social creation and that communication is a social act. In most communities speakers' status depends on their linguistic abilities; their intelligence, personality and even value as human beings may all be judged according to their style of speaking. Because of these factors a socially orientated linguistics is unquestionably of immediate and practical relevance to non-native language learners; sociolinguistic research and themes must be integrated into L2 courses.

In this book a new framework for considering bilingualism was proposed whereby language was shown to often constitute an ethnic boundary which, for a variety of reasons connected to a secondary linguistic-ethnic identity, learners could not always cross (Chapter 2).

Also examined was a realm dangerously neglected by language teachers and theorists involving the interpenetration of language and culture, the significance and workings of which have principally been uncovered by anthropological studies. This interdependence cannot be taken for granted and learners have to be aware of the diverging cultural reality of the target speech-community if they are to attain a satisfying level of proficiency in a non-native language (Chapter 3).

The concept of communicative competence was explicated in terms of socioculturally determined patterns for appropriately framing and symbolizing meaning in accordance with the varying requirements of changing contexts. The fact that different cultural communities employ and expect different patterns can frequently lead to grave misunderstandings in cross-cultural encounters unless the non-native language learner is sufficiently initiated into their subtleties (Chapter 4).

Finally, we saw the non-viability of numerous postulates and practices of traditional, institutional non-native language teaching. The normative ideology which sanctifies only one L2 variety is unrealistic and indefensible in certain cases; investigation has proven that L2 acquisition naturally and necessarily entails error and that linguistic 'deviancy' is much more tolerated by the ordinary members of a speech community than could be supposed from the neurotic obsession with its eradication carried out by L2 teachers. In fact, much of classroom interaction was demonstrated as depriving a non-native language of its vitality and meaningfulness and turning what should be communication into a trial situation. Sociolinguistics, thus, seriously challenges the tenet of absolutist conformity to the norms of the target language (Chapter 5).

In many ways, the sociolinguistics of non-native language learning and using undermines many long-cherished orthodoxies in L2 education. This book, however, does not provide yet another ready-made model for producing greater pedagogic efficiency nor does it wish to advance scientific findings for their own sake. It is, principally, a plea for greater understanding from the educationalist for the social nature of language learning and using, for a more honest and profound conception of its sociolinguistic dynamics. In turn, such understanding is ultimately bound to reap rewards in terms of an increase in learner motivation and proficiency. Language learning is not the mastery of an abstract calculus but a process closely intertwined with satisfying the direct needs of the learner in an authentic context of social experience. Perhaps the classroom cannot fully meet these conditions but that should not prevent it from working towards their provision.

Furthermore, the book offers a review, if not stock-taking of the key themes lying at the crossroads of sociolinguistics and applied linguistics and highlights thereby important areas for future research. Without doubt, a lot more must be carried out but the primacy and profitability of the sociolinguistic perspective should be self-evident. The theoretical validity of the discipline has surely come of age.

The core message is the need for tolerance, support and respect from educationalists and natives towards non-native language learners and from non-natives towards the target community. Such positive attitudes can only lead to an improvement in cross-linguistic and cross-cultural communication, promoting interactional symmetry and satisfaction and thereby encouraging further non-native language learning.

References

Abercrombie, D (1967) *Problems and principles in language study.* Longman, London.
Abrahams, R D and **R C Troike** (eds) (1972) *Language and cultural diversity in American education.* Prentice-Hall, Englewood Cliffs.
Adler, M K (1977) *Collective and individual bilingualism.* Helmut Buske, Hamburg.
Agaar, M (1975) Cognition and events. In: M Sanches and B C Blount (eds), 1975.
Alatis, J E (ed.) (1978) *International dimensions of bilingual education.* Georgetown University Press, Washington, DC.
Albert, E M (1972) Culture patternings of speech behaviour in Burundi. In: J J Gumperz and D Hymes (eds) 1972.
Allport, G W (1954) *The nature of prejudice.* Addison-Wesley, Reading.
Andresen, H (1976) Sprachnormen als Problem für Sprachunterricht und Sprachwissenschaft. *Osnabrücker Beiträge zur Sprachtheorie* **1**, 1-32.
d'Anglejan, A (1978) Language learning in and out of classrooms. In: J C Richards (ed.) 1978a.
Antier, M (1977) Language teaching as a form of witchcraft. *English Language Teaching Journal* **31**, 1-10.
Applbaum, R I *et al.* (1974) *The process of group communication.* Science Research Associates, Chicago.
Applegate, R B (1975) The language teacher and the rules of speaking. *TESOL Quart.* **9**, 271-281.
Argyle, M and **J Dean** (1965) Eye contact, distance and affiliation. In: J Laver and S Hutcheson (eds) 1972.
Atkinson, R E (1975) RP and English as a world language. *International Review of Applied Linguistics* **23**, 69-72.
Bailey, C N (1974) Some suggestions for greater consensus in Creole terminology. In: D DeCamp and I F Hancock (eds) 1974.
Ball, W J (1979) Social hazards in TEFL. *English Language Teaching Journal* **34**, 14-19.
Barker-Lunn, J C (1971) *Social class, attitudes and achievement.* National Foundation for Educational Research, Slough.
Barkowski, I *et al.* (1976) Sprechhandlungstheorie und Gastarbeiterdeutsch. *Linguistische Berichte* **45**, 42-56.
Barnes, D (ed.) (1974) *Language, the learner and the school.* Penguin, Harmondsworth.
Barnlund, D C (1975) *Public and private self in Japan and the US.* Simul Press, Tokyo.
Bauman, R (1974) Speaking in the light: the role of the Quaker minister. In: R Bauman and J Sherzer (eds) 1974.
Bauman, R and **Sherzer, J** (eds) (1974) *Explorations in the ethnography of speaking.* Cambridge University Press, Cambridge.
Bedford, R C (1972) *English experienced.* Michael Wayne State University Press, Detroit.
Bell, R T (1976) *Sociolinguistics: goals, approaches and problems.* Batsford, London.
Beneke, J (1975) Verstehen und Mißverstehen im Englischunterricht. *Praxis des neusprachlichen Unterrichts* **22**, 351-362.

_____ (1979) Fremdsprachenanwendung in real life situations. *Linguistik und Didaktik* **39**, 238–265.

Benton, R (1964) *Research into the English language difficulties of Maori school children.* Maori Education Foundation, Wellington.

Bernstein, B (1971) *Class, codes and control*—Vol. 1. *Theoretical studies towards a sociology of language.* Routledge & Kegan Paul, London.

_____ (1973) *Class, codes and control*—Vol. 2. *Empirical studies.* Routledge & Kegan Paul, London.

Bertukua, J S (1975) An analysis of English learner speech. *Language Learning* **24**, 279–286.

Bertrand-Bocandé, M (1849) De la langue créole de la Guinée portugaise. *Bulletin de la société de Géographie de Paris* 3ᵉ série, **12**, 57–93.

Bickerton, D (1977a) Pidginization and creolization: language acquisition and language universals. In: A Valdman (ed.) 1977b.

_____ (1977b) Some problems of acceptability and grammaticality in pidgins and creoles. In: S Greenbaum (ed.) 1977.

Black, C and **W Butzkamm** (1977a) *Klassengespräche-kommunikativer Englischunterricht.* Quelle & Meyer, Heidelberg.

_____ (1977b) Sprachbezogene und mitteilungsbezogene Kommunikation im Englischunterricht. *Praxis des neusprachlichen Unterrichts* **2**, 115–124.

Bloomfield, L (1933) *Language.* Holt, Rinehart & Winston, New York.

Blount, B G (ed.) (1974) *Language, culture and society.* Winthrop, Cambridge.

Blount, B G and **M Sanches** (eds) (1977) *Sociocultural dimensions of language change.* Academic Press, New York.

Boas, F (1940) *Race, language and culture.* Macmillan, New York.

Bourhis, R Y, N J Gadfield, H Giles and **H Tajfel** (1977) Context and ethnic humour in intergroup relations. In: A J Chapman and R C Foot (eds) 1977. *It's a funny thing humour.* Pergamon Press, Oxford.

Brazil, D, M Coulthard and **C Johns** (1980) *Discourse intonation and language teaching.* Longman, London.

The British Council (1977) *Games, simulations and role-playing.* English Teaching Information Centre, London.

Brooks, N (1960) *Language and language learning.* Harcourt Brace, New York.

Brown, P and **S Levinson** (1978) Universals in language usage: politeness phenomena. In: E N Goody (ed.) 1978b.

Brown, R N and **A Gilman** (1960) The pronouns of power and solidarity. In: J A Fishman (ed.) 1968.

Brown, R and **C Hanlon** (1970) Derivational complexity and order of acquisition in child speech. In: J Hayes (ed.) 1970. *Cognition and the development of language.* Wiley, New York.

Brumfit, C J and **K Johnson** (eds) (1979) *The communicative approach to language teaching.* Oxford University Press, Oxford.

Bublitz, W (1980) Höflichkeit im Englischen. *Linguistik und Didaktik* **40**, 56–69.

Burmeister, H and **D Ufert** (1980) Strategy switching. In: S Felix (ed.) 1980b.

Burstall, C *et al.* (1974) Primary French in the balance. National Foundation for Educational Research, Slough.

_____ (1978) Factors affecting foreign language learning: a consideration of some recent research findings. In: V Kinsella (ed.) 1978.

Burt, M and **C Kiparsky** (1975) Global and local mistakes. In: J Schumann and N

Stenson (eds) 1975. *New frontiers in second language learning.* Newbury House, Rowley.

Burt, M and **H Dulay** (1980) On acquisition orders. In: S Felix (ed.) 1980b.

Butzkamm, W and **C J Dodson** (1980) The teaching of communication: from theory to practice. *International Review of Applied Linguistics* **28**, 289–310.

Cameron, N and **A Magaret** (1951) *Behaviour Pathology.* Houghton Mifflin, Boston.

Cammack, F M and **H Van Buren** (1967) Paralanguage across cultures. *English Language Education Council Bulletin (Tokyo)* **22**, 7–10.

Carey, S T (ed.) (1974) *Bilingualism, biculturalism and education.* University of Alberta, Edmonton.

Cathcart, R L and **T E Olsen** (1976) Teachers' and students' preferences for correction of classroom conversation errors. In: J F Fanselow and R H Crymes 1976. *On TESOL 76.* TESOL, Washington, DC.

Cazden, C B, P J Vera and **D Hymes** (eds) (1972) *Functions of language in the classroom.* Columbia University, New York.

Chamberlain, B H (1904) *Things Japanese.* (Reprinted 1974). Tuttle, Tokyo.

Chapman, R D (1976) *Bilingualism in Birmingham.* In: C E Perren (ed.) 1976.

Chastain, K (1980) Native-speaker reaction to instructor identified student second-language errors. *The Modern Language Journal* **64**, 210–215.

Chaudron, C (1978) A descriptive model of discourse in the corrective treatment of learners' errors. *Language Learning* **27**, 29–46.

Cherubim, D (ed.) (1980) *Fehlerlinguistik.* Niemeyer, Tübingen.

Chomsky, N (1957) *Syntactic structures.* Mouton, The Hague.

_____ (1965) *Aspects of the theory of syntax.* MIT Press, Cambridge.

Christophersen, P (1948) *Bilingualism.* Methuen, London.

_____ (1973) *Second language learning: myth and reality.* Penguin, Harmondsworth.

Clark, R (1975) Adult theories, child strategies and their implications for the language teacher. In: J P B Allen and S P Corder (eds) 1975.

Clyne, M (1975) *Forschungsbericht—Sprachkontakt.* Scriptor, Kronberg.

_____ (1981) Culture and discourse structure. *Journal of Pragmatics* **5**, 61–66.

Cohen, A D (1975) Error correction and the training of language teachers. *The Modern Language Journal* **59**, 414–422.

Connors, K, N Ménard and **R Singh** (1978) Testing linguistic and functional competence in immersion programs. In: M Paradis (ed.) 1978.

Corder, S P (1967) The significance of learner's errors. *International Review of Applied Linguistics* **15**, 161–170.

_____ (1971) Describing the language learner's language. In: *CILT reports and papers,* No. 6, 57–64. Centre for Information on Language teaching publications, London.

_____ (1975) *Introducing applied linguistics.* Penguin, Harmondsworth.

_____ (1978) Language–learner language. In: J C Richards (ed.) 1978a.

Corder, S P and **E Roulet** (eds) (1977) *The notions of simplification, interlanguages and pidgins and the relations to second language pedagogy.* University of Neuchâtel.

Corum, C. (1975) Basques, particles and baby talk: a case for pragmatics. In: *Proceedings of the first annual meetings of the Berkeley Linguistics Society,* pp. 90–99. Institute for Human Learning, Berkeley.

Coulmas, F (ed.) (1979) *Dell Hymes—Soziolinguistik.* Suhrkamp, Frankfurt.

_____ (1981a) *A festschrift for native speakers.* Mouton, The Hague.

_____ (1981b) *Conversational routine.* Mouton, The Hague.

_____ (1981c) Spies and native speakers. In: F Coulmas (ed.) 1981a.

Coulthard, M (1977) *An introduction to discourse analysis.* Longman, London.

The Council of Europe, Council for Cultural Cooperation (ed.) (1973) *Systems development in adult language learning.* Strasbourg.

Craig, C G (1979) Jacaltec: fieldwork in Guatemala. In: T Shopen (ed.) 1979.

Criper, C and H G Widdowson (1975) Sociolinguistics and language teaching. In: J P B Allen and S P Corder (eds) 1975. *Papers in applied linguistics,* Vol. 2. Oxford University Press, Oxford.

Crystal, D (1971) Prosodic and paralinguistic correlates of social categories. In: E Ardener (ed.) 1971. *Social anthropology and language.* Tavistock, London.

Crystal, D and D Davy (1975) *Advanced Conversational English.* Longman, London.

Cuceloglu, D (1967) A cross-cultural study of communication via facial expressions. Microfilmed Ph.D. dissertation, University of Illinois.

Davies, A (1978) Textbook situations and idealized language. *Notes in progress* 11, (Department of Linguistics, University of Edinburgh).

De Camp, D and I F Hancock (eds) (1974) *Pidgins and creoles: current trends and prospects.* Georgetown University Press, Washington, DC.

Diebold, A (1961) Incipient bilingualism. *Language* 37, 97–112.

Dillard, J (1972) *Black English: its history and usage in the US.* Doubleday, New York.

Diller, K C (1970) 'Compound' and 'coordinate' bilingualism: a conceptual artifact. *Word* 254–261.

Di Pietro, R J (1978) Culture and ethnicity in the bilingual classroom. In: J E Alatis (ed.) 1978.

Dittman, J (ed.) (1979) *Arbeiten zur Konversationsanalyse.* Niemeyer, Tübingen.

Dittmar, N and W Klein (1977) *The acquisition of German syntax by foreign migrant workers.* The Heidelberg Project on Pidgin-Deutsch. Unpublished mimeograph.

Dixon, R M W (1972) The Dyirbal language of North Queensland. *Cambridge Studies in Linguistics* 9. Cambridge University Press, Cambridge.

Dodson, C J (1976) Foreign language teaching and bilingualism. In: G E Perren (ed.) 1976.

Doi, T (1977) *The anatomy of dependence* (translated by J Bester). Kodansha, Tokyo.

Doughty, A and P Doughty (1974) *Using Language in Use: a teacher's guide to language work in the classroom.* Edward Arnold, London.

Douglas, M (1973) *Rules and meanings.* Penguin, Harmondsworth.

Dulay, H and M Burt (1978) Some remarks on creativity in language acquisition. In: W C Ritchie (ed.) 1978b.

Dumont, R V (1972) Learning English and how to be silent: studies in Sioux and Cherokee classrooms. In: C B Cazden, V P John and D Hymes (eds) 1972.

Edwards, J R (1977) Ethnic identity and bilingual education. In: H Giles (ed.) 1977.

Edwards, J R (1979) *Language and disadvantage.* Edward Arnold, London.

English Teaching Information Centre (ed.) (1978) *ELT Documents: English as an international language.* The British Council, London.

Erickson, F *et al.* (1973) *Interethnic relations in urban institutional settings.* Final technical report for the center for studies of metropolitan problems. National Institute of Mental Health, Rockville.

Ervin, G L (1977) A study of the use and acceptability of target language communication strategies employed by American students of Russian. Unpublished Ph.D. dissertation. Ohio State University.

Ervin-Tripp, S M (1968) An analysis of the interaction of language, topic and listener. In: J A Fishman (ed.) 1968b.

_____ (1969) Sociolinguistic rules of address. In: J B Pride and J Holmes (eds) 1972.

_____ (1971) Sociolinguistics. In: J A Fishman (ed.) 1971b.

Escure, G J (1979) Linguistic variation and ethnic interaction in Belize. In: H Giles and B Saint-Jacques (eds) 1979.

Esser, J (1979) Zur Beurtellung fremdsprachlicher Korrektheit bei mündlichen und schriftlichen Sprachvarianten deutscher Lerner des Englischen. In: E Rattunde (ed.) 1979.

Evans, E (1976) Bilingual education in Wales. In: G E Perren (ed.) 1976b.

Fathman, A (1977) Similarities and simplification in the interlanguage of second language learners. In: S P Corder and E Roulet (eds) 1977.

Felix, S (1977) Kreative und reproduktive Kompetenz im Zweitsprachenerwerb. In: H Hunfeld (ed.) 1977.

_____ (1980a) Interference, interlanguage and related issues. In: S Felix (ed.) 1980b.

_____ (ed.) (1980b) *Second language development—trends and issues.* Gunter Narr, Tübingen.

Ferguson, C A (1970) The role of Arabic in Ethiopia: a sociolinguistic perspective. In: J B Pride and J Holmes (eds) 1972.

_____ and **C E DeBose** (1977) Simplified registers, broken languages, and pidginization. In: A Valdman (ed.) 1977b.

Filipović, R (1972) The compromise system: a link between linguistic borrowing and foreign language learning. In: G Nickel and A Raasch (eds) 1972. *Kongressbericht der 3. Jahrestagung der GAL.* Julius Groos, Heidelberg.

Fishman, J A (1968a) Sociolinguistic perspective on the study of bilingualism. *Linguistics* **39**, 21–49.

_____ (ed.) (1968b) *Readings in the sociology of language.* Mouton, The Hague.

_____ (1971a) The description of societal bilingualism. In: J A Fishman, R L Cooper *et al.* 1971.

_____ (1971b) The sociology of language. In: J A Fishman (ed.) 1971c.

_____ (1971c) *Advances in the sociology of language,* Vol. 1. Mouton, The Hague.

_____ (1972) *Advances in the sociology of language,* Vol. 2. Mouton, The Hague.

_____ (1976) *Bilingual education—an international sociological perspective.* Newbury House, Rowley.

_____ (1977) Language and ethnicity. In: H Giles (ed.) 1977.

_____ (1978a) Positive bilingualism. In: J E Alatis (ed.) 1978.

_____ (1978b) *Advances in the study of societal multilingualism.* Mouton, The Hague.

_____, **R L Cooper** *et al.* (1971) *Bilingualism in the Barrio,* Indiana University Press, Bloomington.

_____ *et al.* (eds) (1968) *Language problems of developing nations.* John Wiley, New York.

_____, **R L Cooper** and **Y Rosenbaum** (1977) English the world over. In: P A Hornby (ed.) 1977.

Fitzgerald, M J (1980) Towards realistic communication in the cooperative learning of EFL. *IATEFL Newsletter,* No. 63, June, 27–30.

Forster, L (1970) *The Poet's tongues: multilingualism in literature.* Cambridge University Press, Cambridge.

Frake, C O (1975) How to enter a Yakan house. In: M Sanches and B G Blount (eds) 1975.

Friedrich, P (1966) The linguistic reflex of social change: from Tzarist to Soviet Russian kinship. *Sociological Inquiry* **36,** 159–185.

Fries, C C and **R Lado** (1957) *English sentence patterns*. University of Michigan Press, Michigan.

Frith, M B (1975) Second language learning: an examination of two hypotheses. *International Review of Applied Linguistics* **23**, 327–332.

Gal, S (1979) *Language Shift—social determinants of linguistic change in bilingual Austria*. Academic Press, London.

Galloway, V B (1980) Perceptions of the communicative efforts of American students of Spanish. *The Modern Language Journal* **64**, 428–433.

Gannon, R E (1980) Appropriateness and the foreign language learner. *English Language Teaching Journal* **34**, 90–93.

Gardener, P (1966) Symmetric respect and memorate knowledge. *Southwestern Journal of Anthropology* **22**, 389–415.

Gardner, R C and **E R Santos** (1970) Motivational variables in second-language acquisition: a Philippine investigation. Research Bulletin, No. 149, University of Western Ontario.

Gardner, R C and **W E Lambert** (1972) *Attitudes and motivation in second language learning*. Newbury House, Rowley.

Gary, J O (1978) Why speak if you don't need to? In: W C Ritchie (ed.) 1978.

Gaskill, W (1977) Correction in adult native speaker—non-native speaker conversation. MA-TESL thesis, University of California.

Gatbonton-Segalowitz, E (1975) Systematic variations in second language speech: a sociolinguistic study. Unpublished Ph.D. thesis, Linguistics Department. McGill University, Canada.

Geertz, C (1957) Ritual and social change: a Javanese example. *American Anthropologist* **59**, 32–54.

Genesee, F and **N Holobow** (1978) Children's reactions to variations in second language competence. In: M Paradis (ed.) 1978.

George, H V (1972) *Common errors in language learning: insights from English*. Newbury House, Rowley.

Giles, H (ed.) (1977) *Language, ethnicity and intergroup relations*. Academic Press, New York.

_____ (1978) Linguistic differentiation in ethnic groups. In: H Tajfel (ed.) 1978. *Differentiation between social groups*. Academic Press, London.

_____ (1979) Ethnicity markers in speech. In: K R Scherer and H Giles (eds) 1979.

Giles, H, R Y Bourhis and **D M Taylor** (1977) Towards a theory of language in ethnic group relations. In: H Giles (ed.) 1977.

Giles, H and **B Saint-Jacques** (eds) (1979) *Language and ethnic relations*. Pergamon Press, Oxford.

Gimson, A C (1977) Daniel Jones and standards of English pronunciation. *English Studies* **58**, 151–158.

Gladstone, J R (1972) Language and culture. In: H B Allen and R N Campbell (eds) 1972. *Teaching English as a second language*. McGraw-Hill, New York.

Gloy, K (1975) *Sprachnormen. I. Series Problemata* 46. Fromann-Holzboog, Stuttgart-Bad Cannstatt.

Godard, D (1977) Same setting, different norms: phone call beginnings in France and the US. *Language in Society* **6**, 209–219.

Goffman, E (1975) Replies and responses. Working paper. Centro Internazionale di Semiotica e di Linguistica, Universita di Urbino.

Goodenough, W H (1957) Cultural anthropology and linguistics. Georgetown University Monograph series on languages and linguistics. No. 9, 167–173.

Goody, E N (1978a) Towards a theory of questions. In: E N Goody (ed.) 1978b.

____ (1978b) *Questions and politeness: strategies in social interaction.* Cambridge University Press, Cambridge.

Götz, D (1977) Analyse einer in der Fremdsprache (Englisch) durchgeführten Konversation. In: H Hunfeld (ed.) 1977.

Grace, G W (1981) *An essay on language.* Hornbeam Press, Columbia.

Green, J (1941) An experiment in English. *Harper's Magazine* **183**, 397–405.

Greenbaum, S (ed.) (1977) *Acceptability in language.* Mouton, The Hague.

Greenfield, L and **J A Fishman** (1971) Situational measures of normative language views of person, place and topic among Puerto Rican bilinguals. In: J A Fishman, R L Cooper *et al.* 1971.

Griffin, P and **H Mehan** (1981) Sense and ritual in classroom discourse. In: F Coulmas (ed.) 1981b.

Grimshaw, A (1971) Sociolinguistics. In: J A Fishman (ed.) 1971b.

Grittner, F M (1973) The foreign language teacher. *Modern Language Journal* **5/6**, 262–268.

Gulutsan, M (1974) Cultural differences in language learning. In: S T Carey (ed.) 1974.

Gumperz, J J (1976) Language, communication and public negotiation. In: P R Sanday (ed.) 1976. *Anthropology and the Public Interest.* Academic Press, New York.

____ (1977) Sociocultural knowledge in conversational inference. In: *28th Annual Round Table Monograph series in language and linguistics.* Georgetown University Press, Washington, DC.

____ (1978) The cross-cultural analysis of interethnic communication. In: E L Ross (ed.) 1978. *Interethnic Communication. Proceedings of the Southern Anthropological Society,* Atlanta, Georgia.

Gumperz, J J and **D Hymes** (eds) (1972) *Directions in sociolinguistics.* Holt, Rinehart & Winston, New York.

Guntermann, G (1978) A study of the frequency and communicative effects of error in Spanish. *The Modern Language Journal* **62**, 249–253.

Hakuta, K (1975) Becoming bilingual at age five: the story of Uguisu. Unpublished paper, Harvard College, Cambridge.

Hall, E T (1959) *The silent language.* Doubleday, New York.

____ (1966) *The hidden dimension.* Doubleday, New York.

____ (1972a) Silent assumptions in social communication. In: J Laver and S Hutcheson (eds) 1972.

____ (1972b) A system for the notation of proxemic behaviour. In: J Laver and S Hutcheson (eds) 1972.

____ (1974) The organizing pattern. In: B G Blount (ed.) 1974.

Hall, R (1955) *Hands off pidgin English.* Pacific Publications, Sydney.

____ (1972) Pidgins and creoles as standard languages. In: J B Pride and J Holmes (eds) 1972.

Hansen, T L and **E J Wilkins** (1974) *Espanol a lo vivo,* Level 1. John Wiley, New York.

Hanvey, R G (1979) Cross-cultural awareness. In: E C Smith and L F Luce (eds) 1979.

Hardin, G G (1979) English as a language of international communication. *English Language Teaching Journal* **34**, 1–4.

Hartford, B S (1976) A descriptive study of the language of men and women born in Maine around 1900 as it reflects the Lakoff hypothesis in 'Language in Woman's

Place'. In: B Dubois and I Crouch (eds) 1976. *The Sociology of the Language of American Women*. Texas, San Antonio.

Hatch, E (1976) Studies in language switching and mixing. In: W C McCormack and S A Wurm (eds) 1976. *Language and man: anthropological issues*. Mouton, The Hague.

―― (1978a) *Second language acquisition: a book of readings*. Newbury House, Rowley.

―― (1978b) Discourse analysis and second language acquisition. In: E Hatch (ed.) 1978a.

―― (1978c) Discourse analysis, speech acts and second language acquisition. In: W C Ritchie (ed.) 1978b.

―― (1980) Second language acquisition—avoiding the question. In: S Felix (ed.) 1980b.

Haugen, E (1956) *Bilingualism in the Americas: a bibliography and research guide*. (Publications of the American Dialect Society, No. 26.) University of Alabama Press, Alabama.

―― (1977) Linguistic relativity: myths and methods. In: W C McCormack and S A Wurm (eds) 1977.

―― (1978) Bilingualism, language contact and immigrant languages in the US, a research report 1956–1970. In: J A Fishman (ed.) 1978b.

Haviland, J B (1979) The Guugu Yimidhirr language. In: T Shopen (ed.) 1979.

Heaton, J B (1980) Communication in the classroom. *English Language Teaching Journal* 35, 22–27.

Hendrickson, J M (1978) Error correction in foreign language teaching: recent theory, research and practice. *The Modern Language Journal* 62, 387–398.

Henrici, G (1978) Didaktik und Sprechhandlungstheorie. In: R Meyer-Hermann (ed.) 1978. *Sprechen-Handeln-Interaktion*. Niemeyer, Tübingen.

Herman, S N (1961) Explòrations in the social psychology of language choice. *Human Relations* 14, 149–164.

Hester, R (1970) *Teaching a living language*. Harper & Row, New York.

Heuer, H (1978) Using the learner language to model the classroom target language for the teaching of English as a foreign language. In: G Nickel and D Nehls (eds) 1978. *Models of grammar, descriptive linguistics and pedagogical grammar*. Julius Groos, Heidelberg.

Hoijer, H (1974) *The Sapir–Whorf hypothesis*. In: B G Blount (ed.) 1974.

Hornby, P A (ed.) (1977) *Bilingualism: psychological, social and educational implications*. Academic Press, New York.

House, J (1979) Interaktionsnormen in deutschen und englischen Alltagsdialogen. *Linguistische Berichte* 59, 76–90.

Hudson, R A (1980) *Sociolinguistics*. Cambridge University Press, Cambridge.

Hughes, A and P Trudgill (1979) *English accents and dialects—an introduction to social and regional varieties of British English*. Edward Arnold, London.

Hüllen, W and W Lörscher (1979) Lehrbuch, Lerner und Unterrichtsdiskurs. *Unterrichtswissenschaft* 4, 313–326.

Hunfeld, H (ed.) (1977) *Neue Perspektiven der Fremdsprachendidaktik*. Scriptor, Kronberg.

Hymes, D (1962) The ethnography of speaking. In: T Gladwin and W C Sturtevant (eds) 1962. *Anthropological and human behaviour*. Anthropological Society of Washington, Washington.

_____ (1971) On communicative competence. In: J B Pride and D Holmes (eds) 1972.

_____ (1972) Introduction. In: C B Cazden, V P John and D Hymes (eds) 1972.

_____ (1974a) Sociolinguistics and the ethnography of speaking. In: B G Blount (ed.) 1974.

_____ (1974b) Ways of speaking. In: R Bauman and J Sherzer (eds) 1974.

Inhelder, B and **J Piaget** (1958) *The growth of logical thinking.* Basic Books, New York.

Itoh, H (1973) A child's acquisition of two languages—Japanese and English. M.A. thesis. University of California.

Jaramillo, M (1973) Cultural differences in the ESOL classroom. *TESOL Quarterly* **7**, 51–60.

Johansson, S (1973) The identification and evaluation of errors in foreign languages: a functional approach. In: J Svartvik (ed.) 1973.

_____ (1978) *Studies in error gravity.* Gothenburg Studies in English, No. 44. Gothenburg University, Gothenberg.

John, A P (1980) Approximative languages and language learning situations. Internal Review of Applied Linguistics **18**, 209–215.

Joiner, E (1977) Communicative activities for beginning language students. *English Teaching Forum* **2**, 8–10.

Jones, L (1977) *Functions of English.* Cambridge University Press, Cambridge.

Jorden, E H (1980) The sociolinguistics of foreign language pedagogy. *Language Sciences (Tokyo)* **2**, 222–230.

Kachru, B B (1976) Models of English for the Third World: White man's linguistic burden or language pragmatics. *TESOL Quarterly* **10**, 221–239.

_____ (1978) English in South Asia. In: J A Fishman (ed.) 1978b.

Kahane, H and **R Kahane** (1977) Virtues and vices in the American language: a history of attitudes. *TESOL Quarterly* **11**, 185–202.

Kantrowitz, N (1967) The vocabulary of race relations in a prison. Paper presented at American Dialect Society Meeting, Chicago, December 1967.

Kaplan, R B (1972) Cultural thought patterns in intercultural education. In: K Croft (ed.) *Readings in English as a second language.* Winthrop, Cambridge.

Kasper, G (1979) Pragmatische Defizite im Englischen deutscher Lerner. *Linguistik und Didaktik* **40**, 370–379.

Kay, P (1977) Language evolution and speech style. In: B G Blount and M Sanches (eds) 1977.

Keenan, E O (1977) The universality of conversational implicatures. In: R W Fasold and R W Shuy (eds) 1977. *Studies in language variation.* Georgetown University, Washington, DC.

Keenan, E L and **E Ochs** (1979) Becoming a competent speaker of Malagasy. In: T Shopen (ed.) 1979.

Keesing, R M (1979) Linguistic knowledge and cultural knowledge: some doubts and speculations. *American Anthropologist* **81**, 14–36.

_____ and **F M Keesing** (1971) *New Perspectives in Cultural Anthropology.* Holt, Rinehart & Winston, New York.

Keller, E (1981) Gambits: conversational strategy signals. In: F Coulmas (ed.) 1981b.

Kendon, A *et al.* (eds.) (1975) *Organization of behaviour in face-to-face interaction.* Mouton, The Hague.

Kernan, K T, J Sodergren and **R French** (1977) Speech and social prestige in the Belizian speech community. In: B G Blount and M Sanches (eds) 1977.

Kettering, J (1974) *Communication activities.* English Language Institute, Pittsburgh.

Key, M R (1977) Males, females, and linguistic and cultural categories. In: M Saville-Troike (ed.) 1977.

Khan, V (1976) Provision by minorities for language maintenance. In: G Perren (ed.) 1976b.

Khleif, B B (1979) Insiders, outsiders and renegades: towards a classification of ethnolinguistic labels. In: H Giles and B Saint-Jacques (eds) 1979.

Kinsella, V (ed.) (1978) *Language teaching and linguistics: surveys*. Cambridge University Press, Cambridge.

Kirstein, B (1978) Das sprachliche Normenproblem der emanzipatorischen Pragmadidaktik. *Linguistik und Didaktik* **36**, 324–350.

Klein, W (1974) Variation, Norm und Abweichung in der Sprache. In: G Lotzmann (ed.) 1974.

Kleineidam, H (1975) Zum Problem der Sprachnorm in Linguistik und Fremdsprachenunterricht. *Linguistik und Didaktik* **24**, 288–303.

Kluckhohn, C and **A L Kroeber** (1963) *Culture: a critical review of concepts and definitions*. Random House, New York.

Kolde, G (1980) Auswirkungen sprachlicher Fehler. In: D Cherubim (ed.) 1980.

Königs, F G (1980) Der Einfluß interimsprachlicher Systeme auf die Norm im Fremdsprachenunterricht. *Linguistik und Didaktik* **41**, 37–55.

Krauss, R M and **S Weinheimer** (1964) Changes in reference phrases as a function of frequency of usage in social interaction. *Psychonomic Science* **1**, 113–114.

Kunihiro, M (1975) Indigenous barriers to communication. *Japan Interpreter* **8**, 96–108.

La Barre, W (1974) Paralinguistics, kinesics and cultural anthropology. In: T A Sebeok (ed.) 1974. *Current Trends in Linguistics,* Vol. 12. Mouton, The Hague.

Labov, W (1966) *The Social Stratification of English in New York City*. Center for Applied Linguistics, Washington, DC.

_____ (1969) The logic of non-standard English. *Georgetown Monographs on language and linguistics* **22**, 1–31.

Ladefoged, P *et al.* (1972) *Language in Uganda*. London.

Lado, R (1957) *Linguistics across cultures*. University of Michigan Press, Michigan.

Lakoff, G (1973) Fuzzy grammar and the performance/competence terminology game. Papers from the 9th regional meeting of the Chicago Linguistic Society, 271–291.

Lakoff, R (1975) *Language and woman's place*. Harper & Colophon, New York.

Lambert, W E (1967) A social psychology of bilingualism. In: J B Pride and J Holmes (eds) 1972.

_____ (1977) The effects of bilingualism on the individual. In: P A Hornby (ed.) 1977.

Lambert, W E and **O Klineberg** (1964) *Children's views of foreign people: a cross-national study*. Appleton-Century-Crofts, New York.

Lambert, W E *et al.* (1968) A study of the roles of attitudes and motivation in second language learning. In: J A Fishman (ed.) 1968b.

Lang, R (1976) *A Plea for Language Planning in Papua New Guinea*. Boroko.

Laver, J (1968) Voice quality and indexical information. In: J Laver and S Hutcheson (eds) 1972.

Laver, J and **S Hutcheson** (eds) (1972) *Communication in face-to-face interaction*. Penguin, Harmondsworth.

Lauerbach, G (1977) Lernersprache: ein theoretisches Konzept und seine praktische Relevanz. *Neusprachliche Mitteilungen* **30**, 308–314.

_____ (1979) The threshold level—for schools? *Neusprachliche Mitteilungen* **3**, 149–156.

_____ (1980) Zur Relevanz der Konversationsanalyse für einen kommunikativen Englischunterricht. *Englisch Amerikanische Studien* **3**, 366–378.

Lawrence, T E (1940) *Seven Pillars of Wisdom*. Cape, London.

Lawton, D L (1980) Paradox and paradigm. In: P H Nelde (ed.) 1980.

Leopold, W (1954) A child's learning of two languages. In: H J Mueller (ed.) 1954. *Georgetown Monograph series on language and linguistics, No. 7*. Georgetown University, Washington, DC.

Lester, M (1978) International English and language variation. In: English Teaching Information Centre (ed.) 1978.

Levenston, E A (1971) Over-indulgence and under-representation—aspects of mother tongue interference. In: G Nickel (ed.) 1971. *Papers in contrastive linguistics*. Cambridge University Press, Cambridge.

Levine, J (1976) Some sociolinguistic parameters for analysis of language learning materials. *International Review in Applied Linguistics* **14**, 107–133.

Lewis, E G (1972) Migration and language in the USSR. In: J A Fishman (ed.) 1972.

_____ (1977) Bilingualism and bilingual education—the ancient world to the Renaissance. In: B Spolsky and R Cooper (eds.) 1977. *Frontiers of Bilingual Education*. Newbury House, Rowley.

Lewis, G (1978) Migration and the decline of the Welsh language. In: J A Fishman (ed.) 1978b.

Lindsay, P (1977) Resistances to learning EFL. *English Language Teaching Journal* **31**, 184–190.

Littlewood, W T (1974) Communicative competence and grammatical accuracy in foreign language learning. *Educational Review* **27**, 34–44.

_____ (1975) Role performance and language teaching. *International Review of Applied Linguistics* **13**, 199–206.

_____ (1978) Communicative language teaching. *Audio Visual Language Journal* **16**, 131–134.

_____ (1979) Communicative performance in language developmental contexts. *International Review of Applied Linguistics* **17**, 123–137.

_____ (1980) *Communicative language teaching*. Cambridge University Press, Cambridge.

Lotzmann, G (ed.) (1974) *Sprach- und Sprechnormen*. Julius Groos, Heidelberg.

Loveday, L J (1981a) On the not-so-obvious: pragmatics in ELT. *English Language Teaching Journal* **35**, 122–126.

_____ (1981b) Making an occasion: the linguistic components of ritual. *Anthropological Linguistics* **23**, 135–153.

_____ (1981c) Pitch, politeness and sexual role. *Language and Speech* **24**, 71–89.

_____ (1982a) (forthcoming) Japanese donatory verbs: their implications for linguistic theory. *Studia Linguistica*.

_____ (1982b) (forthcoming) The ecology of designatory markers. In: W Enninger (ed.) 1982. *Studies in the Ecology of Language*. Peter Lang, Frankfurt.

_____ (1982c) (forthcoming) Communicative interference: from Japanese to English. *International Review of Applied Linguistics*, February.

Lowie, R H (1945) A case of bilingualism. *Word* **1**, 249–259.

Mackay, D G (1980) On the goals, principles and procedures for prescriptive grammar: singular 'they'. *Language and Society* **9**, 349–367.

Mackey, W F (1968) The description of bilingualism. In: J A Fishman (ed.) 1968b.

_____ (1972) A typology of bilingual education. In: J A Fishman (ed.) 1972.

_____ (1978) The importation of bilingual education models. In: J E Alatis (ed.) 1978.

Maley, A and **A Duff** (1978) *Drama techniques in language learning*. Cambridge University Press, Cambridge.

Macnamara, J (1970) Bilingualism and thought. In: J E Alatis (ed.) *Report on the 20th annual round table meetings on linguistics and language studies.* Georgetown University, Washington, DC.

Marckwardt, A *et al.* (1953) Developing cultural understanding through foreign language study. *Publication of the Modern Language Association of America* **108**, 1196–1218.

Marquez, E J (1979) Contrastive analysis in sociolinguistics. *International Review of Applied Linguistics* **17**, 313–325.

Maruyama, M (1970) Toward a cultural futurology. Cultural Futurology Symposium, American Anthropological Association national meeting, Training Center for Community Programs, University of Minnesota.

Mathiot, M (ed.) (1979a) *Ethnolinguistics: Sapir and Whorf revisited.* Mouton, The Hague.

____ (1979b) Sex roles as revealed through referential gender in American English. In: M Mathiot (ed.) 1979a.

Maw, J (1971) Sociolinguistic problems and potentialities of education through a foreign language. In: W H Whiteley and D Forde (eds) 1971.

Mazrui, A A (1975) *The political sociology of the English language.* Mouton, The Hague.

McCormack, P D (1977) Bilingual linguistic memory: the independence–interdependence issue revisited. In: P A Hornby (ed.) 1977.

McCormack, W C and **S A Wurm** (eds) (1977) *Language and thought—anthropological issues.* Mouton, The Hague.

McCormack, W C and **S A Wurm** (eds) (1978) *Approaches to language: anthropological issues.* Mouton, The Hague.

Mead, M (1964) Comment in discussion session. In: T A Sebeok (ed.) 1964. *Approaches to semiotics.* Mouton, The Hague.

Mehan, H (1979) *Learning lessons.* Harvard University Press, Cambridge.

Meijer, C and **P Muysken** (1977) On the beginnings of pidgin and creole studies. In: A Valdman (ed.) 1977b.

Meisel, J M (1977) Linguistic simplification: a study of immigrant worker's speech and foreigner talk. In: S P Corder and E Roulet (eds) 1977.

Meyers, W E (1977) Can (and should) standard American English be defined? In: D L Shores and C P Hines (eds) 1977.

Miller, R A (1977) *The Japanese language in contemporary Japan—some sociolinguistic observations.* American Enterprise Institute for Public Policy Research, Washington, DC.

Milroy, L (1980) *Language and social networks.* Blackwell, Oxford.

Mitchell-Kernan, C (1972) On the status of black English for native speakers: an assessment of attitudes and values. In: B Cazden, P V John and D Hymes (eds) 1972.

Morsbach, H (1973) Aspects of nonverbal communication in Japan. *Journal of Nervous and Mental Diseases* **157**, 262–277.

Moskowitz, G (1978) *Caring and sharing in the foreign language class.* Newbury House, Rowley.

Munby, J (1978) *Communicative syllabus design.* Cambridge University Press, Cambridge.

Nelde, P H (ed.) (1980) *Languages in contact and conflict.* Franz Steiner, Weisbaden.

Nemser, W (1971) Approximative systems of foreign language learners. *International Review of Applied Linguistics* **9**, 115–123.

Nickel, G (1973) Aspects of error analysis and grading. In: J Svartvik (ed.) 1973.

Nida, E A and **W L Wonderly** (1971) Communication roles of languages in multilingual societies. In: W H Whiteley (ed.) 1971.

Norrish, J (1978) Liberalisation of views on non-standard forms of English. In: English Teaching Information Centre (ed.) 1978.

Obanya, P (1976) Second language learning out of school. *I.T.L. Review of Applied Linguistics* 31, 15–26.

O'Catháin, S (1973) The future of the Irish language. *Studies* 62, 303–322.

Oftedal, M (1973) Notes on language and sex. *Norwegian Journal of Linguistics* 27, 67–75.

Ogasawara, R (1972) Nichibai no bunka to kotoba joron. In: Miyauchi Hideo Kyoju Kanreki-kinen rombunshū henshū iinkai (ed.) 1972. *Nichiei no Kotoba to Bunka*. Sanseido, Tokyo.

Ohannessian, S, C A Ferguson and E C Polomé (eds) (1975) *Language survey in developing nations: papers and reports on sociolinguistic surveys*. Center for Applied Linguistics, Arlington, Virginia.

Oller, J W and D H Obrecht (1968) Pattern drill and communicative activity: a psycholinguistic experiment. *International Review of Applied Linguistics* 1/2, 165–174.

Olson, D (1977) From utterance to text. *Harvard Educational Review* 47, 257–281.

Olsson, M (1972) Intelligibility: a study of errors and their importance. Research Bulletin, No. 12, Department of Educational Research, Gothenburg School of Education. Gothenburg, Sweden (ERIC).

Ong, W (1958) *Ramus, method and the decay of dialogue*. Harvard University Press, Cambridge.

Padilla, E (1958) *Up from Puerto Rico*. Columbia University Press, New York.

Paradis, M (ed.) (1978) *Aspects of bilingualism*. Hornbeam Press, Columbia.

Pattanayak, D P (1978) Language competence and culture transmission. In: W C McCormack and S A Wurm (eds) 1978.

Paulston, C B (1974) Linguistic and communicative competence. *TESOL Quarterly* 8, 347–361.

Perren, G E (1976a) Bilingualism and British education. In: G E Perren (ed.) 1976b.

____ (ed.) (1976b) *Bilingualism and British education: the dimensions of diversity*. Centre for Information on Language Teaching and Research, London.

Philips, S V (1972) Participant structures and communicative competence. In: C B Cazden, V P John and D Hymes (eds) 1972.

____ (1974) Warm Springs Indian time: how the regulation of participation affects the progression of events. In: R Bauman and J Sherzer (eds) 1974.

Piepho, H (1977) Konfiguration authentischer Sprachtätigkeit im Englischunterricht. In: H Hunfeld (ed.) 1977.

Politzer, R L (1978) Errors of English speakers of German as perceived and evaluated by German natives. *The Modern Language Journal* 62, 253–261.

Poyatos, F (1972) The communication system of the speaker-actor and his cultural preliminary investigation. *Linguistics* 83, 64–85.

____ (1975) Cross-cultural study of paralinguistic 'alternants' in face-to-face interaction. In: A Kendon *et al.* (eds) 1975.

____ (1980) The interactive functions and limitations of verbal and non-verbal behaviour in natural conversation. *Semiotica* 30, 211–244.

Prator, C H (1968) The British heresy in TESL. In: J A Fishman, C A Ferguson and J Das Gupta (eds) 1975.

Preston, R C (1962) Reading, achievement of German and American children. *School and Society* 90, 350–354.

Pride, J B and J Holmes (eds) (1972) *Sociolinguistics*. Penguin, Harmondsworth.

192   The sociolinguistics of learning

Raabe, H (1980) Der Fehler beim Fremdsprachenerwerb und Fremdsprachengebrauch. In: D Cherubim (ed.) 1980.

Rabel-Reymann, L (1978) But how does a bilingual feel? In: M Paradis (ed.) 1978.

Rabin, C (1977) Acceptability in a revived language. In: S Greenbaum (ed.) 1977.

Ramge, H (1980) Fehler und Korrektur im Spracherwerb. In: D Cherubim (ed.) 1980.

Rattunde, E (ed.) (1979) Sprachnorm(en) im Fremdsprachenunterricht. Diesterweg, Frankfurt.

Rée, H (1972) A licence to learn languages. *Times Educational Supplement,* 8 December 1972.

Rehbein, J (1978) Reparative Handlungsmuster und ihre Verwendung im Fremdsprachenunterricht. Bochum University (mimeo).

Reisman, K (1974) Contrapuntal conversations in an Antiguan village. In: R Bauman and J Sherzer (eds) 1974.

Richards, J C (1971) A non-contrastive approach to error analysis. *English Language Teaching Journal* 25, 204–219.

____ (1972) Social factors, interlanguage, and language learning. *Language Learning* 22, 159–188.

____ (1974) *Error analysis—perspectives on second language acquisition.* Longman, London.

____ (1978a) *Understanding second and foreign language learning.* Newbury House, Rowley.

____ (1978b) Models of language use and language learning. In: J C Richards (ed.) 1978a.

Rickford, J R (1974) The insights of the mesolect. In: D DeCamp and I F Hancock (eds) 1974.

Ritchie, W C (ed.) (1978a) Introduction: theory and practice in second language research and teaching. In: W C Ritchie (ed.) 1978b.

____ (ed.) (1978b) *Second language acquisition research—issues and implications.* Academic Press, New York.

Rivers, W M (1972) *Teaching foreign language skills.* University of Chicago Press, Chicago.

Roberts, J (1980) Appropriate speaking through cue cards. *English Language Teaching Journal* 34, 285–287.

Robinson, W P (1971) Social factors and language development in primary school children. In: R Huxley and E Ingram (eds) 1971. *Language acquisition: models and methods.* Academic Press, London.

Rosansky, E J (1973) Language acquisition from the Piagetian and the Chomsky-Lenneberg points of view and the implications for second language teaching. Unpublished paper, Graduate School of Education, Harvard University.

Rossner, R B (1980) From control to cooperation in EFL teacher training. *IATEFL Newsletter,* No. 62, April, 29–31.

Roulet, E (1978) The ethnography of communication and the teaching of languages. In: W C McCormack and S A Wurm (eds) 1978.

Rubin, J (1968) Acquisition and proficiency. In: J B Pride and J Holmes (eds) 1972.

Ryan, E B and **M A Carranza** (1977) Ingroup and outgroup reactions to Mexican American language varieties. In: H Giles (ed.) 1977.

Sabsay, S and **T Bennett** (1977) Communicative distress. In: E O Keenan and T Bennett (eds) 1977.

Sacks, H (1972) On the analysability of stories by children. In: J J Gumperz and D Hymes (eds) 1972.

Saint-Jacques, B (1978) Elicitation of cultural stereotypes through the presentation of voices in two languages. In: M Paradis (ed.) 1978.

Sanches, M and **B G Blount** (eds) (1975) *Sociocultural dimensions of language use.* Academic Press, New York.

Sapir, E (1933) Language. In: B G Blount (ed.) 1974.

_____ (1949a) *Culture, language and personality* (ed. by D G Mandelbaum. 1970). University of California Press, Berkeley.

_____ (1949b) The status of linguistics as a science. In: D G Mandelbaum (ed.) *Selected writings of Edward Sapir.* University of California, Berkeley.

_____ (1949c) *Language.* Hart-Davis, London.

_____ (1974) The unconscious patterning of behaviour in society. In: B G Blount (ed.) 1974.

Savignon, J A (1972) Teaching for communicative competence: research report. *Audio Visual Language Journal* **10**, 153–162.

Saville-Troike, M (ed.) (1977) *Linguistics and anthropology.* Georgetown University Press, Washington, DC.

Scanlan, T M (1979) Teaching British and American language and culture with the aid of mail-order catalogues. *English Language Teaching Journal* **34**, 68–71.

Scheflen, A E (1972) The significance of posture in communication systems. In: J Laver and S Hutcheson (eds) 1972.

Schegloff, E (1972a) Sequencing in conversational openings. In: J J Gumperz and D Hymes (eds) 1972.

_____ (1972b) Notes on a conversational practice: formulating place. In: D Sudnow (ed.) 1972. *Studies in Social Interaction.* Free Press, New York.

_____ (1976) *Some questions and ambiguities in conversation.* University of California, Los Angeles.

Schegloff, E, G Jefferson and **H Sacks** (1977) The preference for self-correction in the organization of repair in conversation. *Language* **53**, 361–382.

Schenker, W (1978) *Sprachliche Manieren.* Peter Lang, Frankfurt.

Scherer, K R (1979) Personality markers in speech. In: K R Scherer and H Giles (eds) 1979.

Scherer, K R and **H Giles** (eds) (1979) *Social markers in speech.* Cambridge University Press, Cambridge.

Schnapper, M (1979) Your actions speak louder . . . In: E C Smith and L Luce (eds) 1979.

Schumann, J H (1974) Affective factors and the problem of age in second language acquisition. Unpublished paper, Graduate School of Education, Harvard University.

_____ (1975a) Second language acquisition: the pidginization hypothesis. Dissertation, Harvard University.

_____ (1975b) Implications of pidginization and creolization for the study of adult second language acquisition. In: J Schumann and N Stenson (eds) 1975.

_____ (1976) Social distance as a factor in second language acquisition. *Language Learning* **26**, 135–143.

_____ (1978a) *The pidginization process: a model for second language acquisition.* Newbury House, Rowley.

_____ (1978b) Second language acquisition: the pidginization hypothesis. In: E Hatch (ed.) 1978a.

Schumann, J and **H Stenson** (eds) (1975) *New frontiers in second language learning.* Newbury House, Rowley.

194   The sociolinguistics of learning

Schütze, F (1975-1977) *Sprache soziologisch gesehen,* 2 Vols. Fink, Munich.

Scollon, R and S B K Scollon (1979a) *Linguistic convergence: an ethnography of speaking at Fort Chipewyan, Alberta.* Academic Press, New York.

____ (1979b) *Cooking it up and boiling it down: abstracts in Athabaskan children's storytellings.* Native Language Center, Alaska.

____ (1980a) Literacy as interethnic communication: an Athabaskan case. To appear in: R Scollon and S B K Scollon. *Narrative, literacy and face in interethnic communication.* Ablex Publishing Corporation, Norwood.

____ (1980b) *Athabaskan-English interethnic communication.* Center for Cross-Cultural Studies, University of Alaska, Fairbanks.

Scotton, C M (1978) Language in East Africa: linguistic patterns and political ideologies. In: J A Fishman (ed.) 1978.

Seelye, H N (1977) Teaching the cultural context of intercultural communication. In: M Saville-Troike (ed.) 1977. *Linguistics and anthropology.* Georgetown University Press, Washington, DC.

Segalowitz, N and E Gatbonton (1977) Studies of a non-fluent bilingual. In: P A Hornby (ed.) 1977.

Selekman, H (1973) Communicative interaction activities in the foreign language classroom. English Language Institute, Pittsburgh (mimeo).

Seliger, H (1977) Does practice make perfect? A study of interaction patterns and second language competence. *Language Learning* 27, 263-278.

Selinker, L (1971) The psychologically relevant data of second language learning. In: P Pimsleur and T Quinn (eds) (1971) *The psychology of second language learning.* Cambridge University Press, Cambridge.

____ (1972) Interlanguage. *IRAL* 10, 209-331.

Seward, J (1968) *Japanese in action.* Weather-Hill, New York.

Shapira, R G (1978) The non-learning of English: case study of an adult. In: E Hatch (ed.) 1978a.

Shimanoff, S B and J C Brunak (1977) Repairs in planned and unplanned discourse. In: E O Keenan and T L Bennett (eds) 1977. *Discourse across time and space.* Southern California Occasional Papers in Linguistics, No. 5. University of Southern California, Los Angeles.

Shopen, T (ed.) (1979) *Languages and their speakers.* Winthrop, Cambridge.

Shores, D L and C P Hines (eds) (1977) *Papers in language variation.* University of Alabama Press, Alabama.

Shuy, R W (1978) Bilingualism and language variety. In: J E Alatis (ed.) 1978.

Shuy, R W, A Wolfram and W K Riley (1967) Linguistic correlates of social stratification in Detroit speech. Final report, Cooperative Research Project, 6-1347. Washington, DC: US Office of Education.

Sibayan, B P (1975) Survey of language use and attitudes towards language in the Philippines. In: S Ohannessian, C A Ferguson and E C Polomé (eds) 1975.

Sinclair, J and M Coulthard (1975) *Towards an analysis of discourse—the English used by teachers and pupils.* Oxford University Press, Oxford.

Smith, D (1972) Some implications for the social status of pidgin languages. In: D Smith and R Shuy (eds) 1972. *Sociolinguistics in cross-cultural analysis.* Georgetown University Press, Washington, DC.

Smith, E C and L Luce (eds) (1979) *Toward internationalism: readings in cross-cultural communication.* Newbury House, Rowley.

Sorensen, A P (1967) Multilingualism in the Northwest Amazon. In: J B Pride and J Holmes (eds) 1972.

Southerland, R H (1979) On characterizing communicative competence. In: W C McCormack and H J Izzo (eds) 1979. *The 6th Lacus Forum—1979.* Hornbeam Press, Columbia.

Streeck, J (1979) 'Sandwich. Good for you'—zur pragmatischen und konversationellen Analyse von Bewertungen in institutionellem Diskurs der Schule. In: J Dittman (ed.) 1979.

Strevens, P (1978) English as an international language. In: English Teaching Information Centre (ed.) 1978.

Sumner, W G (1906) (1959) *Folkways.* Dover, New York.

Suzuki, T (1975) *Tozasareta gengo—Nihongo no sekai.* Shinchōsha, Tokyo.

Svartvik, J (ed.) (1973) *Errata: Papers in error analysis.* Lund.

Tajfel, H (1978) *Differentiation between social groups.* Academic Press, London.

Tanner, N (1967) Speech and society among the Indonesian élite. In: J B Pride and J Holmes (eds) 1972.

Taylor, P M (1977) Bilingualism and intergroup relations. In: P A Hornby (ed.) 1977.

Taylor, D M, R Meynard and **E Rheault** (1977) Threat to ethnic identity and second-language learning. In: H Giles (ed.) 1977.

Taylor, L *et al.* (1971) Psychological variables and ability to pronounce a second language. *Language and Speech* **14**, 146–157.

Thomas, A (1978) Dialect mapping. In: J E Alatis (ed.) 1978.

Toelken, B (1975) Folklore, worldview and communication. In: D Ben-Amos and K S Goldstein (eds) 1975. *Folklore-performance and communication.* Mouton, The Hague.

Tottie, G (1977) Variation, acceptability and the advanced foreign learner: towards a sociolinguistics without a social context. In: S Greenbaum (ed.) 1977.

Trivedi, H C (1978) Culture in language learning. *English Language Teaching Journal* **32**, 92–97.

Trudgill, P (1974a) *Sociolinguistics.* Penguin, Harmondsworth.

_____ (1974b) *The social differentiation of English in Norwich.* Cambridge University Press, Cambridge.

_____ and **H Giles** (1976) Sociolinguistics and linguistic value judgements: correctness, adequacy and aesthetics. Linguistic Agency of the University of Trier publication.

_____ and **G A Tzavaras** (1977) Why Albanian-Greeks are not Albanians. In: H Giles (ed.) 1977.

Tucker, G R (1977) Some observations concerning bilingualism and second language teaching in developing countries and in North America. In: P A Hornby (ed.) 1977.

_____ and **W E Lambert** (1973) Sociocultural aspects of language study. In: J W Oller and J C Richards (eds) *Focus on the learner.* Newbury House, Rowley.

Tyler, S A (1969) *Cognitive anthropology.* Holt, Rinehart & Winston, New York.

_____ (1978) *The said and the unsaid—mind, meaning and culture.* Academic Press, New York.

Ubahakwe, E (1980) The dilemma in teaching English in Nigeria as a language of international communication. *English Language Teaching Journal* **34**, 156–163.

Valdman, A (1974) Error analysis and pedagogical ordering. Linguistic Agency of the University of Trier publication.

_____ (1975) Learner systems and error analysis. In: G A Jarvis (ed.) 1975. *Perspective: A new freedom.* National Textbook Co., Skokie.

_____ (1977a) L'effet de modèles culturels sur l'élaboration du langage simplifié. In: S P Corder and E Roulet (eds) 1977.

_____ (ed.) (1977b) *Pidgin and creole linguistics.* Indiana University Press, Bloomington.

van Dijk, T A (1977) *Text and context: explorations in the semantics and pragmatics of discourse.* Longman, London.

——— (1980) *Textwissenschaft.* Deutscher Taschenbuch Verlag, Munich.

Ventola, E (1979) The structure of casual conversation in English. *Journal of Pragmatics* **3,** 267-298.

Vetter, H J (1975) Psychopathology and a typical language. In: D Aaranson and R W Rieber (eds) 1975. Developmental psycholinguistics and communicative disorders. Annals of the New York Academy of Sciences.

Walmhoff, S and **A Wenzel** (1979) Ein Hm ist noch lange kein hm—oder was heißt klientenbezogene Gesprächsführung. In: J Dittman (ed.) 1979.

Weinreich, U (1953) *Languages in contact.* Linguistic Circle of New York, New York.

Wells, R A (1973) *Dictionaries and the authoritarian tradition.* Mouton, The Hague.

Werner, O *et al.* (1975) An ethnoscience view of schizophrenic speech. In: M Sanches and B G Blount (eds) 1979.

Whinnom, K (1971) Linguistic hybridization and the 'special case' of pidgins and creoles. In: D Hymes (ed.) 1971. *Pidginization and creolization of languages.* Cambridge University Press, Cambridge.

White, R V (1974) Communicative competence, registers, and second language teaching. *International Review of Applied Linguistics* **12,** 127-141.

Whitely, W H and **D Forde** (eds) (1971) *Language use and social change—problems of multilingualism with special reference to Eastern Africa.* Oxford University Press, Oxford.

Whorf, B L (1942) Language, mind and reality. In: J B Carrol (ed.) 1956. *Language, thought and reality—selected writings of Benjamin Lee Whorf.* Technology Press of MIT, Cambridge.

——— (1956) *Language, thought and reality* (ed. J B Carrol). Technology Press of MIT, Cambridge.

Widdowson, H G (1978) *Teaching language as communication.* Oxford University Press, Oxford.

——— (1979) *Explorations in applied linguistics.* Oxford University Press, Oxford.

Williams, E (1979) Elements of communicative competence. *English Language Teaching Journal,* October, 18-22.

Williams, F (1970) Language, attitudes and social change. In: F Williams (ed.) 1970. *Language and poverty.* Markham, Chicago.

Witterman, E P (1967) Indonesian terms of address in a situation of rapid social change. *Social Forces* **46,** 48-52.

Wong-Fillmore, L (1976) The second time around: cognitive and social strategies in second language acquisition. Ph.D. dissertation, Stanford University.

Young, R W (1972) Culture. In: R D Abrahams and R C Troike (eds) 1972.

Zydatiss, W (1974) A 'kiss of life' for the notion of error. *International Review of Applied Linguistics* **12,** 231-237.